ART WORLD

The New Rules Of The Game

ART WORLD

The New Rules Of The Game

BARBARA GUGGENHEIM

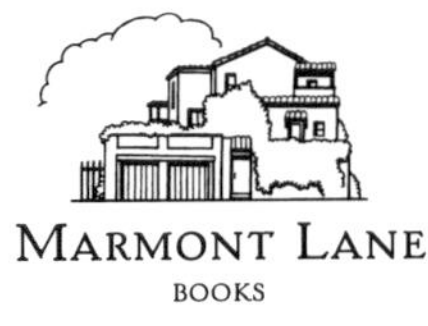

Marmont Lane
BOOKS

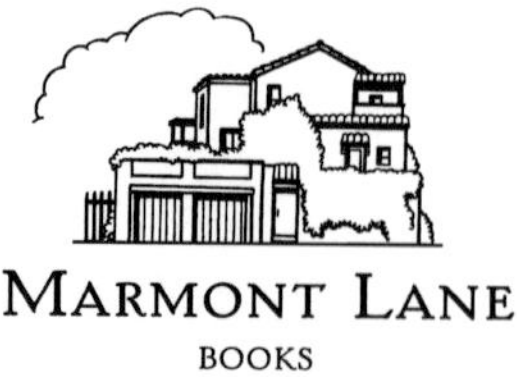

ART WORLD: THE NEW RULES OF THE GAME

For information address Marmont Lane Books
139 South Beverly Drive Suite 318
Beverly Hills, CA USA 90210

www.marmontlane.com

FIRST EDITION

Publisher: Bobby Woods/Marmont Lane Books

Design:

ISBN 13: 978-0-9905602-5-8
ISBN 10: 0-9905602-5-2

Also by Barbara Guggenheim

Decorating on eBay:

Fast and Stylish on a Budget

With Nadine Schiff

The Ultimate Organizer:

Be Your Own Personal Assistant

To

BF

with all my love.

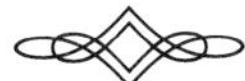

ART WORLD

THE NEW RULES OF THE GAME

BARBARA GUGGENHEIM

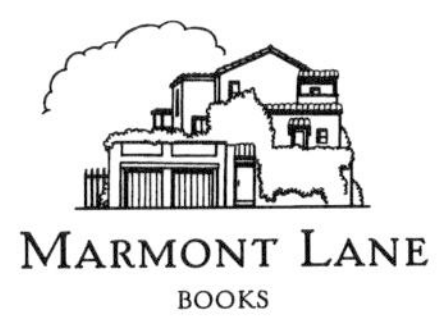

MARMONT LANE
BOOKS

CONTENTS

INTRODUCTION

ART IS MY BUSINESS...MY PLEASURE...MY LIFE. Driving in Los Angeles, I see palm trees against a blue sky and imagine myself motoring through a giant David Hockney painting (ill. 1). In Giverny, a weeping willow evokes Monet's thousand shades of green, and I see the harbor skiffs in Nice as through Matisse's seaside window. A face in a New York crowd looks familiar. I say hello...but do I know him? In a way: he's Philip Glass, the composer. I've seen his portrait by Chuck Close at the Whitney countless times. Call me crazy the way I see art everywhere. But I'll take that kind of crazy anytime.

Images overflow my workdays. In a bank vault, a friend shows me a painting he believes is a Rembrandt. He bought it for a song, certain it's worth a bundle. A pipe dream? Maybe. But it's very good. We stare at it, wondering together.

I leave to meet a client at her apartment. She's considering a Picasso I sent on approval. I don't need to say much; she's transported, and, swallowing hard, she says, "Let's go for it." Next, I check on a large Willem de Kooning painting that's with a conservator. A client's son sent a hockey puck through it, ripping a three-inch gash. It may affect its resale value, but for now, the repair's so good it can't be seen by the naked eye.

I end my day shepherding an anxious client to an evening auction. The crowd radiates money. In the skyboxes, Russian oligarchs are drinking champagne, South American heiresses are chatting, and they're all plotting behind drawn curtains. Our lot comes up. It's a Mark Rothko, and the competition is fierce. New collectors with deep pockets all over the world want one. I whisper to our client, "Be patient." We wait for the right moment to jump in...and it's NOW! I raise my arm calmly, trying to convey inevitability. The hammer comes down. Our client owns the painting. He rises as if to cheer. I tug at his sleeve to sit down; this isn't Yankee Stadium. We watch a few more lots sell, then leave. Reaching the sidewalk and the line of waiting limos, I feel a fierce joy.

Because the art world's exciting and newsworthy, it obsesses insiders and fascinates onlookers. Pick up any magazine or newspaper or click and scroll online, and you'll come across splashy headlines about a record-breaking sale, high-octane exhibition, art fair, or black-tie opening at the museum designed by a big name architect. Leaders like "Christie's has Art World's First $1 Billion Week" rank right up there with "Christie Closes Down Bridge." Who doesn't want to get involved in a world where those things happen? No wonder the numbers are growing daily. In 2014, it was a more than

$66 billion a year business — a mix of dealers, auction houses, art fairs, advisors, museums, conservators, journalists, and critics — all circling the people who make it possible...the artists and collectors.

No question: having an interest in art is life enhancing. Many people get satisfaction casually wandering through museums and looking at art without knowing much about it. Others want to know about the works and what goes on "inside the beltway." A smaller group acquires art and builds collections. Collecting fills their lives with wonderful objects and brings them emotional, intellectual, social, and often financial rewards. Maybe you don't care about money or status, but a lot of people do. Some talk about it freely. Others never say so, but they know that the right painting is a good investment and, hanging in their living room, signals who they are, or who they want to be, more clearly than any Rolex, Bentley, or yacht.

Like D.C. politics and trading derivatives, collecting art is an insider's game. While resources help, high stakes players who shell out tens of millions for Picassos and Pollocks don't always win. You can collect on a small budget and yet reap great rewards if you know how the game is played. Unfortunately, as you'll discover, that's easier said than done. The art world is one of the last unregulated fields. There are no hard and fast rules, no inside lore fathers whisper to sons, Harvard Business School formulas, or a Ouija board to depend upon.

As Pat Altschul, a dealer turned collector says, "The art world could teach the Mafia a thing or two." And yet, what do most people know when they make their first purchase? Nothing. That's also true for many seasoned collectors who've made numerous purchases. What should they know? Well, that's what this book is about.

Think of this book as a backstage pass into the art world, useful for longtime collectors, novices, artists, and curious outsiders. I'll share things people in the field should tell you but often don't. I'll introduce you to the players you need to know and know about. I'll explain how galleries and auction houses work. I'll offer advice for developing a strategy for identifying and finding what you want. I'll use my thirty-five years of experience as an advisor and stories colleagues have shared to explain how to do your due diligence, dodge hidden pitfalls, buy right, take care of your art, and trade up, sell, or give it away. And I promise not to pitch the usefulness of art advisors more than once every chapter.

Before I dive in, allow me to make a few disclaimers. First, although I talk about "paintings" throughout the book, I use the term as a stand-in for works in all media. Secondly, this book is not meant to be an exhaustive study, but rather a compilation of personal observations that I hope will be useful. Thirdly, since the art world runs on secrecy, I've changed the names of individuals and objects to protect the innocent — and the guilty. If you're an insider, you'll probably know who's who, but friends have warned that if I expose too much, "You'll never eat lunch in this town again." I hope they're wrong. I love those lunches.

So, welcome to the wild, wonderful art world. The learning curve may be steep, but the ascent will amuse and reward you every step of the way.

FIRST THINGS FIRST

AT THE OUTSET, it's important to realize that the art world is an equal-opportunity opportunity. Its beauty and excitement are accessible to everyone. Imagine a vast arena where a great spectacle is unfolding, as fascinating to observers as to participants. Art lovers can visit auction houses, galleries, museums, and art fairs, rub shoulders with the rich — and sometimes the very rich — without acquiring a single work. Like plane spotters who collect aircraft sightings but never leave the ground, they collect experiences, without buying a work. Not that there isn't competition and one-upmanship. You might hear 'art world observer A' commenting to 'B,' "Did you see the Magritte show in Paris? I thought it looked so much better there than in New York."

It follows, therefore, that the experiences of those who acquire art vary. Those who have the resources to build world-class collections and enjoy the perks of museum board memberships will have a very different experience from those who need to ferret out affordable works and stand in line to get into museums shows. Nonetheless, who's to say which collector will be more fulfilled and whose collection will be more interesting?

If and when you begin to collect, the earlier you identify your goals and implement a strategy, the more successful you'll be. Even if you're only planning to buy a few paintings, you don't want to make a mistake and look back later and think, "What have I done?" Linda Janger and her late husband Jerry, well-known LA collectors, did just that. Decades ago, on their honeymoon in Italy, they decided to spend the cash they received as wedding gifts on their first work of art. They narrowed down their choices between a small Picasso etching and a big flashy painting by an artist, Pezzoli, which they bought. You know how that turned out.

It takes time to learn the ropes. Subscribing to art magazines is a good start. You probably have a knee-high pile of magazines by your bed you haven't had time to read, and the thought of any more may tip you over. Would you feel better if I tell you that you don't have to actually read them? Flipping through is good enough. General magazines, such as *ARTnews* and *Art in America*, offer a quick way to see images of works by a variety of artists from different periods and movements and get a sense of what art historians, critics, and journalists are thinking about. If your focus is contemporary art, *Artforum* is useful, especially its ads announcing gallery shows. The names of galleries and artists may not mean much at first, but after a few months, you'll start connecting the dots. I also recommend trade journals, like *Art + Auction* and *The Art Newspaper*; they're to the art world what *WWD* is to fashion and *Variety* is to the entertainment business. And if you have time, a number of art websites, such as *Blouin ArtInfo* and *artnet News*, cover daily goings-on.

It may sound old-fashioned in these online days, but you should consider assembling a working library. *Yes, books!* Surveys of a period that interests you, monographs (histories of individual artists' careers), and exhibition catalogues are all useful. And if you become enrapt with a particular artist, you might want to buy his catalogue raisonné. A "CR," as it's called, is a comprehensive list of all known works by the artist, including provenance (succession of owners), literature, and exhibition history. CRs can be expensive, but they're worth every penny. When a dealer offers you a work, you can look it up on the spot and compare it with other works the artist did, see how many the artist made like it, how many are in museums, and how many are still owned privately and may come onto the market. CRs and other books, especially those out of print, can be a good investment, as their value may appreciate along with the art they chronicle. So, you shouldn't feel guilty going on book-buying sprees online at AbeBooks and Amazon or at art bookstores, like Ursus in New York, or Hennessy + Ingalls and Arcana in LA.

Of course, no photo in a book can give you the emotional rush you get standing in front of the real McCoy. By the time I was a teenager, I'd seen so many reproductions of the *Mona Lisa* I was sure if I ever got to see her in person I'd be unmoved. Quite the contrary; standing before her in the Louvre on my first trip to Paris, I cried. For me, she still has the "aura" Walter Benjamin described in his famous 1936 essay, *The Work of Art in the Age of Mechanical Reproduction*, that distinguishes originals from reproductions.

So, your next step is to get out there and look. You probably won't have to go far, as wondrous works can be found in museums close to home. Years ago, I arranged for my entire family to meet in Chicago to see a Monet retrospective at The Art Institute. The logistics were daunting — hotels, restaurants, and vans — but I was glad to do it because my wheelchair-bound dad, who lived near Princeton, was crazy about Monet. As I pushed him through the exhibition, which felt terribly uphill, Dad suddenly pointed to a painting and exclaimed, "That's the *best* painting in the show!" When I read the label, I gasped. It was from the Princeton University Art Museum (ill. 2). I'd spent tens of hours and thousands of dollars dragging Dad to Chicago, and the one painting that bowled him over normally hung ten minutes from his house. But Dad's not alone. Many art lovers make elaborate pilgrimages to museums in Paris, Rome, or London, without realizing that works in their local museum can provide the same take-your-breath-away experiences. Statistics tell us, for example, that Nantucket Islanders visit their local museum, on average, once in their lifetime, and I bet that's on a rainy day. So, don't be an islander. Make visits to your local museum part of your routine. And, while you're there, check out the lectures and gallery tours. Reading and looking on your own are fine, but a gifted lecturer can enhance your appreciation.

Attending shows at galleries adds another dimension to your ongoing art education. If you live in a small city, you'll probably be able to blitz all the galleries in a couple of hours. In a big city, the number of galleries may be so overwhelming that it's hard, especially when you're starting out, to figure out what to see and what to skip. One cold, rainy afternoon, I was making the rounds of New York's Chelsea galleries when I passed a woman standing on the corner in tears, clutching a soggy *New York Times* listing of gallery shows. I asked if I could help. Sobbing, she explained that she'd saved up for months and had flown in from Cleveland to look at art, but had no idea where to go. I took her paper, circled the names of the best exhibitions, and she headed off, smiling. To avoid feeling overwhelmed, like that out-of-towner, start your gallery going by tagging along with friends familiar with the scene or taking some gallery tours organized by your museum or private companies. After a few forays, you'll be gallery hopping like a pro.

You'll also develop your own method for looking at and connecting with the art you encounter. I first realized that "looking" was a skill when, as a teenager, my mother took me to The Barnes Foundation. As we entered the main room, a man was standing in front of Cézanne's *The Card Players* (ill. 3). We walked around the entire room at a leisurely pace for Mom, an eternity for me. As we left, I noticed that the man hadn't moved, he was still looking at the Cézanne. I whispered to my mother, "What's he doing?" "He's appreciating art," she said. I shook my head, "Can't he do it any faster?"

In college, I was impressed by the labor-intensive approach Richard Wollheim described in his prestigious Mellon lecture:

I evolved a way of looking at paintings that is massively time-consuming and deeply rewarding. For I came to recognize that it often took the first hour or so in front of a painting for stray associations or motivated misperceptions to settle down, and it was only then, with the same amount of time or more spent looking at it, that the picture could be relied upon to disclose itself as it was.

Coming from a philosopher who incorporated psychoanalytic techniques in studying art history, I wasn't surprised. Psychiatrists often book double sessions with patients who take the first "hour" to rid themselves of extraneous thoughts before focusing on deeper issues. Wollheim did offer an apology of sorts,

I noticed that I became an object of suspicion to passers-by, and so did the picture that I was looking at.

Hmmm, I wonder if he was the guy I saw at The Barnes staring at *The Card Players*.

Needless, to say, if we approached every painting like Wollheim, we wouldn't be able to do anything else. So, I've adopted a less time-consuming method that the famed collector Baron Hans Heinrich Thyssen-Bornemisza shared with me when I was in grad school. 'Heini,' as he was called, looked at a painting first from a distance, taking in the whole — the subject and the general way it was painted. He'd then move up closer and spend several minutes looking at details, studying the artist's techniques and subject. And finally, he'd step back again to see if the whole came together successfully. Heini's is just one system; it works for me, but you may develop your own approach.

On occasion, when I walk through a museum, I notice someone planted on a bench in front of a painting, seemingly having a deeply-felt experience. I asked a friend, Dr. Antonio Damasio, a neuroscientist, to explain such a reaction in terms of brain physiology. As he described it in his book, *The Feeling of What Happens*, the visual perception in your brain is the simultaneous conduit for both the intellectual interpretation, a decoding in factual, thinking terms, and a visceral activation, provoked by shapes, colors, etc. The latter can be mediated by an individual's past experiences and personal brain design (some of us may be more sensitive to one color, shape, or texture than another). The emotive reactions are what cause changes in our bodies, some perceptible, like increased heart rate, others below consciousness, like an increase in endocrine secretions. The brain processes the new body state as a feeling.

When I was in grad school, I read that Bernard Berenson, the great connoisseur and scholar of Italian Renaissance painting, had an orgasm looking at a painting. I've joked since that that's the reason I went into art history. I'm still waiting, although I've had plenty of profound emotional moments looking at great objects. Without any warning, whether or not I know anything about the artist or the work, I'm transported. If this sounds quasi-religious, so be it. This is my church.

Berenson and I are not alone. A group of Italian doctors have identified a constellation of physical reactions experienced by individuals standing in front of Michelangelo's sculpture, *David*, (ill. 4) in Florence. The symptoms, which they dubbed "The David Syndrome," include rapid heartbeat, nausea, dizziness, and hallucinations, some of which require hospitalization. It helps to have Damasio's explanation of the underlying causes, but, nonetheless, did it occur to the Italian researchers that a number of folks with troubling symptoms were tourists who'd waited hours in long lines in the sweltering heat to see *David*? Did they ever consider heat stroke?

Art can also generate sufficiently negative emotive reactions to make someone disfigure or destroy a work. When the Taliban destroyed the two giant 6th-century Buddha sculptures carved into cliffs (one over 150 feet tall) in Central Afghanistan in 2001, it was an act of violence committed in the name of religion, the obliteration of all non-Islamic sculpture. And when an artist smashed an Ai Weiwei vase in a Miami museum installation, it was political. He was protesting the fact that more local artists weren't being shown.

Peculiarly, two recent episodes of vandalism requiring police intervention revolved around Cy

Twombly paintings. At a museum show in Avignon, a woman wearing bright red lipstick ran up to a predominantly all white Twombly painting and kissed it. A continent away, a different woman was arrested when she disrobed in a gallery of Twomblys and danced nude. For many who think of Twombly as a cerebral artist, these spontaneous incidences must seem quite shocking.

"Alright, already," I can hear you complaining. "Enough reading and looking. It's time to SHOP!" But hold in the reins a little longer. It takes time to develop an 'eye.' I was in high school when I read the line in Joyce Kilmer's *Trees*, "I think that I shall never see a poem as lovely as a tree." "Wow!" I thought, "That's great poetry!" Then, in college, I read Matthew Arnold and T.S. Eliot and, looking back on Kilmer, I blanched, "What was I thinking?" What you like in the beginning is probably not what you'll like after you've been exposed to thousands of works and your taste matures.

Whatever you do, don't depend on beginner's luck. My friend Harvey bought only one painting in his life, decades ago while he was practicing law in Thailand. It was by a drunken local artist who needed rent money. In recent years, the burgeoning interest in Thailand's heritage has kicked in big-time, and Harvey sold the painting for 340 times what he paid. But that was Harvey, and that was Thailand, and I shouldn't have bothered telling the story. In general, acquiring art without adequate knowledge or experience is like paddling upstream, blindfolded, with one oar. Beginner's luck may have worked for Harvey, but it's unlikely to work for you. And it *is* likely to waste a lot of money.

So, take your time, learn how the art world works, experience many different works of art and train your eye. You'll have fun doing it, gain lifelong dividends, and you'll put yourself in a position to get the most out of collecting.

PLAYERS

While collecting is certainly about art, it's not *only* about art. It's also about the people you meet along the way. The art world is like a giant stage on which the players — artists, dealers, auction houses, advisors, museums, curators, critics, journalists, art historians and collectors — all play unique roles. As a collector, you're the focus of the attention...and sometimes wiles... of other cast members determined to be the stars of their own personal dramas. If you don't want them 'stepping on your lines' or creating other problems for you, pay close attention. This chapter introduces the art industry's cast of characters, explains what they do, how they can help you, and, if you're not careful, how they can hurt you.

ARTISTS

The artist is the most important player in the art world...and the least. Without artists there'd be no art, no art world, and no profits. Without artists, I wouldn't be writing this book. Yet, once an artist creates a work and it leaves his or her studio, the work takes center stage, and the artist is relegated to the wings. It's hard to imagine, but it's possible to build a major collection of contemporary art over a lifetime without knowing anything about the artists or ever meeting one. That's the way it works in the music world, too. We all recognize Rachmaninoff's piano concertos, yet many of us know little or nothing about the composer and couldn't care less. In the art world, we all recognize famous works by Cézanne, but we don't stop to think about the man who lived and breathed and stood in front of his easel day after day, applying paint in unforgettable, seminal ways. *He* isn't the point. His art is.

Well, maybe that's an overstatement. Some artists, like Leonardo, Michelangelo, Vincent van Gogh, Pablo Picasso, and Andy Warhol have become as iconic as their work. Today's artists take a page from these greats and understand that creating myth-size personas can call attention to their work and help increase its value. You'd think that in today's celebrity-driven culture, more artists would become household names. But they don't. Charity auctions regularly hawk "lunch with Tom Cruise" or Warren Buffet, but artists don't bring in the bucks. As for endorsements, artists haven't begun to catch up to sports figures as flacks for pricey goods. Although only a few artists have taken advantage of the crossover between art and fashion, such as Takashi Murakami and Yayoi Kusama, who've created designs for Louis Vuitton, and Jeff Koons, whose balloon dog graces H&M handbags, expect more as talent agencies enter the fray to represent artists.

More often than not, artists are sidelined while other art world insiders steal the limelight. The author of a recent book on contemporary art includes interviews with dealers, collectors, and advisors, but not a single artist. It's as if he wrote a book, *Inside Basketball*, and only interviewed people with floor seats. What gives? Was he afraid that, by including some artists and excluding others, he'd be accused of favoritism by his artist friends? Or, if the artists he interviewed didn't pan out five years hence, he'd be slammed for making the wrong prognostication? Or did he believe that a serious discussion of collecting contemporary art should focus on the art and leave artists out? I'm sure he had good reasons, but I think it's worth turning our attention to artists, the artist's practice (a term which refers to art-making in its entirety from the idea to the construction of the work), and how artists function in the art world ecosystem.

Let's begin by looking at how artists become artists in the first place. For centuries, until recently, the answer was — slowly, very slowly. In 19th-century France, it took longer to become an artist than a doctor or lawyer. An art student would enroll at the École des Beaux-Arts, where he spent his first few weeks learning to sharpen pencils. He'd study tracing for six months and then advance to two years of drawing from plaster casts. After that, a student went on to life drawing for another two years, and finally, after four years, he was allowed to paint. Training was rigorous, and teachers could pay surprise visits to students' homes, day or night, to make sure they weren't drawing from life or, heaven forbid, painting when they were still in the pencil-sharpening stage.

If you were male and hugely talented, you'd vie for the golden ticket, the Prix de Rome, a three-to-five-year stay in Rome at the expense of the French king or government. Women were excluded from the competition as they were considered too ladylike to paint male nudes and not intellectual enough to interpret the subjects demanded of a prizewinner. Annually, ten finalists were chosen, and each was given a subject to paint and seventy-two days to complete a work — in isolation. A successful painting was not only the culmination of years of technical training; it required a deep knowledge of history, mythology, the Classics, and the Bible. Imagine having been assigned *The Three Wise Men* and not knowing who they were or what their gifts were. The stakes were high, because if an artist won the Prix de Rome, commissions would come rolling in and his career would be made.

Today, there's little call for traditional skills, and only a few schools, notably the New York Academy of Art, teach figure drawing and anatomy. (Full disclosure: the NYAA was founded by my sister and brother-in-law.) The faculty of the NYAA, which includes well-known figurative artists Eric Fischl and Jenny Saville, believes that students will be well-served by academic training, no matter what kind of art they go on to make. They aren't wrong. Have you seen the exquisite drawings of chrysanthemums by Piet Mondrian? He did dozens, and I can only imagine that the skill and rigor required to create them contributed to the power of his subsequent abstract grid paintings.

Although most art schools have less traditional curricula than the NYAA, a few, like the California Institute of the Arts (CalArts), Rhode Island School of Design (RISD), and Yale University School of Art, have distinguished themselves as hotbeds for the next generation of successful artists. A lot of collectors scan the CV of an artist whose work they're considering, and, if he comes from one of those incubators, it's confidence building, even though the artist may not live up to his potential. Still, many artists, with or without degrees, feel that their best training comes from apprenticing as studio assistants. Abstract painter Josh Smith, for example, worked for Christopher Wool, who had worked for Joel Shapiro.

Becoming an artist requires no degree, no training at all. Many artists are autodidacts, and these days anyone who calls himself an "artist" is an artist, and anything made by anyone who calls himself an "artist" is "art." Not happy about that definition? Join the club. At least you can get some satisfaction knowing that not all "art" has a successful life in museums and galleries.

It turns out that art world professionals are pretty good pickers, and cream tends to rise to the top, fast. It took me a while to understand this. When I moved to LA and met a lot of young writers, I thought there must be thousands of great scripts out there desperately looking for studios to produce them. In fact, the opposite's true. Good screenplays are rare, and studios, desperate for a full slate of releases, including "tent pole" summer and Christmas films to fill their distribution pipeline, are forced to make some of the dreadful films that lead us to question their judgment or sanity. In the art world, it's the same. You might think there are thousands of great artists desperate for representation, overlooked by a cruel art world. Not at all. Gallerists and collectors are quick to snap up quality artists, leaving few good ones, if any, languishing in obscurity. Dealers, like film studios, frantically looking for those few stand-outs, often have to settle for less.

If an artist shows promise and gets gallery representation, what comes next is nothing short of a Herculean task on the part of his gallerist. The dealer must nurture the artist, arrange exhibitions of his work, and get a buzz going. He encourages critics and art magazines to pay attention, gets dealers in other cities to represent him, and pitches his work to museums and serious collectors. All the while, the dealer, or a staff member assigned by the dealer, must keep the artist happy by listening to his complaints about lovers, landlords, and the percentage he's getting on sales. When I asked a dealer why he specializes in old master paintings (works done before 1800), he quipped, "There's no artist like a dead artist. They don't talk back." Nor do they jump ship as living artists often do. As soon as emerging artists start to sell, they're often wooed away from their starter galleries by bigger galleries with an array of promises — huge spaces to create big installations, stipends, signing bonuses (like ballplayers), loans, new price levels, sales to important collectors, etc. It's sad for the smaller galleries that discovered them, took the risk, and poured time and effort into moving their careers along. Sometimes, an artist's move doesn't work out. In a smaller gallery, he may be a star, but in a bigger emporium, he's one of many and may get lost in the shuffle.

The pressure on artists is huge. Because collectors are insatiable in their desire for what's 'new,' an artist must come up with novel ideas and enough saleable works for his dealer to take to art fairs and fill his gallery for shows every couple of years. Blame it in part on Picasso. Before him, most artists would develop a signature style and stick with it, with some tweaking, for the rest of their lives. But Picasso's fertile mind refused to be paralyzed by success, and he changed his style over and over again. Ever since, expectations are high, and artists who don't constantly "evolve" tend not to last long on the art world stage.

Jeff Koons and Damien Hirst, two of the most memorable artists of their generation, are poster children for this 'evolutionary' success. And like Picasso, both have made lots of work to support every new idea. In different ways, they've pushed the limits and challenged our definition of 'art,' creating works which are knock-your-socks-off great.

One Sunday morning decades ago, I was cruising The Metropolitan Museum's 19th-century decorative arts galleries when Koons came in. He was clearly trolling for inspiration to add to his store of influences, already ranging from old masters to Marcel Duchamp, Warhol, and beyond. I'd like to think that looking at porcelains that day inspired him to make *Michael Jackson and Bubbles* (1988). Not only is it one of the largest porcelains ever created, but it's innovative in its breakthrough use of a decorative arts material, the kind we're used to seeing in our grandmother's house, in a fine arts context. At its heart, Koons' sculpture addresses issues of celebrity, fame, and the way we see our icons. As someone who knew Jackson, I'm struck with the way Koons caught the poignancy of a man who grew up without having a childhood, desperate to recreate one, chimp and all. What's particularly astounding about the work is how it's entered our collective consciousness. Young people who don't know Jackson from his videos or concerts, know him from this sculpture. It's no wonder that, when it sold, it broke sales records, as many of Koons' works have before and after.

For his sculpture, *Puppy*, (ill. 5), made a few years later, Koons turned to another non-fine-art medium, garden topiary (plants and flowers over a metal armature), to push the limits of monumental sculpture. Koons says that his use of topiary, which peaks and fades by the season, reminded him of the life/death cycle of 17th-century Italian and Dutch paintings. Koons chose as his 43-foot stalwart, a Westie, which he considers to be the universal symbol for happiness. The breed exudes youth and vivacity, obsessions in today's society, and, since Westies are terminally cute, they evoke in almost everyone who sees one, even in sculpture, waves of sentimentality. (Full disclosure: I own *two* Westies.)

From Koons' early basketballs floating in water-filled vitrines to his mirrored-surfaced sculptures, like *Balloon Dog*, which looks like a twisted balloon memento magicians make at kids' birthday parties, his works are the ultimate shiny baubles we're allowed to love because they come in the form of art. No artist has better put his finger on the pulse of the times with works that reflect, often literally, ourselves, and remind us of society's obsession with narcissism, fame, money, conspicuous consumption, sex, and desire. A collector once confided that he loved his Koons because he could look at the art and himself, and admire both, at the same time.

Koons has crafted his persona with the same meticulous detail with which he's crafted his sculpture, from wearing a business suit while other artists are in jeans, to asking the Whitney to commission Antonio Damasio, the rockstar of neuroscience, to write an essay for his retrospective catalogue. All of this is not just in service of his work; it's an intrinsic part of it. No wonder that whenever Koons switches directions, collectors gasp and pull out their checkbooks.

Hirst, like Koons, has had a tremendous career dealing head-on with the big loaded issues that have concerned artists for centuries, namely the fragility and beauty of life and the terror of death. But he's done it in brilliant, new ways. His preserved animals, such as the shark floating in a tank, *The Physical Impossibility of Death in the Mind of Someone Living* (ill. 6), and his butterfly wing "paintings," are updates of centuries-old memento mori, reminding us that life is short and worldly pleasures fleeting. If the skull is a standard prop in Dutch 17th-century vanitas paintings, then Hirst's 2007 diamond skull, *For the Love of God* (ill. 7) is the ultimate update, done in inimitable Hirst style. If you're Hirst and want to display a $100 million platinum-dipped skull encrusted with over a million carats of diamonds, including a 52.4-carat pink valued at $6.3 million, you give it the Barnum & Bailey send off. And that's just what he did. Visitors lined up around White Cube, his gallery in Mason's Yard, London, to get tickets to see the most eye-popping bling since the Crown Jewels. Security men, with ear wires like Secret Service agents, led visitors upstairs where the skull was on view. All bags and packages had to be left outside the room, which seemed pitch black when you entered. Then, as your eyes acclimated, Hirst's masterpiece, in a glass case in the center of the room, lit from above, seemed to materialize before you. WOW!

Everything, down to the last unscripted detail, was part of the work. It was a performance in which everyone who attended participated, whether they knew it or not.

In September 2008, in the days after Lehman Brothers' collapse, Hirst took on the system and became the first living artist to have a major auction house devote an entire sale to his work. In two days at Sotheby's, 223 works, with an estimate of $122–176 million, sold for over $200 million. Did Hirst's marketing smarts rival his artistic talents, or was the whole sale another performance piece?

A few years later, Hirst accomplished a feat just as daring, a 'retrospective' of more than 300 of his 1400 famous 'spot' paintings, held simultaneously at thirteen Gagosian galleries in eight cities worldwide (ill. 8). Hirst has described the origins of the spot paintings as wanting to paint color without expression, but, as you can imagine, critics have different interpretations. Some, for example, consider the spots to be placebos. If you follow that line of thinking, what Hirst achieved by the paintings' sameness was anaesthetizing or hypnotizing viewers, collectors, and the entire market, at least for the duration of the show. Since then, although prices on some bodies of Hirst's work, particularly the Natural History series (preserved animals floating in vitrines), have remained strong, prices of others, including the kaleidoscope (butterflies) and spin paintings, have suffered from the way he flooded the market with work.

This is a good place to mention the role of studio assistants, as both Hirst and Koons are known for having plenty of them. The word "studio assistant" is something of a euphemism, as an assistant can do everything from stretching the canvases and mixing paints to doing all the work, which the artist may conceptualize but not touch. If that sounds shocking, you should know that Peter Paul Rubens had over a hundred assistants, and plenty of 'Rubens' paintings were barely, if at all, touched by the master. El Greco's assistants made *repliques* of successful paintings in several sizes which the artist supervised, and today, if they're good, they're considered "El Grecos." Roy Lichtenstein's assistants painted his dots, and I always remember that when a friend was a dot-painter, she'd regularly give me updates, such as, "Blue is *in* this month." But artists like Koons, who at one point had over a hundred assistants, and Hirst, who did only the first five spot paintings out of 1400 himself, are the full monty of conceptual artists. Maurizio Cattelan, a compatriot of the two, has been quoted as saying, "I don't design. I don't paint. I don't sculpt. I absolutely never touch my works." These artists believe that it's the idea that counts and that the execution can be done by others. That doesn't mean that the artists don't work hard. Koons is in his studio every step of the way, supervising. In a story told about Hirst, the artist criticized a studio assistant for not applying color at random as he was told to do, instead making a spot painting with five yellow spots in a row. The assistant insisted that, indeed, the selection was random. He eventually won the argument, and the painting exists in Hirst's oeuvre. In another story Hirst tells in *On The Way to Work*,

> *The best person who ever painted spots for me was Rachel. She's brilliant. Absolutely fucking brilliant. The best spot painting you can have by me is one painted by Rachel. Mine are shite compared to hers.*

The way these artists create their works reminds me of filmmaking. A film director doesn't make a single scene by himself. He hires costume and set designers, lighting technicians, cameramen, actors, and others to execute his wishes, and, if he's lucky, they exceed them — and then he stands back and shouts, "Action." It's possible that neither the "producer," nor the writer, who creates the blueprint for the entire film, has ever set foot on the set.

Hirst, Koons, and other well-known conceptual artists may not actually 'make' art, but they do make money — lots of it. As Andy Warhol said in his book, *The Philosophy of Andy Warhol (from A to B and Back Again)*, "Making money is art and working is art and good business is the best art." Koons and Hirst followed in Andy's footsteps as consummate businessmen and yet, as with Andy, none of that takes away from their artistic achievements. For collectors who like to imagine their artists starving picturesquely in garrets, this can be a trifle disconcerting. One evening, I was at Café Boulud on New York's Upper East Side with an older friend who knows nothing about the art world. Koons came in, nattily dressed in jacket and tie, indistinguishable in a sea of upscale businessmen. When I pointed him out to my friend, he grumbled, "Why isn't he hanging out at some grungy bar downtown?" I laughed; I'd have expected someone saying that in the 70s but not today. If my friend had the preconceived notion that all great artists were destitute Bohemians, then *he* — not Koons — had a problem. Of course, many artists probably live on the edge, act unreliably, and do drugs to excess, and we romanticize them and give them a wide berth to behave badly. Unfortunately, the myth of Van Gogh (think Kirk Douglas in the film *Lust for Life*) has colored our expectations of artists' behavior. Even the Van Gogh Museum in Amsterdam has tired of that to the point that they've recently rehung their Van Goghs in a way that plays down his madness and personal problems, focusing on his artistic intentions instead.

Contributing to the legend of Van Gogh is the fact that he had almost no success in his life and became famous after death. (He sold only one work and got one good review which he said ruined him.) Frankly, I can't think of another artist who's made it into the history books without having had some recognition while alive. Today, one thing's certain. Artists don't live in a parallel universe unfettered by money and the material world. In fact, some collectors like the fact that the artists they collect make more money than they do. An artist, aged 32, who's doing well but hasn't become a multi-millionaire confided that he was deeply depressed because he felt it was already over for him.

Many collectors may not care whether the artists they collect are rich or poor, but they do care about the way they talk. A Harvard *summa* friend told me that he'd just bought a work in a gallery when the artist wandered in. He asked some questions about the work, and the artist's answers were such drivel, he nearly cancelled his purchase. After that, he vowed to skip any meet and greets with artists. Maybe he was wise, but I think he was unrealistic. You don't expect a quarterback who can throw a 65-yard pass to quote Shakespeare, do you? So why expect an artist to be eloquent? The work speaks *for* him. As poet and artist Jean Cocteau famously said, "An artist cannot talk about his art any more than a plant can discuss horticulture."

On the other hand, plenty of artists are splendid talkers and writers. David Hockney has given superb lectures, and his close friend, Ron Kitaj, was asked by the Tate to write the wall text for his 1994 retrospective. The critics lambasted Kitaj on the grounds that his descriptions were too dense, but his work *is* dense, so what'd they expect? I know many museums are doing away with texts on the basis that they're obtrusive. I like them, and I wish more museums and galleries would display labels with the artist's own observations. Wouldn't it be great if we had Leonardo's own musings on the *Mona Lisa*? We wouldn't have had centuries of conjecture about who she is (the latest has it she's a Chinese slave) or why she's smiling (she's wearing clothes worn by pregnant women). Institutions, such as the Smithsonian's Archives of American Art, the Museum of Modern Art in New York (MoMA), and the Getty in Los Angeles, are recording oral histories and videos and preserving papers of living artists. They're marvelous ways for us to learn what artists were thinking when they created their works.

Of course, there's no greater way to learn about the creative process than visiting an artist's studio. But how do you get in? Advisors and dealers regularly take collectors, art tour companies provide access, and museums arrange visits for their supporters. A studio visit can be an eye-opening, mind-expanding experience. In fact, talking to artists about their work, in front of the work, is one of the great perks that comes with an involvement in contemporary art. And, if the artist lives where he works, and you're a lifestyle queen and love to see the way other people live, as I am, the voyeuristic pleasure is irresistible. Of course, I admit that ogling Julian Schnabel's in-bedroom bathtub isn't reason enough for a studio visit, but it's certainly memorable.

Don't be disappointed if the studios you visit don't resemble those you've seen pictured in books — ateliers with standing pointy easels and platforms covered with oriental rugs. Times have changed. The once essential large windows with northern exposure that provided coveted cool light, found in the double height studio apartments in the Hotel des Artistes and along West 67th Street in New York, are no longer of interest to most artists.

Artists used to be studio-centric, and the physical constraints of the studio impacted the work produced, if for no other reason than size. The rabbit warren of small rooms in the San Francisco house Wayne Thiebaud transformed into one of his studios was the perfect environment for him to produce intimate scale still life paintings, while Willem de Kooning's airplane-hangar-sized studio in Long Island enabled him to paint large-scale. But the art most artists produce today no longer draws on what goes on within the studio's four walls or its environs as it did for Picasso and Matisse. If you visit Doug Aitken's studio in a string of Venice, California houses, you'll find room after room of assistants working on computers creating videos and photos. They could be anywhere.

One day, when I was a graduate student, I took a group of out-of-towners to Hannah Wilke's second-story SoHo loft. Wilke, a feminist artist, regularly used her body as the subject of her work, and that day, as we entered her studio, she passed out sticks of gum, which she asked everyone to chew and spit into a large bowl. Then, as I recall, Hannah created a work by sculpting the wads into tiny vaginal shapes and sticking them at random onto a large photo of herself, nude. We all sat, totally entranced. At the end of our visit, a woman pulled me aside and whispered, "She can't be a good artist." I braced myself for a harangue about Hannah's X-rated subject. Instead, she pointed to the ceiling and frowned, "No skylight. Everybody knows that important artists have skylights."

Most artists without gallery representation try hard to accommodate visitors, as selling to them is their lifeblood. In 2003, when collectors Don and Mera Rubell bought out the studio of Nate Lowman before he became hot, the $20,000 they paid him enabled him to give up his day job and devote full-time to painting. Similarly, when a client of ours bought two paintings on a studio visit, the artist wept, explaining that the money would enable him to buy a plane ticket home to Alabama to see his ailing mother.

Once, I took Jackie Onassis, hiding behind dark glasses, and her longtime companion, Maurice Tempelsman, to an artist's studio. When I introduced them to the artist, he was so anxious that a sale could be looming, he paid no attention. While Jackie and Maurice looked at the work, the artist cornered me in the kitchen. "That woman looks so familiar. Is she a big collector?" When I told him who she was, he turned, and, without a word, opened the fridge, pulled out a beer and chugged it down. It was ten am.

If you *do* manage to get in the door, you have to assess the work you see. You may instantly connect with it, but you'll want to figure out if it's just appealing or really good, if the artist is just going over familiar turf and doing it well, or whether he's pushed the limits beyond what anyone else has done. Here are a few questions to ask:

1. *What were you thinking about when you made this?*

2. *What were your goals in creating this body of work?*

3. *What got you started on this series?*

4. *What was your earlier work like?* (Ask to see some or photos to better understand the roots of the current body of work.)

5. *In what direction do you see your work going?*

6. *Which artists have influenced you?*

7. *In what ways do you think you've pushed the envelope?*

No matter how many questions you ask, sooner or later, the artist is going to have one for you, "What do you think of my work?" At least, he'll expect a reaction that signals positive reinforcement. That can be sticky if you dislike it. If that happens, let me share a few useful "compliments" I've learned from my husband, Bert, a Hollywood lawyer, who's sat through many disappointing films made by or starring his clients. "It's *you*," is one of his favorites, or, "You've done it again!" But these work only if you know the artist. If you don't, try "The work is so powerful, I haven't had time to properly take it in yet." The thing is, that's probably true.

If you want to buy something you see, that's great. But if you want something in a specific size or color range and start talking about a commission, it could mean trouble. The artist may feel he's being asked to compromise his integrity for money.

An older, more commercial abstract painter told me that fifty years ago, when he was starting out, he took a cynical approach. If a collector was looking for a work that's smaller, bigger, more this color or that, the artist would say, "Funny, I just finished one exactly like that. It's out being framed, and I can send it to you on approval when it gets back." Then of course, he rushed to paint one. At least, it was his choice.

With any luck, you buy something that increases in value tenfold. If you sell, please be aware that the artist may not be thrilled about the profit you'll be pocketing on his work. The 1973 Sotheby Parke-Bernet auction of works from Robert and Ethel Scull's Pop Art collection was a watershed moment in that regard. Throngs of people attended to witness the first commercial success of Pop Art, a total of $2,242,900, a staggering sum in those days. John Schott and E.J. Vaughn, documentarians shooting *America's Pop Collector: Robert C. Scull—Contemporary Art At Auction*, caught Robert Rauschenberg in the salesroom after the sale railing at Robert Scull over the price he got for the artist's *Double Feature*. Scull had bought it for $2,300, and it sold for $90,000. "I've been working my ass off just for you to make that profit," an inebriated

Rauschenberg snarled at Scull, who snapped back that he'd made Rauschenberg rich by making the world aware of the artist's worth. And it wasn't just Rauschenberg who took Scull to task. Protestors and critics, including Barbara Rose, who wrote a scathing piece in *New York* magazine, "*Profit Without Honor*," criticized the Sculls' unabashed, crass efforts to make a profit and catapult themselves into the social limelight by buying and selling contemporary art. Certainly, Rauschenberg knew that paintings were bought and sold. He could have taken the risk of holding the work rather than taking Scull's money. Scull took the risk Rauschenberg wasn't willing to take, and it paid off. Rauschenberg had no right to be angry and neither did Rose. What was considered "dishonorable" then, using art collecting for social gain and profit, is totally acceptable today.

Subsequently, Rauschenberg spearheaded an effort for artists to get a 'piece of the action' on re-sales. England and the EU countries have an artists' resale rights law, called the *droit de suite*, which, like copyright laws for books and songs, mandates that when a work is resold, the seller must pay the artist or the artist's heirs a percentage of the sale on a sliding scale which maxes at 4%, capped at 12,500 euros. California had a similar law, struck down in 2012, that mandated that 5% of the gross sale of 'fine art' by a resident of California go to artists or artists' estates. It narrowly defined 'fine art' as "painting, sculpture, or drawing, or an original work of art in glass," which ridiculously excluded photography and other media. Did that mean that Mark Bradford, the painter, should get royalties but not Bill Viola, the renowned video artist? But what would happen if an artist's work goes down in value? Why wouldn't the artist have to recompense the collector for 5% of his losses? The law also based the artists' royalties on the gross sales price, which seems crazy. If you bought a work for $95 and sold it for $100, the artist would get the entire $5 profit. What about interest and shipping and other costs? The law didn't stand because the District Court determined that it tried to control sales out of the state. Other states are studying similar legislation, but they should profit from California's mistakes. Those against a law argue that art is chattel, free to be bought and sold. But if you buy the argument in favor of artists receiving a percentage of resale profits, what would be useful is an organization that does for artists what ASCAP does for composers — keeps track of the transactions and collects and distributes royalties.

In the end, artists are like the rest of us — some cranky, others inarticulate, loquacious, charming, or all of the above in turns. Caravaggio committed murder (maybe twice), and Rembrandt stole his wife's dowry, but those things don't affect our appreciation of their works. As W.H. Auden wrote in his elegy to W.B. Yeats, "You were silly like us; your gift survived it *all*."

DEALERS

When you're acquiring art, galleries will likely be your first port of call. There's a plethora to choose from, all free to enter and browse. According to recent statistics, there are close to 400,000 galleries worldwide, although only a small fraction is responsible for most of the dollar volume of art sold. And the dealers who run them are as varied a lot as the galleries and what they show. Some operate splashy public spaces with changing exhibitions and scheduled viewing hours. Others, called 'private dealers,' conduct business out of apartments or offices, receiving clients by appointment only. Some dealers specialize in works by artists who've been dead hundreds of years, while others focus on art that's existed only a few weeks. Some are naughty. Others are nice. But we'll get to that later.

When I was in grad school, exploring careers, I asked Serge Sabarsky, a German Expressionist art dealer and co-founder of the Neue Galerie in New York, how I could become an art dealer. "It's easy," he said, "Go to Hutton, my competitor. Get a painting and bring it to me. If I buy it, you're an art dealer." If only it were that simple. Still, Serge was telling me the basics of art dealing; there are no rules. In fact, it's like the Wild West, and collectors must learn to tell the Good Guys from the Bad Guys — those who know what they're doing from those who don't, those who are straight shooters from those who aren't. Fortunately, the good guys are in the majority. In this chapter, I'll explain what art dealers do, how they do it, what they can do *for* you, and what they might do *to* you if you're not quick enough on the draw.

All belong to a profession unlike any other. Multimillion-dollar transactions take place, yet, there are no tests to pass, no educational requirements for joining the ranks. Dealers need no license to practice, and there are no industry standards policed by a higher authority like the Bar Association or the AMA. As a result, some dealers are highly educated and have tremendous expertise, whereas others know little and are flying by the seat of their pants. Iwan Wirth, who owns the gallery Hauser & Wirth, described the situation to Dodie Kazanjian in *Vogue*,

> *The best thing about the art market is that it's unstructured and unregulatable.... Things that would put you in jail in another industry are not bad in this wonderful world.*

As long as there's been art, there've been art dealers. When the first caveman scratched a design on a gourd, his brother-in-law probably traded it to a neighbor for a side of mastodon. According to Pliny, there was a great demand for "luxury goods," and the desire of Romans to own Greek art fueled a healthy interplay between dealers and collectors. Even in Medieval times, someone had to purvey all of those ivories and reliquaries to kings and nobles. And by the Renaissance, plenty of art was being commissioned, including frescoes and tomb sculpture for churches, but because much of it was site-specific, there wasn't a significant resale market. That changed, especially when a resurgence of interest in Greek and Roman culture in the 15th century created a secondary market for antiquities.

After the Sack of Rome in 1527, the subsequent economic decline in Italy boosted the art market, with artists acting as intermediaries/dealers between poor Italians and the wealthy north of the Alps. Vasari's book *Lives of the Artists*, published in the mid-1500s, also invigorated the market. Its dramatic description of Michelangelo and others helped popularize the idea of the artist as genius, replacing the "anonymous craftsman" who'd supplied most of the art made for churches to date. That gave the dealers the ability to market personalities and sell "hot" names to clients across Europe, such as Charles I and Philip II of Spain.

In 17th-century Holland, a new middle class passed up overtly religious art in favor of small-scale landscapes, genre, and still lifes for their homes. They loved paintings and treated them like furniture, hoping that they'd increase in value over time. During the so-called Golden Age of Dutch painting, it's estimated that between 5 and 10 million paintings were created, and dealers happily supplied collector/speculators with works by artists such as Frans Hals and Pieter de Hooch, who they hoped would 'hit the big time.' Meanwhile, the French cleverly developed an export business for tapestries, furniture and silver.

A hundred years later, in Venice, dealers lay in wait for wealthy Brits on the Grand Tour and sold them the obligatory Renaissance drawings, some forged, the ubiquitous *vedute* (views) by Canaletto, some also forged, and cheaper look-a-likes by minor artists we see on the walls of stately British homes.

Stateside, dealing hit its stride in the late 19th and early 20th centuries. America's new millionaires, such as Henry Clay Frick and J.P. Morgan, craved the appearance of 'old money,' and the great dealer Sir Joseph Duveen raided the houses of impoverished European aristocrats to provide them with the essentials. The titans competed shamelessly for the old masters that Duveen dangled before them, squabbling over the Rembrandts and Gainsboroughs that greased their entrée into high society. Meanwhile, more avant-garde American collectors, like Henry and Louisine Havemeyer and, later, Walter and Louise Arensberg, looked to a new breed of advisors and dealers to supply them with the avant-garde Impressionist and Cubist works they favored.

Today, every big city boasts a long list of dealers in a variety of fields, and it helps to know that some cities specialize in particular areas. London is the epicenter of the old master painting market, Beijing is ground zero for contemporary Chinese art, and New York is the mecca for contemporary art. Not that the Big Apple isn't equipped to serve collectors in other fields. The capital of American commerce is also the capital of art dealing in almost every area. And while its riches may seem daunting and its gallery scene labyrinthine, it's actually surprisingly easy to navigate.

Here's a thumbnail map of the New York action. Simply put, the further downtown you go, the newer the art. Galleries uptown, from 60th Street to 80th Street, on or near Madison Avenue, generally show antiquities, Medieval Art, old masters, Impressionism, and classic 20th-century masters. A few high-end contemporary art galleries are mixed in, with more along 57th Street, between Sixth and Park Avenues. Chelsea, a several-block area on the West Side, between 17th and 27th Streets and 10th and 11th Avenues, is the largest arts district in the city, filled with galleries principally showing mid-career and emerging artists. And lower-priced, extreme cutting-edge art is sold out of storefront galleries on the Lower East Side, the Bowery, and in the outer boroughs, like Brooklyn's Williamsburg, Bushwick, and Red Hook neighborhoods.

Wherever you go, gallery décor sets the stage for the art. Galleries offering old master and 19th-century art frequently occupy opulent period townhouses decorated with antique furniture and brocade wall coverings. Dealers create this old world/establishment look because it suits the paintings (the dark walls makes paintings in elaborate gold frames 'pop') and delivers the clear message, "Collecting this kind of art is a classy thing to do."

Contemporary art galleries, on the other hand, generally present as stark white boxes, to the point that a well-known London gallery calls itself "White Cube." Typically, these galleries have cement or wood floors, little or no furniture, and are so sterile-looking they could double as operating rooms. This look says, "It's the art, stupid," and, "We're not so mired in the useless past that we have to obscure our works' visual power with decoration."

Isabel Wilkinson, in a *Daily Beast* article, questioned how much of our appreciation of art relies on context. You could see works in a grungy studio and not like them, but if the same works were hanging in a plush gallery or museum, beautifully lit, you'd be more likely to give them a chance. Remember when Joshua Bell, the famed violinist, played on a Washington, D.C. subway platform with an open violin case on the ground to collect donations? Music lovers pay hundreds of dollars a ticket to hear him at Carnegie Hall, but in the subway, most everyone rushed by save a few who paused, and only one person recognized him. Banksy made the same point when he set up a table in a lineup of other vendors on the edge of Central Park. He stocked his stand with paintings worth hundreds of thousands of dollars and had an older gentleman sell them for $60 apiece. Even with discounts, the man sold only eight all day and grossed $420.

Gallery décor does more than predispose us to like specific works. Whether galleries are decorated in over-the-top velvets or painted flat industrial white, they're telegraphing the message that communing with art is an uplifting, spiritual experience. Just as 15th-century French peasants got a bracing shot of awe when they left the sun-lit fields and entered the dark, majestic cathedral in Chartres, visitors to galleries are provided with a soothing escape from the hustle and bustle of big city life. What better place to take a deep breath and relax than the sheltered sanctum of an art gallery hung with transporting works of art? And dealers are careful not to break the spell by even hinting that the works are for sale. There are no cash registers, price tags, or other signs of commerce. If works are sold, galleries eschew putting red dots on the wall as they once did. Although they're mandated by law to make price lists available, they're usually inconspicuously placed on the front desk, and you have to ask receptionists to see one. And have you noticed that receptionists are invariably dressed in black — like clerics?

Those receptionists are the first staff members you'll encounter and the gallery's first line of defense. Whether the gallery is selling Rubens or Rauschenberg, the reception desk is usually manned by young, good-looking, well-dressed women (and men) that Danielle Ganek calls "gallerinas" in her art world send up *Lulu Meets God and Doubts Him*. Most generate cooler-than-thou vibes and barely give you the time of day. It may be because gallerists want to convey an elitist air, but I don't blame them if they're just plain bored, answering phones, sorting mail, and tactfully fending off lookie-loos all day. Imagine how often they must have to direct people to the nearest restroom. Their plight reminds me of that dreadful joke about the guy shoveling elephant dung in a circus. When asked why he doesn't quit, he answers, "What? And leave show business?" Overeducated and underpaid, many gallery assistants do it because they love being at the center of creativity and/or hope to learn the ropes and become dealers themselves.

If receptionists barely look up when you enter, it can be a good thing if all you want to do is enjoy the exhibition in peace and quiet. But what if you want to buy? A lovely Texas couple became clients of ours after a receptionist gave them the cold shoulder. They walked into a gallery, fell in love with a Lichtenstein hanging on the wall and wanted to buy it. When they asked the price, the receptionist ignored them, and the couple left empty-handed. Remember how Julia Roberts' character in *Pretty Woman* told off the snotty Rodeo Drive salesperson who snubbed her, "BIG mistake...BIG...HUGE"? Same thing. The couple called us, and we helped them build a major collection that put them on every art magazine's list of 100 Top Collectors. But the gallery that had the Lichtenstein isn't one they'll patronize.

If a receptionist senses you could be a buyer or recognizes you or your name, he buzzes a salesperson, director, or the gallery owner who comes out and walks you around the show. Most gallerists are quick studies. If they don't know you, they'll engage you in what may seem like idle chatter, asking questions like, "Where do you spend your summers?" "What country club do you belong to?" and "Do you know so-and-so?" Those questions are designed to help them quickly assess your taste and spending power. Accordingly, they'll tell you that they have something 'special' for you to see and usher you into a private viewing room, what old-time dealers called a 'sting room.' Viewing rooms are intimate, pleasant spaces, simply appointed with a sofa, coffee table, and a couple of chairs. There may be an empty velvet easel, which looks rather like a *prie-dieu* (that's right, a kneeling bench in church), and the walls are pictureless so that no other art distracts you from what the dealer wants you to focus on. Once you're comfortably seated, handlers wearing white gloves to avoid marring the painting's surface will materialize out of a backroom and silently place a painting on the easel or hang it on the wall.

Since a first impression can make or break a sale, dealers go to great lengths to make sure it's a jaw-dropping experience. Older paintings are shown cleaned, well framed, and at the perfect height against a flattering, neutral background. Some dealers use sophisticated combinations of pink and white lights that can be dimmed, depending on the 'needs' of the work being shown. Before he retired, Ira Spanierman, an

American art dealer, experimented with the lighting of every new painting that entered his inventory. When he got it right, handlers would tape lighting instructions to the side of the frames. That way, they could turn on the optimum wattage before the painting was brought into the viewing room, and it would look perfect the minute the client laid eyes on it. You could have almost heard the silent, "Ta Da!!!" as the works were set down.

Of course, as frequently happens, all these theatrics are in vain. You may take one look at the painting... and hate it. No worries. If it's not for you, just say so politely. Don't waste your time or the dealer's. He'll invariably have other works for you to consider, and, if you're lucky, he'll show you something you love. When that happens, the atmosphere changes. You may ask a few questions about the work, but they're usually preludes to finding out the price. Instead of asking, "How much is it?" savvy collectors use the more nuanced, "What are you asking?" That sends the message that they presume the price is negotiable. If the dealer answers, "I'm asking X," that translates as, "Make an offer." If the price is in the collector's ballpark, the chitchat will cease, and a focused conversation between the dealer and buyer begins.

Below are a few questions you, as a buyer, may pose to a seller:

1. Ask for a photo of the work, a "doc sheet" which lists provenance, literature, and exhibition history,

and other documents he may have, including letters of authenticity, bills of sale, and a condition report describing damages and/or repairs.

2. Ask the dealer to see other works by the artist he may have, photos of similar works they sold, and ask what prices they sold for. Think of it like asking your realtor for comps on a house you're considering (I discuss this in my *Due Diligence* chapter, under *Price and Negotiation*).

3. If the work is on the "secondary market" (a resale), ask if it's come up at auction and whether he owns it or has it on consignment.

4. Ask how the work fits into the artist's oeuvre.

5. Ask which artists have influenced the artist and which artists he's influenced.

Although you may not get definitive answers, and you'll have to do your own research, listen carefully to the dealer's responses. They'll enable you to better understand the work, the artist, the dealer's relationship with the work, why the dealer's asking what he's asking, and how flexible he'll be in negotiating. Some dealers offer full disclosure and will tell you that a work you're considering is on consignment, went to an art fair, didn't sell, etc. Others say very little and don't feel that they have any responsibility to tell you they bought it six months ago at a small auction in Italy for half of what they're asking. Remember; the dealer's not there to teach you Art History 101. No matter how honest he is, almost everything he does and says is a seduction, calculated to get you to buy the work for as close to his asking price as possible. And everything you're experiencing is 'the sell.'

As a colleague once chided me, "Paintings don't sell paintings, people do." Unlike jewelry or cars, here the 'product' is a piece of canvas with paint on it. It has none of the intrinsic value of gold or silver and has little usefulness. You can't live in it, yet its price can be more than a house or the GNP of a small country. Obviously, works by proven artists who've found a place in art history have recognized value and market performance. But to make a sale, whether the artist is young or fabled, the dealer must stir the passions of the buyer by invoking hard-to-quantify qualities like importance, the prestige of ownership, and investment potential. No one did it better than Ira Spanierman, who literally sold a houseful of paintings to a blind man. The man, who had once had sight, kept buying from Ira because Ira could evoke a scene and stir passions about art better than just about anyone else in the field.

Dealers may position themselves in any number of ways. They can be, like Ira, interpreters of the art, pioneers in the field, discoverers of talent, or idealists. And depending, their "sell" can take many forms. Some dealers will fold their arms, stare at the painting and say almost nothing. They're sending the message that explanations are unnecessary for masterpieces like the one you're looking at and that you're clearly unworthy of it if you don't agree to buy it on the spot. The late Leo Castelli was a man of few words, especially when he showed clients work in an artist's studio. The artist would bring out several works for them to see, and, if the client asked Leo which one he liked, Castelli would say, "You tell me what *you* think." Whichever work the client pointed to, Castelli would smile and nod approvingly at the client's wonderful eye. "Yes," he'd say, "*That's* the one." Like all dealers, he wanted to make the sale.

Today, serious dealers of the caliber of Castelli don't "sell" at all. They believe that they're responsible for the way the world perceives art and their artists. As gatekeepers for their artists, they want to work with collectors who'll create important collections and play a role as a conduit between their artists and the collectors' communities. They don't want to sell to clients who are buying to decorate their house or wanting "investment art." So, please be aware, especially when you're starting out as a collector, of your obligations as a collector. Dealers are interviewing you as a custodian of their artists' works, and getting yourself accepted can be harder than getting your child into private school. At Art Basel Miami in 2014, Hauser & Wirth brought two Mark Bradford paintings. Collectors who inquired were told that they were taking names for an "interest" list. They were looking for the "right" collector who'd buy two at $850,000 each (the first with a 10% discount and the second with 20%), keep the first, and give the second to the "right" institution in the "right" community.

On the other hand, some dealers use some pretty standard sales techniques. They refer to every work they sell as a "masterpiece," suggesting that the art establishment is aware of the object's greatness. That's overworked, to say the least. Others barely draw breath describing the art, artist, and anything they can think of until it sounds as if they live and breathe for art — and they probably do — and that making money doesn't interest them. It doesn't mean that they're phonies, but sitting through their endless litany can be tedious, when you're already convinced and just want to know the price. It reminds me of the famous interaction between Samuel Goldwyn, the legendary film producer, and George Bernard Shaw. Goldwyn, who wanted to get the rights to George Bernard Shaw's plays, spent several hours impressing Shaw with the idea that he was motivated by art. Finally, Shaw responded, "Well, Mr. Goldwyn, there is not much use going on. There is a difference between you and me: You are only interested in art and I am only interested in money."

If you're considering a work on the secondary market and think it might be 'the one,' there's serious work ahead. Your advisor or you will do whatever due diligence that seems necessary. While you're still in the gallery, however, take the opportunity to carefully look at the painting. Use the condition report the gallery gives you as a guide, knowing that if you're spending a significant sum, you'll have to have your own conservator examine it later. Ask to see the painting in daylight — the way you'll be seeing it at home, away from the flattering lighting in the gallery. You might be able to see damages or repairs you didn't see under artificial lighting. Then ask to see it in a darkened room under a black light — an ultra-violet bulb, the kind used to grow marijuana — which causes changes and repairs typically made after the artist varnished the work to fluoresce. Later, after your conservator examines the work, he'll explain any problems and treatment. Also turn the painting around and snap an iPhone photo of the back so you can look more closely at the labels and other markings when you get home.

For primary market works, those that have never sold before and come directly from the artist or the artist's gallery, there's no due diligence necessary. There's no provenance, no literature or exhibition history, and you don't have to worry about condition. And there's not much you can do about determining or negotiating the cost of a painting on the primary market. Paintings are usually priced by size, with larger paintings more expensive than smaller ones. What you must do, however, is to pick the best of the artist, as later, when works hit the secondary market, the works that are better sell for more, regardless of size.

The dealer and artist split the sale price in an agreed-upon ratio, depending upon which one of them is more important to the relationship. Early in an artist's career, the dealer is in the driver's seat, typically taking 50-60%

of the sale price. As the artist becomes more successful, the ratio tilts in his favor. At the time Richard Prince was sued by a photographer for appropriating his photos of Rastafarians for a series of million dollar paintings, court filings revealed that Prince was receiving 60% and his gallery, Gagosian, 40%. I've heard that Damien Hirst in his heyday squeezed his galleries down to a 20% share.

What about discounts? There was a time when anyone could walk into a gallery cold and get a hefty percentage off any work. That's no longer the case. Typically, 10-20% is pretty standard, but if an artist is hot, dealers may not discount the work or they'll reserve discounts for a small circle of gallery regulars, advisors, big collectors, museums, and museum trustees. Whereas befriending dealers — inviting them to dinner, weekends at your beach house, or vacations on your yacht — used to be the way collectors got bigger discounts, today's collectors charm dealers hoping to jump the line for the gallery's next hot artist or the next great resale work that comes into the gallery.

Before you start fuming about paying full freight, consider the expenses dealers bear out of their share of sales — rent, staff, phone, utilities, framing, shipping, insurance, installation, ads, mailings, website, entertaining, and travel. And don't forget that dealers pay over $100,000 a pop to participate in art fairs. That's why some dealers live on the edge and rely on profits they make selling more expensive resale (secondary market) works from their back rooms to make their businesses work.

Aside from a staggering financial commitment, being a gallerist requires a tremendous commitment of time and energy. Finding the right artists to represent, handling them, placing work in museums, courting collectors, and hunting for and selling secondary material is a 24/7 occupation. It's more like taking the veil than a job.

Because the competition between dealers to attract clients and the right artists to their stable is so tremendous, dealers must constantly think up creative ways to brand themselves. Sometimes, a single show can put a gallery on the map. White Cube was already well known when it installed Hirst's *For the Love of God* (the diamond skull) in 2007, but the show catapulted the gallery into the center of that season's cultural conversation. As well, Hirst became more famous than ever, and the royal jewelers, Bentley & Skinner on Bond Street, got to put a sign in their window announcing to the world that they had sold Hirst the diamonds he used.

Dealers of secondary market material also look to brand themselves. Julius Weitzner, a leading old master dealer for over fifty years, quietly conducted business from a house off Berkeley Square in London. He held salons several afternoons a week where, over cocktails and finger sandwiches served by a waiter in a white jacket, he'd discuss art with clients, colleagues, scholars, and curators. Especially on the days leading up to old master sales when the *cognoscenti* were in town from all over, he'd pick up 'insider' information, such as which works catalogued as "attributed to" were actually by the hand of a master, partner-up with other dealers, buy at the sales, sell, and turn a handsome profit.

Some dealers, in an effort to achieve an air of venerability, mount museum-quality exhibitions filled with loans from museums and private collections and curated by well-known scholars. The Braque show at Acquavella and the Monet show at Gagosian subliminally put the two galleries on a cultural par with The Met or MoMA and demonstrated their status, financial stability, and generosity to the public. Of course, dealers hope to sell the few things they may have for sale or can shake loose from lenders. But the real benefit is long-term; They become the go-to place for individuals wanting to buy or sell the artist's works.

Another way a dealer can get a lock on an established artist's market is by sponsoring the catalogue raisonné. That means underwriting an art historian or hiring a scholar and staff to do the work in-house. Being the clearinghouse for an artist's oeuvre ensures that the dealer will learn the comings and goings of every work by the artist in private hands. Like the galleries which hold museum-quality exhibitions, they become the obvious source for buyers or sellers of works by that artist. Preparing CRs is expensive and takes years, but dealers don't mind. They have no incentive to finish, since doing so might exclude some highly saleable works yet to be discovered or yet to come onto the market.

While professional tactics are crucial to a dealer's success, many feel that the way they dress is an effective sales tool. They believe that if their clients come to them for an aesthetic experience, the way they present themselves is a part of it. For a *New York Times* article, Ruth La Ferla interviewed gallerists who wear designer clothes or choose an offbeat hairdo or big glasses that becomes their trademark and increases their visibility at events.

In the current hot-as-a-firecracker primary market, a few dealers have become as great 'stars' as their 'star' artists. 'Star' dealers get to sell out shows "sight unseen" and decide who gets a work and who doesn't. By "placing" (upscale word for "selling") work in important collections and museums, they create demand and are able to raise prices. It's no different today than it was for Duveen. If a client bought a Rembrandt, he might have told friends he bought a 'Duveen.' Recently, when I asked a collector, "What was the last thing you bought?" he answered, "I just got something from Hauser & Wirth." This man clearly felt that his status as a client of a star gallery known for its seriousness and intellectual artists trumped any status conferred by owning a particular work.

The power of star dealers tends to self-perpetuate to the point that when they open an exhibition for an artist, according to Jed Perl in *The New Republic*, "[a] show has all the trappings of a coronation." And if the star dealer's next artist isn't the real McCoy, big clients may not know the difference or may not admit it. They may be too heavily invested in keeping the dealer in power. The phrase, "too big to fail" comes to mind.

Collectors who buy all their art through one dealer may get priority treatment, including first choice of works that become available at that gallery. The downside is that most gallery loyalists don't develop confidence in other dealers and might turn down the *Mona Lisa* if it was offered to them by anyone else. Certainly, they wouldn't buy it without getting 'their' dealer's blessing, and, too often, "dealers-in-charge" will try to kill sales from other dealers to their clients. Once when Duveen was asked by a client to come to his house to look at a religious painting another dealer offered him, he went, looked, and said, "Very nice dear fellow, very nice. But I suppose you are aware that those cherubs are homosexual." Dealers may also be afraid that the collector's dealer will move in on their secret sources so they won't offer such collectors works. As a collector once reasoned, "I'd rather be #2 on every dealer's list than #1 on one dealer's list and dismissed by others." No dealer minds, however, if a collector shows their works to an art advisor, and most dealers follow the protocol of offering works to a collector's advisor, who passes them along to the principal.

Dealers may be friends and buy works together as a way of spreading their capital and making works available to a bigger pool of potential buyers. It's also not uncommon for dealers to offer works belonging to other dealers to their clients. That means that there are two dealers between buyer and the seller. If three or more are involved, it's called a 'daisy chain.'

Dealers in secondary market material are under pressure from the competition of other dealers and the auction houses in taking advantage of the 3Ds — death, divorce, and debt. Remember the truism, "Where there's an undertaker there's an opportunity"? Duveen had moles in the household staffs of the very rich, so that he'd be the first to know when a collector was ill or dying. Today, dealers and auction houses shamelessly troll the obituaries and are in constant contact with trust and estate lawyers.

A rather unscrupulous dealer I know calls the family of the deceased, and, pretending not to have heard the sad news, asks for the person who died. Told by the survivor that his/her spouse has just died, he apologizes and explains that the deceased had called a few weeks earlier to discuss selling a particular painting in their collection. The grieving spouse, in a weakened state, often jumps to the conclusion that if his/her lost love had wanted to sell the painting through this dealer, that's what ought to be done.

Ira Spanierman took a unique approach in finding material. One summer, he rented a house in rural

Connecticut, which surprised me because Ira hated the country. On the only night I went out to the house for dinner, he was miserable, brandishing a fly swatter wherever he went. Nevertheless, he spent every weekend driving around looking at houses for sale. One day, he called to tell me that he'd bought one. I thought he'd gone crazy — crazy like a fox, it turned out. The house came furnished with a superb collection of saleable Hudson River landscape paintings, which he cleaned, reframed, and sold for as much as he paid for the house. Then he sold the house for a small profit and never spent another night in Connecticut.

Some dealers make "cold calls" to collectors they may or may not know to get paintings out of them. There's nothing wrong with that. But sometimes, they offer more money than a painting is worth and have no intention of getting the owner an over-the-moon price. It's a form of "bait and switch." Once they pry the work loose on consignment and it's out of the owner's house, they figure that the owner will become less attached and soften on his price. Meanwhile, the dealer calls potential buyers until he gets an offer, often substantially lower than what he told the owner he could get. After considerable back and forth, getting the seller down and buyer up, misleading both sides, the dealer may strike a deal.

Old master dealers do what other dealers do to get material, but they also do something different and special — they make attributions. They buy dirty, unsigned or misattributed paintings in auctions, out-of-the-way galleries, antique shops, and from a network of "runners" who find old paintings in small towns and sell them to city dealers. OM dealers can look at a work and instantaneously compute its identity — country, period, city, the artist who painted it, and whether it's autographed (by the hand of the artist), school of, circle of, or a period or late copy. To them, the way the brushwork, the style, or the subject is handled distinguishes one artist from another the way handwriting distinguishes individuals. Even if dealers aren't sure of the attribution but feel that a work is by "somebody" good, they buy it. Cleaning it, if it's dirty, often leads to disappointment. But if it still looks promising, they'll research it, come up with the name of an artist, and ultimately try to get the reigning expert on that artist to accept their discovery.

Some discoveries are made by accident. When the late London dealer Edward Speelman was starting out, he had so little success that he decided to spend a last weekend in Brighton before changing careers. He stayed in a rooming house, and in the hall to the bathroom were two drawings he immediately recognized as being by Rubens. He bought them inexpensively from the proprietor, and his career was re-launched. Speelman became a major dealer, but for the rest of his life, he was called "Lucky Eddy" by friends who knew him back when.

Like Speelman, London dealer Derek Johns has made numerous discoveries in his long career. Once, while vacationing in Malindi (Kenya), he went into a sweet shop looking for tobacco. The owner said he'd order some, so Johns went round to the back of the cabin to write his name and contact information. Pinned to the inside of the door was a full-length portrait of a man in Arabic costume, complete with a jewel-encrusted sword hilt and scabbard. Johns bought the portrait and tobacco in a package deal. Back in London, he worked out that the portrait was of the Wahli of Zanzibar, the grandfather of the then Sultan of Oman, to whom Johns sold the portrait. As Derek says, "Smoking can damage your health, but can improve profitability."

Other discoveries are made by a special breed of "hunters" who've anchored their careers by looking for works that have fallen out of the literature or are listed in the CR as "whereabouts unknown." For a series of articles written between 1929 and 1932, published posthumously as a book, *Homeless Paintings of the Renaissance*, in 1969, Berenson assembled photos of missing works hoping to get owners to come forward and make their works available to scholars and the public. It sent plenty of hunters searching. When I was in graduate school, a friend took me to meet one, Tommy Grange, in his Eaton Square apartment/office. At that time, I didn't understand Grange's business model and was perplexed that he had nothing there to sell, nothing for us to even see. After we left, my friend explained how he worked. Living on Eaton Square, he obviously did it well.

Alain Tarica, a Paris dealer, had his own special twist on ferreting out works. In the backs of some CRs, scholars list works no longer accepted as being by the artist. Tarica understood that scholars make mistakes, so he'd pore through that section and, if he thought a painting had a chance of being 'right,' he'd track down the current owner, who was probably only too happy to offload his "worthless" painting on Alain — for very little. Tarica would do the research necessary to prove that the painting was right and then present his case to the expert, often the same person who compiled the CR. If he convinced the expert and got a letter of authenticity, Tarica was able to sell the painting at a handsome profit. Although Tarica made a lot of money that way, that wasn't why he did it. His real enjoyment came from outwitting the experts.

While finding and selling art are central to a dealer's career, dealers can often make money not selling. Unlike inventory in other businesses which depreciates over time, art generally does the opposite — it appreciates. If you're in the women's clothing business, and you're stuck with leftover dresses at the end the season, you have a sale to get rid of them. But if a work of art doesn't sell, and the dealer can afford to stash it away and wait, he may find years later that its value has risen enormously. There's an old saying: "Dealers make a living on what they sell and get rich on what they keep." That certainly was true for Ernst Beyeler and Heinz Berggruen, dealers in classic 20th-century European art. Both became extremely wealthy by holding important inventory. To their credit, each left a major collection to a museum. Unfortunately, inventory doesn't always go up. Dealers who filled their backrooms with run-of-the-mill American paintings or 19th-century European commercial paintings of cardinals in red robes have watched their markets flatten or erode.

Although dealers are important players in the art world, the old 'gallery-centric' system is changing, especially in the contemporary art sector. Although artists still want galleries to hold big exhibitions of their work, there are fewer collectors regularly out and about, like Si and Victoria Newhouse, who used to spend every Saturday religiously in the galleries. Some find that it's easier to buy at fairs and auctions than take the time to develop relationships with dealers. Galleries have to adjust their MO to this new event-driven art world, particularly by participating in more fairs.

Galleries also have to develop a stronger internet presence. Collectors all over the world can now cruise a gallery's inventory online. A Lower East Side gallery can sell to a collector in Bombay it's never heard of as easily as it can sell to someone who lives on Houston Street. One dealer told me that he's never even met his best client or spoken with him, and doesn't know his name or address. The client chooses tens of millions of dollars of Picassos a year from the dealer's website, has a lawyer in Chicago negotiate, draw up and sign the bills of sale, funds are transferred, and the paintings are shipped to a warehouse in Texas. Is the client laundering drug money, or is he just shy — or both?

I have mixed feeling about all this online action. Sites like Artsy, Artspace, Paddle 8, Saatchi Online, eBay, and Amazon offer outlets for dealers, artists without galleries, and collectors who are looking for an outlet to offload mistakes or unwanted works. Some of these websites even have iPhone apps which make it possible to buy art anywhere you can take a cell phone. I thought that the ones which advertise that they have an algorithm for finding the kind of work you like would be popular. On one, I filled in the blank, "If you love __________," with the name EGON SCHIELE and it came back, "Then you'll love MARGARET KEANE." I don't think so. Although there've been a number of reported sales for over $100,000, the companies target the under $15,000 market. So, in the grand scheme of things, no one is going to get too hurt.

The internet may be great for locating and researching works, but acquiring art from a digital image seems as unfulfilling as cyber-sex. That probably makes me a dinosaur, but how else can you feel that "zing" and know you've found the right one? By collecting over the net, you also lose the opportunity to interact with dealers and other art world players. To me, that's a shame, as they do so much more than sell. They add immeasurably to your store of knowledge and collecting experience.

So, troll the internet all you want but please take the time to create and nurture in-person relationships with interesting dealers. There's nothing like sitting in dealers' comfortable viewing rooms, and, under the soothing pink lights, enjoying their knowledge, patter, and the works on display.

AUCTION HOUSES

An Aladdin's Cave of endlessly replenished treasure, the auction house is the "department store" of the art world compared to the dealer's "boutique." It offers one-stop shopping plus anonymity. You can drop in, check out the goods, and hit the exit without anyone trying to sell you anything or speculating on your net worth. You feel 'at home' there. You've seen their salesrooms so often on the evening news ("Another painting brings a record price!") that their podia and electronic bid boards are as familiar as the set of *Modern Family*. Since every sale is conducted in public and every price appears to be the result of multiple bids, you feel you pay 'fair market value' for items you buy there and that auction purchases are safe purchases. If you're nodding along to all of this, wake up and smell the seduction. Auctions may be a great way to buy art, but only if you know what you're doing. If you don't, you can find yourself sliding off your own fiscal cliff before the auctioneer says

"Sold!" In this chapter, we'll go backstage at the auction house and look at some of the things that happen before, during, and after the sales. I guarantee that this "tour" will help you maneuver the salesrooms with finesse.

There are thousands of auction houses worldwide, but the two big kahunas, Christie's and Sotheby's, got their start in 18th-century England. A century later, they were selling the property of every land-rich, cash-poor duke and earl in the British Isles and beyond. At about the same time, the first generation of mega-collectors on this side of the Atlantic began to pass on, and new auction houses popped up in major cities across America to sell their estates.

By the early 20th century, New York City had half a dozen successful auction houses, but they bore little resemblance to the houses of today. Until the 1970s, they worked on a business-to-business model. Upcoming lots were hung in the salesrooms salon style, floor to ceiling, higgledy-piggledy. No attempt was made to clean or repair them, catalogues were little more than checklists, with few, if any photographs and, whether or not the works were signed, they were catalogued only as "school of" or "X century." Old master drawings were sold in bundles tied with string. The whole thing screamed, "Buyer beware," or, as my husband, Bert, would say, "Caveat emptor," pretentiously pronouncing the "v" as a "w."

Auction prices in those days had little to do with true 'value.' Few private collectors were bidding, and dealers would buy works inexpensively, clean and reframe them if required, and sell them on to collectors, making a good profit. Some dealers formed 'rings' to avoid bidding against each other and paying unnecessarily high prices. Participants in a ring would decide in advance which objects they wanted to go after, designate a person to bid, while the rest sat it out. After the sale, they'd hold a 'knock out,' a sort of round-robin auction amongst themselves, in which one dealer would wind up owning the object, and the others would get paid varying amounts as they dropped out. Although rings were illegal, the auction houses knew about them and turned a blind eye. I remember, after a sale at Sotheby's in LA in the 70s, a ring used Sotheby's conference room for its post-auction knockout. And a few years later, after a jewelry auction, the ring was so large that the dealers rented a hotel ballroom and hired an auctioneer to conduct a post-auction auction. Some experts and cataloguers at the houses weren't much better than ring members; they miscatalogued lots, calling authentic works copies and attributing works to lesser artists, so that they could buy them cheaply themselves. The plot of a 2013 film, *The Best Offer*, revolves around an auctioneer who built a secret collection that way.

By the 1980's, Sotheby's had taken over Parke-Bernet, the major New York auction house, Christie's had opened in New York, and both realized that, with a little effort, they could make the material collector-ready and sell directly to privates. By eliminating the middleman, the dealer, the houses could make bigger profits, *much* bigger profits. As more privates bought and prices increased, the rings lost their power, a few ringleaders went to jail, and fewer dealers could compete with privates. The modern auction era had arrived.

In 2013, the worldwide total of sales at auction was approximately $12 billion, a number that's growing annually. Yet, two sets of sales, the Impressionist and Modern Art and the post-war and contemporary art sales held twice a year in New York and in London, gross more money than all other sales combined and are considered 'bellwether' economic indicators. In May, 2015, Christie's contemporary art sales topped $1.5 billion.

Preparations for the big sales begin months before the auctioneer mounts the podium. Each house must lock in hundreds of millions of dollars worth of saleable art, which, contrary to popular belief, almost never walks in off the street. Of course, people do cart their goods in all the time, but they're usually toting worthless flea market finds or worthless family heirlooms they're convinced are extremely valuable. Staffers spend a lot of time examining this dreck and do their best letting the owners down gently. "Very decorative" is a phrase often used. Of course, discoveries do happen. During a routine valuation in Dorset, England, a local auctioneer told a couple that a Chinese vase they were using as an umbrella stand was worth $750,000. But that's unusual.

Most material that goes on the block comes from estates, collectors, and dealers, and there's vicious competition among the houses to get the best of it. Like dealers, auctions are on point for the 3Ds. An estate can make a house's season, and a single major painting can form the backbone of a sale and attract other consignments. So the major houses work every angle to attract fresh material at reasonable prices. House experts and business getters nurture relationships for decades, remembering birthdays and anniversaries of potential consignors. As the story goes, when Steven Murphy, who hadn't worked in the art field prior to his arrival as CEO of Christie's (he's no longer there), asked an expert how he got a particular collection for sale, the expert answered, "It's simple. I met the collector thirty years ago, wined and dined him ever since, and finally got the collection for sale."

With Sotheby's, Christie's, and Phillips locked in battle for market share in the contemporary art sector, there's a willingness on their part to sacrifice profitability by making tremendous financial concessions to consignors of important lots. I discuss this in my chapter *Exit Strategies*, but, in brief, the biggest draw for potential consignors is the guarantee (a pre-arranged minimum the house agrees to pay whether the bidding reaches that level or not). In volatile times with a changing market, most sellers, risk adverse, feel comfortable with a set minimum and are willing to give away some of the upside. The houses may do the guaranteeing, but since both majors lost a bundle on guarantees in the wake of the 2008 crash, they often bring in third-party guarantors (usually collectors or dealers) to offload the risk. For consignors without guarantees, the house suggests an estimate (a two-number range between which the house thinks the hammer will fall) and a reserve (the minimum amount the consignor agrees to accept). Depending on the importance of the item, they make other concessions, like waiving the seller's premium, the percentage of the hammer the seller pays the auction house. They also offer sellers of coveted lots an "enhanced hammer," a percentage of the "buyer's premium," the commission the house charges buyers on top of the hammer price. The buyer's commission is calculated on a sliding scale, which starts at the moment at 25% for lots that sell for $250,000 and under, to almost 15% for lots over $3,000,000. It's not uncommon for sellers of important works to receive an enhanced hammer of as much as 111%. The house can also waive buy-in fees consignors are supposed to pay if the work fails to meet the reserve. As a result, auction houses make a very small percentage on top lots and rely on the high volume of mid-range material in which they don't have to give away the seller's and buyer's premiums, as their bread and butter.

Sometimes, when the wooing is done and the financial packages offered by the top houses are almost indistinguishable, a consignor's choice of house boils down to a personality contest. A major Lichtenstein went to Sotheby's in 2012 when its owners heard that Christopher Burge, Christie's principal auctioneer, was retiring. They felt that since Christie's had no successor with the firepower of Burge, they were better off at Sotheby's. Ironically, Burge did take the podium for that sale. It was his swan song performance and the biggest-grossing post-war and contemporary art sale Christie's held to date. As for the Lichtenstein, it did fine at Sotheby's, selling over the $30-40,000,000 estimate, for close to $45 million. And speaking of Burge, when Billy Wilder, the film director, couldn't make up his mind which auction house to use, he chose Christie's because he could imagine Michael Caine playing Burge. But the choice can be totally random. When a Japanese collector with several paintings to sell found himself unable to select an auction house, he suggested that representatives from Sotheby's and Christie's play "Rock, Paper, Scissors" — winner take all. Nic Maclean, a Christie's expert at the time, remembered his young daughter saying, "Everyone knows, Daddy, you start with scissors," so he passed that advice along to his Japanese representative. The Christie's rep did what Nic's eleven-year-old suggested. Evidently, the Sotheby's expert went with paper, and since, "scissors cuts paper," Christie's won the game and the consignment — a Cézanne, an early Picasso, and a Van Gogh, worth more than $20 million.

Once the material is gathered, estimates and reserves established, and contracts signed, the house prepares a catalogue. That's no easy task. Although a sale revolves around its important lots, specialists try to structure it to appeal to a broad range of buyers. Showstoppers are great for media attention, gross sales figures, and attracting future consignments, but a sale filled with nothing but objects in the high eight figures would scare away a lot of potential bidders, especially beginners. So, like a Vegas show, most auctions lead off with an opening act — a few less expensive lots. The headliners come up further in the sale, when the audience is warmed up and the auctioneer has hit his stride.

Even so, contemporary art night sales are fast becoming too rich for many people's blood. As a collector I know laughed, after many years of buying in the night sales, "I guess I have Part One taste trapped in a Part Two body." Phillips seems to be filling the void with less expensive works that make buyers feel they can be in the game.

"Imp and Mod" and "Post-War and Contemporary" sales consist of two parts each, part one night sales, comprised of forty to sixty higher-priced lots, and part two, day sales, with several hundred low- and medium-priced lots.

The catalogues for the night sales usually describe each lot in a two-page spread. On the right is a full-page photo of the work and opposite is the information about it — the name of the artist, his dates, the name, date, size of the work, medium, and, if signed, where. Below is the provenance, literature, exhibition history, and lastly the estimate. Auction houses don't publish reserves, but they're somewhere between two-thirds low-estimate and low-estimate, which, by law, is the most they can be. That means, if a Matisse drawing has an estimate of "$1,000,000 - $1,500,000," the reserve is likely between $700,000 and $1,000,000.

Top lots have pages of essays tacked on, explaining the work's art historical significance. These essays don't talk about market, but make their appeal on the basis that the object is the kind of cultural icon that will go down in the history books. It's clever marketing, because most buyers who spend big money want to feel that they're getting something that matters to society long-term. Essays often include photos of the work in the artist's studio, sometimes with the artist standing next to it, reminding the buyer of the artist's celebrity status and the importance of the work to the artist. Photos of more famous works by the same artist or other well-known artists are included. I had to laugh, when, in a 2012 sale catalogue, a good, but not great Picasso was compared with a Duccio and, if you can imagine, the *Mona Lisa*! It reminded me of something Christie's Christopher Burge once told me. "Whatever you do, remember, we work for the seller."

If that isn't enough, catalogues often contain pages of photos and stories of the sellers, most of whom you've never heard of before. Invariably, they're portrayed as savvy collectors, philanthropists, and distinguished citizens. Why? It's a perk the house can offer the seller (Who doesn't want a day in the printed sun?). But how does a photo of a tanned owner in shorts standing on the deck of his yacht make someone want to buy his works? It's an implied warranty: if you buy, people will see you as one with the yachtsman in the picture. So, the catalogues keep getting thicker and heavier to the point that you can barely lift the damn things: pre-sale weight training is advised. Thank heaven the houses provide pocket versions to carry to the sales.

Once the catalogue is completed and printed, the house posts it online and sends hard copies to subscribers and good clients who are 'comped.' Before the sale, star lots travel to major cities worldwide to garner publicity and entice collectors who aren't inclined to travel to bid on the phone. House specialists call buyers on their "interest lists" to offer advice and bidding assistance and to urge them to view and bid. An ad for Christie's following their November 2013 sale boasted that Brett Gorvy, Chairman of its post-war and contemporary art Department, logged in 3400 hours on his cell phone (not including time spent on his office phone) talking to clients prior to the sale.

Several days before the auction, the sale goes on public view. Houses spare no expense for the installation — moving and repainting walls, adjusting lights, and hanging the works in the company of others in ways that make the sale look like an important museum show and every work 'institution-worthy.' On occasion, an artist will show up to make sure his work is installed to its best advantage. I've seen Schnabel at Sotheby's, and Koons once came to Christie's to inspect his bourbon-filled stainless steel Jim Beam sculpture before it went on the block. Now, he sends a studio assistant to polish works, should they need it.

During the several-day viewing, house experts work the floor to answer clients' questions and drum up interest. They're extremely knowledgeable about the items they're selling, and they're happy to opine on condition, rarity, quality, provenance, and investment potential. And if they tell you to stay away from this or that lot, you may be flattered, thinking that they care about *you*. Maybe they do, but they certainly will try to get you to bid on *some* lot — and bid high. After all, their job is to make as much money as possible for their consignors and themselves. The public wanders in and out, free of charge, and collectors walk through intently looking for something they can't live without. Jack Nicholson, who has a terrific collection of late 19th- and 20th-century art, told me that he loved going to pre-sale exhibitions where he waited for one great work to jump out at him from a sea of mediocrity.

Calling many of their employees "specialists," offering condition reports, and providing coffee table catalogues, are some of the ways the houses make you think that everything's transparent, has been vetted, and that you have no worries. All of that may be true sometimes, but you still have to do your due diligence as you would buying anywhere else. To begin with, since auction "specialists" are generalists and not scholars on particular artists, the veracity of information given cannot always be taken for granted. As for condition reports, since those provided by the house are commissioned by them (the seller), you should have your own done. That's particularly true for works on paper, as most condition reports for works on paper are done without taking the works out the frames. Once, in London, when I was checking out a Picasso in a Works on Paper sale for a client, I had the feeling it was a print and not a drawing as catalogued. I told the department head, who assured me I was overreacting and that the drawing came from "a fine English family." Maybe, but I asked the expert to take it out of the frame, and when he did, what that "fine English family" had hanging on their wall all those years was a print. Was the auction house trying to palm a print off as a drawing? Of course not, but they did have to withdraw the work from the sale. Staffers are so busy cataloguing hundreds of items in rapid succession that mistakes in authenticity, provenance, literature and exhibition history are made. Most are minor and have no impact, like listing a wrong date or omitting an entry in the literature, but some errors can be serious.

When your advisor or you have completed your due diligence and determined the right price to pay (turn to the chapter section on *Price and Negotiation*), don't be surprised if that number is less or more than the estimate listed in the catalogue. An estimate is supposed to reflect the experts' opinion of the work's fair market value, but often that's not the case. If the material comes from a consignor who needs money or just wants out or from an estate lawyer who's up against a deadline to close out the estate, the estimate may be unrealistically low. This suits the auction house, because, if the work sells above the high, day-after-sale headlines will read, "Sale Exceeds Expectations." But, if a house has to win a desirable work away from a rival or is dealing with a greedy consignor who wants the moon, estimates may be unrealistically high. When that happens, the work may sell at the low end or not at all. That's why buyers can't pay any attention to estimates and must come up with an independent assessment. I've heard people say, "Estimates don't matter; the market will take the piece where it wants to go." That certainly seemed to be the case when, in the same season a day apart, two identical Cindy Sherman photos, "*Untitled 94*," came up, one at Phillips with a $1,000,000 - 1,500,000 estimate, and the other at Christie's, with a $300,000 - 500,000 estimate. Both brought the same amount — $722,500. But, does that mean you should bid to buy in all cases and not stop until you get the lot? Of course not.

On top lots, the house may not assign an estimate in the catalogue, but, instead, substitute the cryptic phrase, "Estimate on request." A number will be verbally floated by word of mouth to potential buyers. By the time the sale takes place, though, everyone knows what the house expects.

Once you have your number, the number you want to pay all in, you have to work backwards and deduct the buyer's premium, artist's resale rights and sales and/or use tax if applicable to arrive at your maximum hammer price. Keep it to yourself, as disclosing it to any of the house's personnel doesn't help you. Before every sale, executives hold daily 'interest meetings' to share information about which clients are "on" which lots and how high they plan on bidding. I once saw a staffer's catalogue with names of future bidders written in by each lot number. If you tell them what you're willing to bid, they'll use that information to get other potential buyers to raise their bids. For example, if you tell a specialist you're bidding up to $800,000 on a Matisse drawing estimated at $400,000 - 600,000, he'll tell the next interested party who comes along that he has to bid more than $800,000 to get it. If the other guy still seems keen, the auction house will come back to you, warn you that you've got competition, and suggest that you raise your bid. Next thing you know, you're on a steep, upward spiral. Keep your own counsel, decide how high you want to bid, and shut up about it.

Sticking to your highest bid also prevents 'auction fever.' If you really love a work, however, you should be flexible enough to go an extra increment or two.

Years from now, when the work triples in value, you won't remember that you went a little over what you'd originally planned. If, say, the Basquiat drawing of your dreams comes up, how would you feel if you set your ceiling at $2,000,000 and it sells for $2.1 million? Would you kick yourself for not reaching a bit, perhaps to $2.2 million? On the other hand, if you reach to $2.4 million and someone else gets it at $2.5, you might not have any regrets. So, add ten to twenty percent for "the love factor."

You should also decide whether you want to go one more bid in case you get in 'on the wrong foot' or if the auctioneer is calling bids at different increments than you thought. For example, if you decide to go up to $2,000,000 on a Basquiat, and during the bidding, the auctioneer takes someone else's $1,800,000 bid, you raise your hand and he takes your bid at $1,900,000. If someone else bids $2 million, you can't say, "I'll bid $2 million, too." Either you bid the next increment, which could be 2.1 or 2.2 or you have to let it go. If someone's bidding for you, you must be clear and tell them whether or not they have the discretion to go "plus one."

Auction houses are notorious for not making the financial structures of their deals public, so it's often difficult to know what's really happening. You may find symbols to the left of some lot numbers in the catalogues — small circles, triangles, etc. — denoting the lot's financial arrangements. They're almost invisible because auction houses prefer not calling attention to them. You have to page through the 'boilerplate' at the back of the catalogue to find out what a symbol means, but it's a step you have to take as it could seriously affect your decision to bid and the amount you bid. One symbol means that the lot has a guarantee, another tells buyers they have to pay Artists' Resale Rights, etc. While you're at it, please study the entire 'Condition of Sales,' especially the ways in which the house limits its liability. Authenticity is warranted for only five years, and if you sell a work on, you can't assign your rights. Also, don't assume that if you find out in year one that the house made a mistake and the work you bought is a forgery they're going to take out their checkbook without a fight. The onus of proof is on you. All of these are good reasons for you to do your due diligence *before* you bid.

If you haven't bid before, you must register in advance of the sale by providing bank references, account numbers, etc., all of which gives the house confidence that you can come up with the cash. That way, on the night of the sale, when you step up to the registration table and ask for a bidding paddle, you'll be 'on the list.' Your paddle will have a number on it, which will be entered in the auctioneer's book if you're successful, and the information will be sent to the billing and pick-up departments, allowing you to pay for and claim your prize.

Finally...Showtime!! Impressionism and Modern Art and Post-war and Contemporary Art night sales are the ultimate spectator sport. Think of them like the Circus Maximus of the 21st century. Today's gladiators, dressed in designer clothes rather than armor and brandishing paddles instead of swords, do battle over multi-million-dollar works of art, while an audience of the world's wealthiest cheers them on. This is where the elite of the social and art worlds meet, and everybody who's anybody attends, if for no other reason than to show the flag or to be seen as a prominent player. There's a lot at stake, and the air crackles with suspense as everyone waits to see what will happen — who will buy which treasure at what price, which artists are trending up or down, and whether the market is buoyant or not.

As the room fills up, dealers and collectors mill around up front flashing their paddles and whispering to each other for everyone in the room to see. Even those with no intention of bidding posture like big time players, and those who saw each other that afternoon greet each other as if they were long lost relatives. I recently overheard one dealer ask a colleague, "Who was that woman I just kissed?"

Don't laugh...perception is power. A veteran Parisian dealer reminisced about a trip he made to New York when he was a neophyte to offer a painting to Nate Cummings, then chairman of the Sara Lee Corporation. Cummings offered him less than he paid for it, they failed to strike a deal, and he was crushed. That evening at Sotheby's, before the sale started, Cummings, who was seated in the first row, motioned for the young dealer to come up front. He whispered, "Being seen talking to me is so valuable for you that you should sell me the painting for what I offered." The dealer returned to his seat shaken by Cummings' arrogance, only to be buttonholed by the couple seated next to him, "You know Nate Cummings? Do you have anything for us?" He sold them two paintings that week, and Cummings got the painting he wanted at his price.

Evening sales are ticketed and seats assigned; the closer to the front, the greater your perceived spending power and art world importance. Skyboxes, high above the salesroom floor, are, as in sports arenas, reserved for big spenders or sellers of important property. Hors d'oeuvres and drinks are served in the boxes, softening many a buyer's resolve, and bidding is done by phone to staffers or advisors in the salesroom below. At Christie's, the boxes have one-way glass so that those seated inside can see the room below, yet remain totally anonymous. At Sotheby's, the boxes are equipped with curtains that can be drawn...or not. The scene reminds me of Pierre-Auguste Renoir's *La Loge* (ill. 9) in which a woman in a theater box has lowered her opera glasses so that other spectators can see her, while her male companion looks through his glasses at others in the audience. For Renoir, the real drama in the theater was played out in the audience, and that's how it is in auction rooms, too.

When the auctioneer of a major sale, invariably impeccably dressed in a bespoke suit or black tie, mounts the rostrum, the gabble of voices dies down and everybody takes a seat...everybody, that is, except Mr. Green. Five minutes after the start of every evening sale I've attended over the last thirty-five years, Mr. Green — now white-haired and slightly stooped, but still attractive — has wended his way down the center aisle pretending to look for his seat. He's had the same seat all those years, so who does he think he's kidding? Apparently, he's just not happy unless the entire art world knows he's arrived.

Mr. Green was probably still in the aisle when Sotheby's began its May 2004 Impressionist and Modern evening sale, but nobody cared. Picasso's *Garçon à la Pipe* (ill. 10), a painting that some said would be the first to bring more than $100 million, was about to be sold. Since then, I've sat through auctions in which paintings and sculptures have brought more, but that night was a landmark evening I'll never forget. The room was packed to the rafters. Promptly at 7:00 pm, Sotheby's auctioneer mounted the podium with an air deftly projecting the seriousness of the occasion. A silence settled over the room. A client of ours was interested in the first lot, a painting by Degas. We were hoping everyone would be so distracted by the Picasso that we'd get it at a bargain price. No such luck. The Degas went way past its estimate and what our client wanted to pay, and we never got our hand in the air. It was business as usual until the auctioneer announced in a more dramatic tone than usual, "Lot 7, the Picasso." Slowly, the stage revolved and the *Boy with a Pipe (Garçon à La Pipe)* came into view. There was a collective gasp and a palpable change in the temperature of the room...as if the heat had suddenly been turned up. Then everyone fell silent. In a voice betraying no excitement at all, the auctioneer announced that the bidding would start at $50 million, an unprecedented amount. Fifty million dollars to start? Bids immediately sprouted from everywhere in the room...$52 million...$55 million...$58 million. There seemed no end to them. It was as if collectors were impelled to bid by the sheer impact of this superb image.

Once the bidding reached $75 million — 'the nosebleed zone' — it narrowed into a tense, *mano a mano* duel between mega-dealer Larry Gagosian and Warren Weitman, Chairman of Sotheby's North and South America. Gagosian, sitting on the center aisle, was on his cell phone, relaying bids from a would-be buyer. Weitman, who never bids for clients, was making an exception. He stood in front of a phone bank to the auctioneer's left. Was he bidding for someone in the room or executing an absentee bid he'd received before the auction? Nobody knew, nor would they ever find out.

The bid was now $80 million, and the audience was mesmerized. Then, at $82 million, Gagosian's cell phone suddenly went dead. He turned a ghastly white. The auctioneer, in a moment of sang-froid, simply waited, his face calm. Gagosian grabbed the cell phone of the woman sitting next to him. She was a colleague, but there's no doubt that, at that critical moment, Larry would have ripped the phone from a total stranger's hand. He reconnected with the bidder, and with every eye in the room trained on him, he resumed bidding.

Finally, the auctioneer announced a bid of $93 million from Weitman. Gagosian remained silent. The auctioneer leaned toward him and asked, "Are you sure?" Gagosian nodded sadly. The audience held its breath. The auctioneer paused, emphatically restated Weitman's last bid, and brought down the gavel. With shining eyes, he announced, "Sold, for $93 million." He turned to Weitman and with a slight bow from the waist, thanked him for his bid. The room broke into wild applause. Everyone knew that, if you add the $11 million buyer's premium, the painting sold for over $100 million, $104 million to be exact. They had witnessed auction history.

Great auctioneers have an extraordinary skill set, and you should think of them as highly paid entertainers. In less than ten seconds, a star auctioneer can foster a 'relationship' with a bidder that makes the bidder want to bid again, just to please him. When Christopher Burge leaned over Christie's podium and coyly asked, "Just one more bid, sir?" even the toughest auction veteran found it hard to resist. While a good auctioneer makes 'taking a sale' look easy, he's actually performing a juggling act of epic proportions. As every new lot comes up, he checks his 'order book' where he's noted the reserve, guarantee or other financial arrangements, absentee bids, and bidding signals. Once he opens the bidding, he takes bids from individuals on the floor and staff members at long desks to his left and right. They're bidding for buyers who have either left bids or are on the telephone. Generally, absentee bidders use the same staffers for every sale, so the pros in the room have a pretty good idea who's bidding on what. The auctioneer continues to execute bids, including those coming from online bidders. At a recent sale, the auctioneer joked: "Not yours, computer," when someone outbid an online buyer.

While the auctioneer's doing all that, he'll change the increments, the spread between two bids, to keep up the pace. The progression by which he raises the bids is his discretion, and it's an extremely important decision. The fear, if a sale lags, is that bidders may lose interest, so, if there's active bidding, he'll increase the increments and speed the sale along. If a lot isn't doing well, he'll reduce the increments and baby it along, hoping it will catch fire. Generally, for lots below $100,000, the auctioneer goes in $5000 or $10,000 increments, above $100,000 he switches to $10,000 increments or he can jump $20,000 or $30,000, to $120,000, $150,000, $180,000, $200,000, and so forth. At some point, he may change to $50,000 increments and, when a lot tops a million, he takes bids in $100,000, $500,000 or $1,000,000 increments.

Sometimes a bidder will make a sideways chopping gesture signaling that he wants the auctioneer to split the next increment, or he'll call out a number less than the auctioneer is asking. The auctioneer can accept or reject the bid. If the lot comes up late in the sale and it's lagging, he may go for it. If the lot's early in the sale, it's unlikely the auctioneer will take it, as he doesn't want to break the rhythm he's set in motion. I always wonder how consignors feel if an auctioneer doesn't take a split bid and the bidding stops at the lower number. Wouldn't they have wanted the extra money a bidder was willing to pay?

Meanwhile, the auctioneer ad libs to relieve tension, pauses to add drama, and cajoles and seduces bidders to go higher. He can even decide to sell a work slightly shy of the reserve, knowing he can make up the difference from the buyer's premium. All of this takes place within the two minutes or so it takes to sell a lot. When the gavel comes down and the object is sold, the auctioneer barely draws breath before he goes on to the next lot. No wonder auctioneers are considered superstars. Like great athletes, they function under enormous pressure at the very top of their game, all the while making it look effortless.

Bidders in the room generally exhibit one of two distinct bidding 'styles.' Some call attention to themselves early on, waving their paddles wildly in the air or holding them up until they succeed or drop out. Exhibitionist bidders may also 'jump the bid' to intimidate competitors, calling out "$100,000!" when the bidding is still at $70,000. How do they know that the individual bidding against them wasn't about to drop out? Other bidders take a different tact and wait until the auctioneer seems ready to bring down the hammer. With a single nod or gesture, they get the auctioneer's attention and hopefully the lot.

Extremists in the low profile camp use pre-arranged signals with the auctioneer or other staff members. They may be bidding as long as their glasses are on, they're touching their chin, or they have their pen in their mouth. Norton Simon, known for the eponymous museum in Pasadena, was notorious for using convoluted bidding signals. At a Christie's London auction in 1965, he almost outfoxed himself. Simon was planning to bid on Rembrandt's famous *Portrait of a Boy*, once thought to be a portrait of the artist's son, Titus (ill. 11). As related in his biography, *Collector Without Walls*, Simon sent Christie's his bidding instructions: "When Mr. Simon is sitting down he is bidding. If he bids openly when he's sitting down he is also bidding. When he stands he has stopped bidding. If he then sits down again he is not bidding until he raises his finger. Having raised his finger he is continuing to bid until he stands up again." How'd you like to be the auctioneer having to remember those instructions? When the sale began, Simon remained seated. By the time the bidding hit the $2 million range, the auctioneer, seeing no action from Simon despite looking directly at him, knocked the Rembrandt down to Marlborough Gallery (on behalf of Stavros Niarchos).

Simon stood up, screamed, and pulled a copy of his bidding instructions out of his pocket — all while TV cameras were rolling. Christie's reopened the bidding, and Simon got the painting for $2,200,000, which was, to date, the second highest price ever paid for a work of art at auction (Rembrandt's *Aristotle Contemplating the Bust of Homer* was the highest at $2,300,000). The problem may have occurred not out of confusion, but because the auctioneer was worried that if Simon backed out, there'd be no witnesses and that the house would be left holding the bag. As it turns out, several weeks later, Niarchos offered Simon a profit, but Simon turned it down.

In recent auctions, an increasing number of bidders are on the phones, calling in from all over the world. Instead of watching two titans of industry duke it out, the audience will turn their heads in unison, as if at a tennis match, watching two staff members manning phones on opposite sides of the room. Sometimes, I imagine that the phone bidders are on a yacht in the Med, dining at the White House, or, dare I say, in the midst of having sex.

During the sale, the audience follows along in catalogues poised on their laps like hymnals. Professionals are on point, aware of everything that goes on — who's bidding, who's not, what's selling, what's not. They jot down the prices lots bring in their catalogue, as well as the names of buyers and underbidders, if they can see who they were. When a work sells for a record price, everyone applauds. I'm never sure if they're cheering for the artist, the seller, the buyer, or congratulating themselves for being in such a lucrative business. If you miss any of the action, Josh Baer's online newsletter, *The Baer Faxt*, comes out the day after the sales and lists bidders and underbidders. Dealers find it useful, particularly because the underbidders are potential buyers for similar things they have or may come across.

Before every sale, I guess what every lot will bring. I'm not the only one. Ladbrokes, the English bookmaking chain, takes odds on big-money lots. For Edvard Munch's *The Scream*, which sold in May 2012, the odds were 3-to-1 the week before the sale it would bring between $150 and $200 million and 3-to-2 that it would become the most expensive art object ever sold at auction. At $119.9 million, it was the most expensive work of art sold at auction to date.

Not every lot is met with a fusillade of bidding. If there are no bidders, the auctioneer minimizes the damage by taking "chandelier bids," fake numbers pulled from the air. It's not always easy to spot, so here's a clue. If the auctioneer remains vague and doesn't point to a particular bidder or avoids specifics like, "I have $50,000 from the gentleman in the second row," he may be taking 'bids' from a large light fixture. As Patty Hambrecht, who was chief Business Development Officer at Phillips, reminded me, it's perfectly legal for the auctioneer to take chandelier bids up to the reserve because he's trying to stimulate bidding and protect the consignor's reserve. Sometimes it works. Some bidders may be waiting to jump in at the end, or a single bidder may enter, and the auctioneer will 'run him up' to the reserve price and sell him the lot. If there are no bids and the auctioneer takes the lot up to a number just shy of the reserve, he'll bring the hammer down with a crack and very quietly mutter, "Pass," which he hopes nobody will hear.

'Buy-ins' can be disastrous. If a work by a living artist doesn't sell, it usually means that the artist's dealer isn't supporting the work, and that could trigger a crisis of confidence among the artist's collectors. It may be the result of a weak economy in general, or simply greedy consignors wanting too much or auction specialists overzealously assigning estimates and reserves.

Whatever the reason, buy-ins aren't good for anyone. Consignors are stuck with unsalable works, the houses suffer because the sale's success statistics are lowered, and the journalists report market weakness, which may not be true. That's why, when a lot fails to sell, the auction house will immediately ask the seller to lower his price and offer it to underbidders, other collectors who'd expressed interest during the viewing, and bottom fishers. If they can consummate a sale quickly enough, the results will be included in the official stats. The higher the sale's success rate, the better everyone feels about the market.

In addition to the action in the auction room, auction houses are now focusing on private treaty sales as an important profit center. The staff likes doing them, too, as they make substantial commissions. In 2012, Sotheby's and Christie's combined private sales added up to about $2 billion, a number that's increasing yearly. The majors have opened galleries where they mount sales exhibitions, have openings, create catalogues, and do all the things galleries do. I imagine that soon they'll represent artists. Dealers scream that these sales encroach on their business and that the auction houses are squeezing the life out of them. They're not wrong. We could be facing a future art world comprised of two major auction houses and only a handful of star galleries.

Even if you understand how chandelier bids, guarantees, and reserves work, and how the "Conditions of Sales" favors the seller, auctions are still plenty opaque. If you buy at auction, the old adage, "Buyer Beware," still applies. That doesn't mean that auction houses are the devil to be avoided at all costs. Far from it. As long as you're careful, auctions are a great way to acquire art. Each season some of the best material on the market goes through auction, and if the painting of your dreams is one of them, go for it. If you've paid attention to this chapter, your purchase won't be an unfortunate seduction, but a lasting love match.

ART ADVISORS

Making your way through the art world is like picking wild mushrooms: it's not always easy to differentiate what's okay from what's deadly. You pick a mushroom, find a photo in your field guide that looks just like it, and, satisfied that it's edible, you bite into it. Then you turn the page and see one that looks more like the one you ate – labeled "extremely poisonous." Gulp! In the art world, collectors can prevent fatal errors like that by engaging an art "mycologist," aka an art advisor. Yes, I'm an art advisor, so it shouldn't come as a surprise that I advocate using one. But I promise, it's one of the best things you can do to protect yourself and improve the quality of your experience. It goes without saying that some advisors are better than others, and although I speak about advisors throughout this book, please note, I mean "good advisors."

Bottom line: advisors are hard-wired to shortcut the process of building good collections and making it look easy, which, as you'll quickly discover if you go it alone, it isn't. They can do or help you do everything that I describe in this book as needing to be done. If you're collecting, they'll save you time and money, prevent terrible mistakes from happening, and get you in front of the right paintings you might never find on your own. Whether you're just starting out and need education and introductions, or you're a sophisticated collector looking for specific works or to refine your collection or change directions, advisors can make a difference to the outcome. Advisors spare you the tedious parts and allow you to focus on the things you enjoy. And because advisors watch your back, you can sleep nights without worrying that you made a bad decision. And if you're selling, they lend the expertise to know where, when, and how to best part with your works. Collecting is a long journey, and if you work with the right advisor, the pleasure you'll have will grow exponentially.

I can already see some of you shaking your heads, certain that advisors aren't for you. Perhaps you think you're not spending enough to warrant professional help or you don't want anyone imposing his taste on you or pushing you into buying something you don't want. Maybe you're a do-it-yourself type who relishes a challenge. Or, you just don't want to pay extra fees or commissions. I've heard it all. But please read this chapter before you decide to fly solo in the art market's sometimes not-so-friendly skies. Then, if you still want to go it alone, "Go with God."

As you become involved in collecting, you'll soon discover that the skills and experience that serve you well in your own business aren't as useful in the art world. Why should they be? If you were a doctor, would you drill for oil without a geologist? Of course not. Well, without an art advisor, a new collector is like a doctor standing in a field, wearing a white coat and stethoscope, blindly plunging expensive drilling equipment into unknown ground.

Collecting has a lot of moving parts. It requires looking, listening, researching, and evaluating the information you gather about a perspective "buy." It requires an investment of time and skills that can only be developed over years, including a working knowledge of art history, an ability to identify the right objects to buy and which way taste is going, knowing the questions to ask, and figuring out the right price to pay. All of this reminds me of my first scuba diving lesson in a small Mexican town. The local instructor, non-certified to be sure, got me suited up and began firing commands in Spanish that I only half understood. I think he was screaming, "Hold this cord!" "Breathe in!" and "Kick this way!" while I kept protesting, "No entiendo." He then pushed me backwards off the boat into the deep. If I'd failed to do any one of the things he'd 'taught' me, I'd have drowned. Luckily, I didn't, but I remember thinking I'd have been better off with a good interpreter. You see where I'm going with this: a competent art advisor will make sure you don't wind up at the bottom of the sea. Collecting is much easier, safer, and more fun when you have someone at your side translating the mountains of elusive, specialized, and complicated intel that go into making a wise purchase.

Plenty of art advisors are Johnny-come-latelies who've popped up looking to make an easy buck in today's overheated art environment. But, there are many serious professionals who've stood in front of hundreds of thousands of works and have extensive knowledge of art history. Long ago advisors may have had day jobs as artists and/or may have been called agents, but their role was virtually the same as advisors today. In about 1490, the Duke of Milan wrote to his Florentine agent asking for "hot" artists he might commission for a particular job. The advisor provided the names of some candidates — Botticelli, Filipino Lippi, and Perugino. Not a bad line-up. A couple of decades later, Isabelle D'Este wrote her advisor in Venice, asking for a Giorgione. He answered, sadly, that she was too late, Giorgione had died (in 1510), and no one who owned one wanted to sell. *Plus ça change*.

In the mid 18th century, Russia's Catherine the Great decided that forming a great art collection might soften her profile as a ruthless despot. She called on Denis Diderot, the great French encyclopedist and art critic, who helped her buy entire collections en masse, such as 150 prime works owned by the Duc de Choiseul, at discount prices. Thanks to Diderot, her acquisitions became the nucleus of the fabulous Hermitage Museum in Saint Petersburg.

Early 20th-century American mega-collectors Henry and Louisine Havemeyer and Albert Barnes relied on artists (Mary Cassatt and William Glackens respectively) to scout potential purchases in Europe. And decades later, Impressionist scholar John Rewald performed the same service for a new generation of collectors, including John Hay Whitney and Paul Mellon.

In the 1970's and 1980's, galleries proliferated, auction houses powered up, and as prices rose exponentially, buyers were less comfortable relying on "I love it!" as their guiding principle. They wanted assurance that they weren't throwing their money away, and they needed guidance to make their way through an increasingly complex field. The art advisory profession came of age. Some collectors kept their advisors under wraps, along with their hair colorists and plastic surgeons. Perhaps they wanted the world to think all of those brilliant collecting moves were theirs alone. Today, it's different. Most serious collectors not only use advisors, they flaunt them. For many collectors, cruising galleries, auctions, and art fairs with an advisor by their side is like bringing along a pit bull lawyer to a serious business meeting. It sends a clear and powerful message, "I'm serious. Don't mess with me."

But what exactly do art advisors do? I can't speak for all art advisors, or any others for that matter. I can only tell you what I might do. Let me go over it all in shorthand. If you were starting from scratch, for example, I'd spend a lot of time with you helping you learn some art history and acquire a familiarity with the workings of the art world. We'd go to museums and galleries, sit down and go through books together, etc. After that, I'd help you identify an area you love and can afford. Connccting a collector with the right collecting field is like being a great matchmaker, and when I succeed, it's enormously satisfying.

Years ago, a young East Coast couple came to me with a limited budget and no clear direction in mind. For the husband, a management consultant, 'process' was at the core of his profession. I thought about it and suggested they collect sculptors' drawings. They loved the idea, and today they own drawings by every major sculptor from Auguste Rodin to Richard Serra. Their collection has been the subject of a catalogue and two museum exhibitions, and, for not a lot of money, they've gotten a big bang for the buck. Over the years, as their business flourished, so did their collection, with the couple expanding it to include sculptures for which their drawings are studies.

A Texas couple called with a similar dilemma. "We like Renoir and Monet, but we can't afford them," the husband told me. If French Impressionism was too costly, I reasoned, they might like the American Impressionists, whose works are as colorful and light-filled as their French counterparts, but not as pricey. On our first day making the rounds of New York galleries, sensitive to price point, I showed the couple second-tier American Impressionists. They bought a beautiful Venetian scene by Jane Peterson for around $20,000. I was delighted that we found a direction and went home to plan the next day's itinerary. That night, the husband called and, in a thick drawl, asked sheepishly, "Hon, y'all think you could show us something a little more expensive?" No problem! Over the next few days we looked at works by first-tier American artists John Singer Sargent, Childe Hassam, and William Merritt Chase. The couple bought the best of what they saw that week, and over the next several years. Today, their collection is one of the greatest in the field in private hands.

My next task would be to search for the best things that fit your taste and budget. Since many of the great works on the market aren't hanging in the public spaces at galleries, I'd get you into the right back rooms and offices of dealers and private dealers. That's where a good advisor is worth his weight in Warhols. Why? Getting in the door is easy. Getting access to the best stuff — not so easy. Let's say that Mr. Smith walks into a gallery for the first time, alone. Any assistant or dealer could easily ignore him. If, however, Smith walks into the gallery with a well-respected art advisor, all that changes. The advisor's presence signals that Smith is serious, and every dealer wants to help form a collection. The dealer also feels confident that if he shows Smith something he wants kept under the radar, Smith and the advisor will keep the confidence. So, what would have been a missed opportunity for Smith becomes a significant collecting moment. The lights come up in the private viewing room and, there on an easel, is Mr. Smith's dream painting. It doesn't always happen, but a skilled advisor makes it far more likely that it will.

Recently, a Midwestern couple came to New York, one step ahead of Mr. Smith. They were armed with an introduction from their local museum director to an upscale Madison Avenue gallery. When the gallerist invited them into the gallery's back room and showed them several paintings, they were thrilled. The problem was that they didn't have a clue whether anything they were shown was worth considering or priced fairly. Fortunately, mutual friends suggested they call me, and they asked me to go to the gallery with them the next day. Of the six works they'd been shown, only one, a small jewel of a Franz Kline, was an appropriate buy, though it was too small for any of their walls. While we were there, however, I asked the dealer to bring out a beautiful Fernand Léger he'd shown me the week before. He'd clearly sized up the couple and decided that the Léger was out of their league, but he was wrong. They flipped for it and ultimately bought it. They've been clients of ours and the gallery ever since.

If advisors thrill when a client connects with a certain area, the moment an advisor lives for is when a client finds a work he loves and can't live without. I know I do. It's also the moment I switch gears. If the work is on the primary market, there's little to do; there are no condition problems, no issues on authenticity, provenance, etc., and the price is set, with, perhaps, a little room for negotiating. But if the painting is on the secondary market, there's work to be done.

To begin, I'll choose a conservator to examine the work and explain to clients in lay terms his findings. If conservation is required, I explain the prognosis, treatment plan, and translate all that into market terms — whether the condition impacts the price and by how much. A few years ago, I was called by a man who'd only bought one painting in his life, a de Kooning that someone sold him for investment. He asked me to sell it for him. The condition report supplied by the seller, a dealer, mentioned "a thin line of inpainting," and that the painting was relined. My friend, unaccustomed to reading conservation reports, didn't realize that meant there was a problem. Anyone could see under black light that the line of restoration was at least 12 inches long, the likely result of a gash. Worse, the relining was done so badly that thick paint layers were squashed down, leaving the work flat and lifeless. If the de Kooning owner had had an art advisor look at the painting or explain the report to him, he might not have bought it in the first place. As a result, when he sold it, he didn't get as much as he hoped.

Checking works by certain artists necessitates unique steps. For one, did you know that when you're buying a Matisse drawing, you may need to get an original letter of authentication from the expert, Wanda de Guebriant? And if the seller offers to give you a copy, that's not good enough? Or, if you're buying a Tintoretto, you may be happy to have found it in the CR, but did you know that a new study of Tintoretto's portraits excluded your work?

Advisors do not opine on authenticity. But if there are any questions as to a painting's authenticity, advisors follow up with reliable experts.

Discerning whether a work is a fine example and whether the price is right are also important, and an experienced advisor, who's stood in front of enough paintings by the artist you're considering knows instinctively how it rates, what it's worth, etc. Nonetheless, if you were my client I'd show you 'comps' from auction and private sales to explain how I arrived at my conclusion. Sure, you can slog through online databases of auction sales for comps yourself, but it's easy to get it wrong. You may think "yours" is like one that brought a low price and decide that you shouldn't pay a dime over that price, without realizing that that one was in horrible condition and would have brought more if it was in better state. Whenever possible, I'd fill you in on the backstories. I'd then go through the catalogue raisonné with you, if there's one on the artist. Because I notate my CR, I'd be able to show you which works are in museums, which are in private hands, and how many and which might come out onto the market. From my notes, I might even be able to tell you how much various owners turned down. Wouldn't you like to know, if you pass up the Rothko you're considering in colors you love, whether or not you'll be able to get another? And whether the trajectory for an artist's prices is going up? An advisor can answer these questions and others you'll have.

If everything checks out, and the "Buy!!" button lights up, it's time to negotiate with the seller. "Aha!" you say. "No problem there. I've negotiated lots of business deals, and I'm great at it." No doubt you have, but your advisor can be an important weapon. If the work's coming from a dealer he's negotiated with before, he knows how to read the tea leaves. He knows when the dealer's bluffing or can't stretch any more. He knows if the dealer's short of cash or if he'll take a long payout, and he knows if the dealer will get insulted and blow the deal if you make too low an offer. Since your advisor is a source of clients to the dealer, the dealer is incentivized to keep him happy, which is good for you. When the smoke clears, you'll usually have the right painting at the right price.

At auctions, an advisor can lead you through, start to finish. When auction season rolls around, and pounds of catalogues arrive on your desk, it could take hours to sift through them and identify promising lots. An advisor does that for you. Then, once you've identified objects you want to pursue, an advisor will make sure you see them early and do the necessary checks, because, as I've mentioned, auction houses can — and do — make mistakes. Lastly, an experienced advisor will know what similar works are or have been on the market and what might become available — all of which is relevant in figuring out how high to bid. And then, of course, an experienced advisor is well known by the auctioneers and can execute your bid.

If all that sounds promising, wait until you see your advisor in action at an art fair. It's easy to become paralyzed by the volume of works on view and the hellish need to make quick decisions or go home empty-handed. An advisor can show you the heavenly side of art fairs: he'll find out in advance what exhibitors are bringing, so you can buy or put the work on reserve ahead of time. If the latter, your advisor will rush you in as soon as the doors open and take you to booths where you have works on reserve or where there are things he wants you to consider. Your advisor will then walk you through the rest of the fair, giving you an on-the-spot commentary on what you're seeing. If you want to buy something, your advisor will negotiate the price.

Once you buy a work, it's not the end of the journey. While acquiring art is wonderful fun, the work required by art ownership, including conservation, framing, shipping, installation, lighting, lending, record keeping, etc., can be less interesting. Many collectors use advisors for all that. If you buy an outdoor sculpture, for example, installing it could take a village — from engineers and shippers to conservators and installers and perhaps even the artist himself. Last summer, I found myself in an empty field in Virginia, in 90-degree weather, supervising the installation of an outdoor bronze. The team of installers sweated it out for hours, literally and figuratively, because the epoxy required to adhere the piece to the base wouldn't set in the heat. An electrical storm moved in, and as the lightning flashed around us,

I realized that standing next to a large metal sculpture in an empty field wasn't a great idea. Luckily, our client didn't have to experience this.

Most advisors love supervising the installation of paintings, and they're good at it. They know that whenever a collector buys a new work that's joining others, re-hanging entire rooms may be necessary to create a meaningful dialogue between works, taking into account color, size, style, and subject matter.

When it comes to collection management, computer programs only go so far. When a request comes in for a loan, an advisor who's been through it all many times can save you a big headache. He knows whether the museum or gallery asking is a worthwhile venue, and he'll take care of the paperwork and lending logistics, including insurance, packing and shipping. And while we're on the subject of conservation, an advisor will arrange and supervise a conservator to come to your home periodically to check the condition of your paintings and maintain outdoor sculpture.

Advisors can also provide clients with services that have nothing to do with the art itself but have everything to do with the collecting experience. If you want to maintain anonymity, your advisor has potential purchases sent to warehouses or your home for you to see. He can arrange for you to preview works coming up at auctions after-hours in a private room, and, if you attend the auction, he'll arrange for you to bid from a skybox and slip in and out through a side door. For celebrities and the very wealthy, these precautions are not just for personal comfort – they're practical. You can negotiate better deals if a seller doesn't know you're Mr. Big. One of our clients guards his privacy so much that we don't use his real name even when we're alone in our office. On the other hand, if you're interested in making a 'splash' in the art world and want to make a life out of collecting, an advisor can orchestrate that handily. Making sure you get prominent seats at auctions and invitations to the right openings and dinners at art fairs is an art advisor's métier. Anonymous or famous, it's your choice.

And finally, advisors help in the end game – determining what and when you should give your art away, trade, or sell. If you're interested in giving works to a museum, an advisor can help you choose one where they'll have the greatest impact and not be buried in the basement or sold off. If you're selling, an advisor will determine the price you can realistically expect and the best venue. And if you're parting with one work to acquire another, and you're eligible for a 1031C like-kind exchange, advisors can orchestrate that, too. A more detailed description of all this is found in my chapter, *After You Own It*.

Looking back at all the things advisors can do for you, electing to use one seems like a no-brainer. But how do you choose the right one? When the word gets out that you're starting to collect and could become a serious player, eager dealers, auction house experts, museum curators, and even other collectors may try to convince you that you don't need an art advisor, because *they'll* advise you—gratis. It's a nice thought, but it seldom works out. Since you might be tempted, let's take a quick look at these alternatives.

Dealers have been advising clients since the dawn of the dealing profession. Nothing new about that. But what is new in recent times is that, as paintings increase in value, more of them can't afford inventory. That leads them to become dealer/advisors. Some are impeccably honest and are able to switch roles with ease. Others can't make the transition as seamlessly and allow their dealer hat to trump their advisor hat. They're so used to making the maximum on every transaction that they naturally want you to buy a work from their inventory or one they get from a colleague in which they have a participation. The thought of helping you buy a work that takes you out of the market for a small advisory commission goes against their very fiber. As well, some couldn't bring themselves to tell you that their competitor has a better, cheaper example than they have. If you think they would, there's a bridge I'd like to sell you.

Another danger of dealers acting as advisors is that they believe and will press hard to make their specialty yours. When a woman banker moved into a new country home, a neighbor, an old master dealer, came calling and suggested he act as her art advisor — for free. She was flattered and agreed. One weekend when she was away, he pulled a truck up to her house, unloaded and hung a dozen old masters from his inventory. She hated them all, hated the dealer for thinking she'd accept them without asking questions, and felt dumped on. She returned the paintings the following day, called us, and bought a houseful of contemporary art in a few months. She couldn't wait to invite her dealer/neighbor for dinner.

What about auction house experts? They're knowledgeable, know the market, and are eager to serve. But, like dealers, they have demanding jobs and don't have the time to scour the world on your behalf and do all the things advisors do. And besides, they have a vested interest in steering you into buying what they're selling.

Museum curators or directors may seem to be a good choice — at first. They know a lot, and they're not pocketing any money. But they too may have an agenda that puts their interests ahead of yours. They may be thinking what's best for the museum and how they can get you to give works or support a program. Or, they like being big man on campus, and squiring you around galleries and art fairs adds to their luster. An additional danger relates to price. Most don't have the market savvy and day-to-day knowledge required to make the right decision.

Several years ago, a curator of a Western museum, attempting to curry favor with a big supporter of theirs/ client of mine, had a landscape by Martin Johnson Heade, a 19th-century American painter, flown out from a New York gallery for him to see. When our client called for my opinion, he told me that the curator recommended the purchase at the dealer's $1.6 million asking price. I explained that I'd seen the painting a month earlier at a private dealer's for $900,000, but I hadn't thought to offer it to him because he already had one better. He understood but thought a pair in his entry could be fun. Fair enough. Rather than cut out the intermediary dealer, who likely had it on consignment from the private dealer who'd offered it to me (and tacked on a $700,000 profit), we decided to make him a generous offer of $1.2 million. The dealer refused, feigning outrage, "I won't accept a penny less than $1.6 million." We instructed the museum curator to return the painting, and we bought it from the private dealer the next day at the $900,000 price.

Lastly, another collector may offer to advise you, but they'll want you to see the world in their terms and buy what they have. They also may introduce you to "hot"dealers hoping for the payback of being offered something great before anyone else. The moral of the story? Dealers, curators, and other collectors may be knowledgeable, but they're not in a position to take the time, step back, and to think about what's best for your collcction and you.

What *will* you pay an advisor? It depends. Some advisors work on a retainer, some charge a percentage of the retail or negotiated net price of each object purchased, and others charge a combination of retainer and commission. In short, there's no one way all art advisors charge, and, as long as both collector and advisor agree, any arrangement can work. The one thing advisors shouldn't do is "double dip," i.e. collect commissions from seller and buyer. When I was starting out, a veteran art advisor told me that if a new client complains about fees, he'd tell them, "Just pay me for all the work I do on all objects you *don't* buy."

When you're in the market for an art advisor, choose carefully. Enthusiasm and amiability aren't enough. Since the field has no regulatory requirements, it's crawling with self-stylized 'art advisors' with no credentials and no expertise. Every Park Avenue lady who once called herself an interior designer is now calling herself an art advisor. And it's not limited to those in the United States. Sometimes, they're Parc Monceau ladies.

Look for an advisor or a team with experience, deep knowledge, a good eye, street smarts, a sprawling web of connections and access to good material, a solid grasp of the market, an uncompromising attitude about due diligence, negotiating skills, respect and trust of others in the field, diplomacy, and unshakable honesty.

Personality is also important. Since you're going to be spending a fair amount of time together, you have to pick an advisor whose personality meshes with yours. Although Diderot did a great job for Catherine the Great, she felt uncomfortable with him and switched her allegiance to Frederich Melchior Grimm, a lesser talent, someone with whom she felt more at ease.

When interviewing an advisor, ask other collectors or your museum director or curator for recommendations, or get a list from the APAA, the Association of Professional Art Advisors. Below are some questions you might ask candidates:

1. *What's your educational background?* (An advanced degree usually indicates a broader perspective.)

2. *How long have you been an art advisor? Do you have other art world experience?*

3. *How many people work with you or for you? What do they do?*

4. *How many clients do you work with at a time?* (Too few or too many could signal a problem.)

5. *What do you do if more than one client wants the same painting or works by the same hard-to-get artist? If you're offered a painting that two clients might like, how do you decide which one to offer it to?*

6. *Do you keep an inventory?*

7. *How do you charge? Is there a minimum a client must spend?*

8. *How do you charge at auction?*

9. *Can you provide references from other clients and people in the trade?*

Don't settle until you find one who offers everything you need. Then sit back and let your advisor show you how much fun collecting can be.

ART FAIRS

Publicity flacks tout art fairs as the coolest places on the planet. "Stroll on over," they tell you. "See lots of interesting art, buy something you love, hang with a glamorous, cultured crowd, and attend swell parties." All of this is true, and then some, but don't forget: art fairs aren't much different from other trade shows, whether they're selling cars, boats, or medical equipment. Galleries rent booths in a big convention hall, show their wares, and hope that visitors who come to browse and party will check out their art, pull the trigger, and buy.

There is, however, one big difference between art fairs and all the other trade fairs: sex appeal. Art fairs have it in spades. Of course, I haven't been to any appliance conventions; maybe they throw some really wild parties. But art fairs are unquestionably seductive. The works on view are a feast for the eyes, and the whole scene — aisles filled with carts selling champagne and chatting, air-kissing socialites and celebrities — is enormous fun. You can't blame neophyte collectors for wanting to join this dazzling insider's club. "If all it takes is buying some art, where do I sign?" There's nothing wrong with chasing that rainbow, but it's important not to get so caught up in the excitement that you end up making expensive mistakes.

Not all art fairs are created equal. More than 300 take place annually, but only a handful tower over all others in artistic and social significance — including Art Basel, held every June in Switzerland, Art Basel Miami in December, The European Fine Art Fair (TEFAF), called "Maastricht" after the city where it's held in March, and Frieze London in October. The two Art Basels specialize in art from the early 20th century to the present and attract mostly collectors of contemporary art. Maastricht features a wider range of material, from the Medieval period on up. And Frieze in London specializes in works by emerging artists, although it's now added "Frieze Masters" which offers a contemporary look at historical work. If you aspire to be a serious collector, or you want to be seen as one, these are the fairs to attend. I suggest booking flights, hotels, and restaurants early.

Art fairs have proliferated like film festivals. Remember when there was only Cannes? Now, it seems, every town has one, from Malibu to Leh, Kashmir (at 11,000 feet, it boasts being the highest altitude film festival). The same is true for art fairs. The tremendous success of the big four (in 2014, nearly 75,000 people went through Art Basel Miami, just a little less than the 90,000 who attended the Super Bowl, and bought 3 billion dollars' worth of art) has spawned copycat fairs in cities as far flung as Madrid and Shanghai.

Many large fairs have fostered smaller, specialized fairs that cluster around the mothership and piggyback on its drawing power. Over two dozen satellite fairs orbit Art Basel Miami, all showing affordable art, such as PULSE and Aqua Art, which feature emerging artists, Focus Miami Photo Fair, and DesignMiami, where collectors can find furniture and decorative arts. And there are also dozens of pop-up galleries, exhibitions, and performance works.

A number of fairs focus on specific collecting areas. Fans of works on paper can check out the Salon du Dessin in Paris or drawings fairs in New York, and Asian art collectors can revel in Asia Week fairs in New York, London, and Hong Kong. Consult *The Art Newspaper*, for a list of fairs (as well as gallery and museum shows). If you've got the money and the energy, you could fair-hop every weekend of the year.

Why are there so many art fairs? Simple answer: because dealers want to be there. Why do dealers want to be there? Even simpler answer: they can sell work and market themselves to individuals who'd probably never set foot in their galleries. How else can a dealer in San Francisco make inroads with a budding collector from Indonesia? Although the overhead for a gallery's participation in a fair is staggering (booth rental, construction and décor, lighting, airfare for all employees, hotel, city transportation, and insurance, not to mention the cost of parties and dinners to entertain clients), most find that the $100,000 or more they pay per fair is worth it. In Basel 2015, almost 300 galleries from 33 countries participated, and a number of dealers said that the sales they made accounted for as much as half or more of their annual income. So, for the best fairs, getting a booth is like getting into a tony country club.

Unfortunately, the quality of the art shown at fairs can be uneven. Galleries used to hold back their best material all year to ensure that their booths were extraordinary. Nowadays, a shortage of desirable material and the growing number of fairs in which dealers participate have taken their toll. Another change is that the action has moved away from secondary market material, and the primary market is the new growth area. You see it clearly when the doors open at Basel, Switzerland. The majority of the waiting horde, which used to run to the first floor booths of galleries showing established artists, now rushes upstairs to galleries selling works by emerging artists. And it's not just because that work is more affordable. That's where the fun is — and the profit.

I've heard collectors compare art fairs to speed-dating, and it's true. It's easy to fall in love with a different work every time you round the corner at a fair. Fairs are also a great way to indulge in speed-shopping. An article in *The New York Times* by Patricia Cohen, *A Collector Bets his Eye and His Gut*, chronicled the buying spree of a Louisville couple, Steve Wilson and Laura Lee Brown, at Art Basel Miami in 2013. The two, accompanied by the curator of their private museum and a videographer, whizzed through the fair, and in a few hours made about 25 purchases, including two works comprised of piles of bricks by two different artists! The total they paid for all 25 works was an amount that is less than what many collectors pay for a single work. Ms. Brown, whose grandfather founded the company that makes Jack Daniels and Southern Comfort, clearly could collect established artists, but chose young artists instead. She and her husband have bought over 1600 works so far which they've housed in their chain of 21c Museum Hotels, and received museum discounts to boot!

Dealers see fairs as a way of branding their artists, their galleries, and themselves. They hope they can parlay one well-placed sale of a hot artist into many by letting the jungle drums of an art fair spread the word. When rumors circulated at an art fair in 2010 that Stevie Cohen, a billionaire hedge fund manager and mega-collector, had bought Adel Abdessemed's $300,000 world map made of tin cans, other collectors hurried to dealer David Zwirner's booth to buy one.

Another way dealers brand themselves at fairs is by showing unusual, controversial works. At Art Basel

Miami in 2006, Gavin Brown showed an Urs Fischer sculpture — a crumpled cigarette pack mechanized so that it appeared to dance or drag itself across the floor — that was the hit of the fair. The piece, which speaks to the lengths addicts will go in chasing their vice, attracted more attention than any other work and put Fischer and Gavin Brown on everyone's radar.

On the rare occasions dealers gather the best of the best for a thoughtful installation, their booths can be as enthralling as a visit to a world famous museum. Again, it's a way of setting them apart from the rest of the pack. At one fair, Matthew Marks put on a terrific Ellsworth Kelly mini-retrospective. At another, Pace mounted a museum-quality installation by Agnes Martin. More often, though, dealers bring a smorgasbord of works by the artists they represent. For seasoned collectors who know what they're looking at, that works, but for beginners, seeing only one work by an artist previously unknown to them may not do its magic.

There are so many fairs, that fair organizers are trying to come up with ways to brand their fairs, including "curating" them. At Turin's 2013 fair, there were five different sections, including one called "Back to the Future," curated by a committee showing works by 32 artists made from 1960-1990 it considered undervalued. At Frieze, there was a "Live" section for performance art.

Art fairs are almost always worth attending. Where else can you see a vast number of works for sale in one place in a short period of time? At a dealer's, you might see a couple dozen works, at an auction a few hundred, but at an art fair, there are thousands. And not only is the viewing great, so is the talking. A good fair puts you within chatting distance of extremely interesting dealers. If you give it time, it can be like taking a crash course in contemporary art 101, while getting an update on the art market. Pull up a chair in a gallery's booth (most bring great mid-century chairs), ask the gallerist or staffer questions, and *listen*. They'll pull out their computers and books they keep in their tiny back rooms and they'll make an artist's work come to life. And don't miss peeking into those back rooms; that's where dealers keep small gems set aside for important collectors. But, please be respectful. People working the booths are exhausted from standing eight hours a day shaking hands, kissing people with colds (remembering what country they're from and how many kisses they get on which cheek), and answering the same questions over and over ("How much is that?" "What's it made of?" "What's it about?"). So, if you're not really interested in buying, don't monopolize their time.

After a once around an art fair, you'll be in a position to make your own observations about the art market, or at least how the fair's going. If a dealer tells you he's had a great fair because he's made a lot of connections, that probably means he hasn't made a lot of sales. Sold works are often removed overnight and new ones installed in their place. So, if you return the next day and you think you're at a different fair, that signals a high volume of sales, that the market's healthy, and that there's a high level of buyer confidence.

Since dealers bring what they know they can sell, a fair gives you a sense of what the marketplace is favoring and what it isn't. One year, there may be an abundance of photography; the next, by contrast, lots of sculpture. If many works by the same artist or a related group of artists are sold, that suggests a "hot" or at least fluid market for that market segment. And if works by an artist who once had a strong presence are absent, that speaks to a diminished interest in that artist. Every art fair tells a different story.

One thing art fairs don't offer, despite all the advertising to the contrary, is a sure-fire way to bypass dealers' waitlists for hard-to-get works. Before the fair, dealers may tell you that everything they're bringing is available on a first-come, first-served basis. Rubbish. By opening day, many of the best things are pre-sold or are on reserve. To beat the crowd, some buyers resort to drastic measures. One year at Basel, dealer Philippe Ségalot donned a wig and Coke bottle glasses and, with the help of a professional makeup artist and a fake ID, slipped into the fair while dealers were setting up, reserving some of the best works for his clients.

Galleries representing hot artists may bring works that aren't readily for sale. Remember my mentioning the approach of Hauser & Wirth in regard to Bradford?

They took two of his paintings to an art fair and were taking "names" for an interest list so they could carefully place the work. That was the case with Christopher Wool sculptures, too, at Luhring Augustine's booth in Basel 2015. It may seem frustrating if you can't get what you want, but it's understandable and admirable from the dealer's point of view. He's working for the artist and will do what's best for him.

This year in Basel, I ran across a collector who was shell-shocked that he didn't get the work he came to buy. He'd seen a Mark Bradford on resale in an email blast from an obscure Swiss gallery. The gallery assured him that the work would be available at the fair. He'd studied the fair's layout, plotted the quickest route to the gallery's booth, and made sure he was first through the doors when the fair opened. He sprinted across the hall to the booth, and, as he related to me, "There it was, like a mirage — the painting of my dreams — hanging on the outside of the booth." But when he reached the gallery and spoke to a salesperson, he was told it was sold. "How could that be?" he whined. "There wasn't a soul in sight." Sadly, he didn't understand the unwritten rules of art fairs. Despite what the gallery said, it had pre-sold the work to an important collector. In 2011, Adam Lindemann, a collector, gallery owner, and journalist, brought attention to the problem by calling for a boycott of Art Basel Miami, saying, "The whole place has been cherry picked before I even walked in. I am left wasting my time inspecting a pile of leftover *chazerai*."

Maybe so, but Lindemann went anyway and probably had a great time. Art Basel Miami has become a hundred-hour party. Galleries give private dinners, and banks, fashion houses, and other luxury brands sponsor lavish, invitation-only events for celebrities and art world movers and shakers. Young hipsters flock to the parties that attract other young hipsters. All of this is an aphrodisiac for some collectors and would-be collectors. Who wouldn't like being invited to fancy parties and mingle with famous models, socialites, and entertainers?

Art fairs have become the favored watering holes for jet setters who used to make the pilgrimage from Gstaad in February, to London for 'the season' in June, to Saratoga for the races in July, and so forth. Now they flit from one fair to the next. As Becca Cason Thrash, a Texas socialite, told a *New York Times* reporter, "We all collect art. We all love to travel. We all love being together on the circuit. You see your friends and it's like, 'Same time, next fair.'" It's not surprising that the airports near fairs are so clogged with private jets that securing a landing time is harder than getting a reservation at a hot new restaurant. The last time I arrived in Basel in a client's G5, we were sandwiched between two Saudi 757s, probably one for passengers and the other to carry home the art they intended buying.

For many, the often-asked question, "What'd you buy?" has been replaced by, "What party did you go to last night?" When I bumped into Eli Broad at Art Basel and asked what art he'd bought, he said, "I didn't come for the art; I came for the parties." He was joking, but a lot of people really do come for the parties. In *Page Six* of *The New York Post*, journalist Mara Siegler described a party given by real estate mogul Aby Rosen, at the 2014 Miami fair and what would-be crashers did to get in:

> *There were literally billionaires waiting on line to get in. Someone showed me bank statements to prove he was a billionaire, and he was, but he still wasn't allowed in. I saw pictures of people with presidents, and everyone was Aby's best friend, or Aby's cousin, nephew, mother or garage attendant...The most inventive ruses included one crasher who arrived with Starbucks and an ear radio saying they were making a delivery to a guest inside. Somebody else said they were another guest's spiritual healer and needed to give an urgent consultation.*

So how do you make an art fair work for you? To begin, realize that with miles of aisles, it's an endurance contest. Although a few memorable attendees look like they're trying out for the cover of *Vogue*, a fair is one of the few art world events where you can put comfort before style and wear sneakers and carry a water bottle and power bars.

It's important not to succumb to a fair's now-or-never pressure to buy. At a gallery, you can usually have a work sent home on approval and live with it a few days. At auctions, a pre-auction viewing lasts several days during which you can decide what to go for and how high to bid.

At an art fair, even if you're "connected," a gallery may only allow you a couple of hours or a day max to keep a work on reserve, and most dealers won't even do that. If you don't make a decision pronto, you risk losing the work to someone else. Part of the pressure for some is not to come home empty-handed. They've travelled a long way, made a big effort, and they may want to be seen as a "player" or have something to talk about at that night's party. Don't feel desperate, please. It can lead to a big mistake.

If you're considering a primary market work, the price will be the same as it is in the artist's gallery, but your ability to negotiate may be less. The dealer may believe he can sell it to any number of collectors who'll file by without having to extend a discount. If you can't strike a deal and want to risk it and wait, get the dealer's cell number and do what bottom fishers do, call him the last day of the fair. If he hasn't sold the work by then and is faced with paying to ship it home, he may be ready to accept an offer.

The downside of buying secondary market works at a fair is that you're hampered by your inability to do your due diligence. You might be able to figure out the right price to pay by ducking around the corner and pulling up an art price database, like *Artnet*, on your phone. It will tell you if the work or others like it came up at auction, and what it/they brought. But you won't have time to check authenticity. Many buyers assume that, because fairs are vetted, and the dealers are major players, they don't have to worry anyway. That's true, and it's true that a committee of dealers walks around the fair every morning weeding out fakes, but realize that those dealers aren't experts in every artist. You might do what I did when a client wanted to buy a Magritte. We committed with the understanding that we'd only pay after the work was sent to the committee and accepted.

Art world insiders wonder if art fairs can continue to be successful in their current form. Although significant numbers of collectors prefer buying at fairs over galleries, brick-and-mortar fairs may soon be replaced by virtual fairs. But virtual fair organizers will have to learn to deal with virtual stampedes. When the VIP Art Fair opened online in 2011, so many people rushed the site at once that it crashed. Meanwhile, as long as fairs take the form they're in now, here's my closing advice: wear sensible shoes, keep your eyes open, ask lots of questions, and enjoy the parties.

MUSEUMS

Unless you're a Mellon, Rockefeller, or you've come from another family fortunate enough to live with paintings at home, your first encounter with art was probably in a museum. Maybe you were dragged there by a well-meaning teacher or parent to 'get some culture' and were bored stiff. But despite your yawns, something got through the *medulla oblongata*, and maybe that *something* has made you return over and over again. Museums not only put us in front of great works of art, they also allow us to learn about other times and other cultures. For aspiring collectors and anyone interested in art history and history in general, museums are essential.

Museum-going has become a major pastime for people of all ages. The most obvious reason is that most people enjoy looking at art, particularly in the company of others. They go back because, as their understanding grows, they see things they haven't seen before, and they connect anew. Many visitors go to see 'blockbuster' exhibitions so they can say they've been or so they're not left out of the conversation at the water cooler at work or at the next cocktail party. Guys go to pick up girls and vice versa: it's classier than a bar and cheaper than the movies (many museums offer free general admission). Parents go to give their kids a taste of "culture" and to keep them occupied on a rainy day. Tourists go because museums are usually ranked four stars in their guidebook or they house a famous work everyone knows they should see. Anything that gets people in the door is a good thing. As Victoria Newhouse says in her book, *Towards a New Museum*, we should encourage whatever makes "...art once again a vibrant part of life..."

In the late 19th century, early patrons of major city museums in the US, like The Metropolitan Museum of Art in New York and the Museum of Fine Arts in Boston, hoped that a brush with art of the past would imbue the 'great unwashed' with a sense of history and moral values. Most museum collections started off small, and few people paid much attention. In Edith Wharton's novel, *The Age of Innocence*, set a few years after the 1870 opening of The Met, the married Newland Archer and his lover, Ellen Olenska, hold a clandestine rendezvous at the museum because they know they'll be alone there. Archer observes, "Ah well...someday, I suppose, it will be a great museum." He was right about that, and it's probably still a good place for a romantic tryst — although the planetarium across the park might be better; it's totally dark.

By the early decades of the 20th century, the big city museums outgrew their modest quarters and moved into the Beaux Arts extravaganzas they inhabit today. Designed to emulate the Louvre and the Prado, The Met, the National Gallery of Art in Washington, and others were ponderously equipped with stone columns, classic pilasters, gigantic entrance halls and grand staircases. Meanwhile, a generation of newly-minted American millionaires who'd taken the Grand Tour and bought vast amounts of art was dying off, and their treasures were making their way into those hallowed halls. The American museum as we know it was born.

During the first half of the 20th century, these museums remained airless ivory towers whose sole mission was collecting and preserving art of the past. Curators mounted esoteric shows, and directors had little interest in bringing in the general public. All of that changed in the late 1960's, when Thomas Hoving became the director of The Met. His friend and former boss, Mayor John Lindsay, couldn't understand why he wanted the job. Lindsay laughed. "Seems to me the place is dead. But Hoving, you'll make the mummies dance." Hence, Hoving called his memoirs *Making the Mummies Dance*. Hoving's goal was to turn everybody — rich or poor, young or old — on to the joys of art. To this end, he unleashed his unique talents as impresario and procurer, transforming The Met from a preserve of pedants into the popular mecca it is today.

To make the collection grow, Hoving realized that it was more efficient to go after whole collections rather than single works. In hunting for big game, nothing beat Robert Lehman's collection in terms of quality and breadth. Lehman had already decided to convert his home on West 54th Street into his own private museum, but that didn't stop Hoving. Finally, in 1969, when Lehman was practically on his deathbed, Hoving persuaded him to donate his massive collection of paintings, furniture, and decorative arts — about 2600 objects in all. To seal the deal, Hoving promised to replicate every room in Lehman's home and exhibit all the objects exactly as they were placed in 54th Street. In effect, he promised Lehman to build a museum within a museum. Best touch? In the Lehman Wing, there's a staircase which leads nowhere.

During his tenure, Hoving, who had a Ph.D. from Princeton, spearheaded many thoughtful shows designed to elevate the conversation between the public and art. He also ramped up The Met's attendance by inventing the 'blockbuster.' His famous "King Tut" show of 1978 and other wildly popular exhibits, like "Inca Gold," generated long lines along Fifth Avenue. Today, museum directors all over the world have taken a page from Hoving's playbook. For example, a one word show, "Caravaggio," at the Los Angeles County Museum of Art (LACMA) in 2012, was enough to bring the public out in large numbers. Hoving also turned his attention to the museum's gift shop. His father, Walter, had been CEO of Tiffany & Company, and Tom followed his dad's lead by beefing up The Met's shop and making it a destination itself. Not a night went by that he didn't call his dad to tell him the day's 'take.'

While Hoving was working his wonders at The Met, museum architecture was undergoing a transformation. Frank Lloyd Wright's Guggenheim Museum (1959) and Louis Kahn's Kimbell Art Museum in Fort Worth (1972) dealt deathblows to the hermetically sealed, tomb-like edifices favored by the Beaux Arts gang. The Guggenheim's ramp and irregularly-shaped interior spaces were different from anything museum visitors had ever encountered, making it reason enough to visit. And Kahn's Kimbell, with its unprecedented use of natural light and courtyards, gave visitors the ability to remain connected with nature while looking at art.

The ultimate game-changer was the Guggenheim Museum in Bilbao, Spain. In a Hail Mary pass to attract tourism, the city bought a franchise from the Guggenheim in New York for $20 million and spent $89 million on a wildly adventurous museum by "starchitect" Frank Gehry. Never mind that the museum, which opened in 1997, had no art collection of its own. The envelope was the star, more important than almost anything that could be shown in it. It made Bilbao a top tourist destination overnight, and four million visitors flocked there in the first three years it was open. They spent so much money, that the city collected over 100 million euros in taxes — more than they paid for the project.

Cities all over the globe chased after the "Bilbao effect." More than $16 billion was spent on new museums and museum expansions between 1994 and 2008 in America alone. In Roanoke, Virginia, the director of the local museum wagered, "If we build it, they will come." The community, which up to that time had put all its money into social services, pushed through the construction of the Taubman Museum of Art, designed by Gehry acolyte, Randall Stout. Like Bilbao, the building has become a vibrant destination for locals and tourists, yet financial success didn't follow.

Of all the American museum directors who've followed Hoving, a few stand out, including Kirk Varnedoe at MoMA and Philippe de Montebello, Hoving's successor. De Montebello, who presided over The Met for thirty years, was brilliant, urbane, and articulate, and had an impact on generations of museumgoers by striking just the right balance between scholarship and showmanship. He even recorded the museum's audio tours himself in the six languages he spoke fluently *and* mellifluously. Everyone who visited The Met when it was under de Montebello's stewardship felt educated and entertained, never stupid or silly. His exhibitions were never dull, but they weren't crazy carnivals that overwhelmed the art either. He often said that he wanted the art to speak for itself, and that simple premise worked. During his tenure, The Met attracted enormous crowds to its galleries and huge dollars to its coffers.

Thomas Krens, who led the Guggenheim from 1988 to 2008, took a different path to fame — for his institution and definitely for himself. A Yale MBA, Krens thought of the Guggenheim as a Coca-Cola franchise and attempted to internationalize the brand by opening branches all over the world. Bilbao, the first, worked brilliantly, but some, like Berlin and Las Vegas, failed. Krens' detractors worried that he was turning the Guggenheim into the art world's Planet Hollywood, that famous constellation of restaurants that multiplied like crazy and then collapsed like a house of cards.

When my husband and I contemplated selling a money-losing Paris nightclub he inherited on the Ile Saint-Louis, he laughingly suggested that, because I go by my maiden name, *Guggenheim*, in business, we install my collection of over a thousand sets of salt and pepper shakers at the club and call it 'The Guggenheim Museum." That way, if Krens wanted to build a Guggenheim Museum in the City of Light, he'd have to buy us out. Alas, Krens never opened a Guggenheim in Paris, and we sold the club to our tenant. The latest Guggenheim is a Helsinki branch designed by a Parisian firm, Moreau Kusunoki. I've heard Krens is working for a for-profit institution building a "space" in the Berkshires, whatever that means. I'm sure it's something 'big.'

Of course, not every museum director is a de Montebello, a Nicholas Serota from the Tate, Nicholas Penny from the National Gallery in London, or another of the handful of greats. It's hard work. Recognizing that the director's role in the 21st century requires a complex skill set, Buffy Easton, a former curator at the Brooklyn Museum, and Agnes Gund, President Emerita of MoMA, founded the Center for Curatorial Leadership (CCL) to train curators for positions of leadership. They learn to deal head-on with issues like providing a new context for works in the collection, growing the collection, cultivating supporters, connecting with the community, and raising an endowment.

Like directors, curators have a tough job. They're expected to contribute to the scholarship in their field by writing books, articles, and catalogues on shows they produce. At the same time, they must find the best works to acquire and spend time cultivating constituents, who often come to them for advice, to pay for acquisitions and programs. For years, Reba White Williams and Dave Williams had a close relationship with The Met and contemplated leaving it their collection of over 5000 American prints. But after curator Bill Lieberman, their chief contact there, passed away in 2005, no one on staff voiced any interest in the collection. It was only when Reba and Dave gave it to the National Gallery that a curator from The Met called to arrange a visit. Too little, too late.

As an aside, reading wall texts is always fascinating, as they give us much more than a description of the work and an essay on the work's importance. They also tell us when and from whom a work was acquired. Like the Dewey Decimal System libraries use, museums usually list a date followed by a colon and another number. For example, "1968:14" means that the work was the 14th acquired by the museum in 1968. If there are three numbers: "1968.14.17", it may mean the work is the 17th, given by the 14th donor that year. But today, in an effort to keep the "looking experience" pristine, many curators omit wall texts and make the information available on apps, in leaflets, etc. At MoMA's 2015 Picasso sculpture show, an available diagram located works so unsatisfactorily they had to add numbers.

Mounting exhibitions is an extremely complicated activity. Curators have to come up with a thesis and fresh focus that distinguishes their exhibition from earlier shows on an artist or subject, get their director on board, and then develop it in a way that's community friendly and will attract a sponsor. They then have to decide which works to borrow and determine the feasibility of getting pivotal paintings. Sometimes diplomacy with other museums takes years, at the end of which the lending institution will extort loans of major works in return. It's not easy convincing other prestigious institutions and collectors to lend and often plans cannot go forward without securing the anchor loans. Only then can curators raise the funds, get a sponsor, and write a catalogue. Finally, they must work with the museum staff responsible for installing shows to refigure rooms to ensure that visitors flow through at the right pace, build vitrines, if necessary, and design rooms down to choosing colors for the walls that enhance the works on view and that reinforce concepts advanced in the show. It's a huge undertaking by any standards.

Acquiring major works for the collection and mounting shows are important, but anything the public sees on a drive-by or before they even enter the building has as great an impact. No director understands that better than Michael Govan, of LACMA. The first highly-visible outdoor piece he enlisted donors for when he arrived on the job was Chris Burden's *Urban Light*, a forest of 202 restored antique Los Angeles street lamps. It's become a mecca to selfie-seekers 24/7. Burden said that the idea for the piece came to him after a visit to the Rose Bowl flea market. He came across a street lamp laying on the ground and bought it. Later, realizing what he wanted to create, he went back to the seller and asked if he had any more. The dealer told him he had over a hundred, and that, "I knew you'd come one day." A more recent addition to the museum's outdoor sculpture collection is the $10 million *Levitated Mass*, by Michael Heizer. It's comprised of a 340-ton boulder seemingly precariously perched over a below-ground-level walkway. The feeling of threat one feels walking under it turns to exhilaration as one ascends. Recently, Govan championed a Swiss architect, Peter Zumthor, to create a new facility that will further brand LACMA from the outside. The dramatic biomorphic-shaped building will replace others on campus, extend over Wilshire Boulevard, and attract tourists for certain.

SHOPPING, SLEEPOVERS AND iPHONE APPS: THE MUSEUM TODAY

Interactive programs are increasingly important in making a museum community-friendly. The Tate, for example, has teamed with a video game company to create Tate Worlds, in which players use paintings to create their own environments and activities. In 2010, the Walker Art Center in Minneapolis went to the public with "50/50," a show of works on paper from its own collection. The chief curator posted 180 photos of works from the museum's collection on its website and asked the public to vote on which they thought should be in the show. Nineteen hundred people took part. The curator mounted the show, putting the crowd-pleasers chosen by the public on one side of the gallery and her picks on the other. Everyone who voted brought friends and families. It was a brilliant move on the curator's part, demonstrating that interactivity can get people in the door. Museums are not just about art; they're about self-discovery through communal activities. I worry, however, that in making use of all the technology, curators will demystify works that are meant to challenge and provoke the viewer. I'm also concerned that a lot of information available digitally, including what things cost, will color visitors' experiences in negative ways. I hope that museums will be able to strike a balance between new approaches and old-fashioned interaction of the visitor and works — through reflection.

My earliest museum memory wasn't interactive. It was straightforward and indelible — a mummy at the Academy of Natural Sciences in Philadelphia. Well, that and the gift shop. Clearly, I'm not the only one who likes a good gift shop. Museums are now dedicating more of their square-footage to selling goods. The Met even has satellite shops in airports and department stores all over the world. Doesn't it seem strange to be able to buy something in a museum shop without having to see any art? Yet, none of the outlets compare to The Met's "mothership" on Fifth Avenue which a few years ago grossed a whopping $40 million, including over $1 million in *postcards* alone.

These days, small shops are embedded in and at the end of exhibitions to ensure that no one escapes the gift shop experience. As my husband and I were leaving the SFMOMA exhibition, "The Steins Collect," an assemblage of works which once belonged to Gertrude Stein and her brothers, Bert commented, "Exit from the gift shop." I laughed and told him that graffiti artist Banksy beat him to the punch by using that line as a title of a film. Unfazed, he joked, "Aren't there any Gertrude Stein dolls for sale?" I laughed again, "If the Morgan Library sold Van Gogh dolls with a removable Velcro ear, there's got to be a Gertrude Stein doll somewhere."

In 2007, The Museum of Contemporary Art in Los Angeles (MOCA) offered visitors the ultimate museum gift shop experience, a Louis Vuitton retail shop smack in the middle of the Takashi Murakami retrospective. Murakami, the hugely popular Japanese artist who'd designed bags for Vuitton, may have meant the shop to serve as a metaphor for the culture of conspicuous consumption. If so, the lesson was lost on most visitors who, like me, shopped up a storm. The museum made a point of saying it made no money from the shop, but obviously someone did. Was it Murakami? Vuitton? One or the other, or both, took that metaphor straight to the bank. As a result of that combination, the link between art and fashion became all the closer, as wearing 'art' became an obvious sign of wealth and the ability to get something as hard-to-get as the work of a hot painter.

A number of museums have been beefing up their costume departments, capitalizing on this growing intersection of art and fashion. Of course, they hope to reel in wealthy donors who make their money in the fashion business. In the summer of 2011, the *Alexander McQueen: Savage Beauty* show at The Met generated the longest lines the museum ever had. Nearly 25,000 people became museum members just to jump the sometime 5-hour-long queue. Similar shows followed, like Yves St. Laurent at the Denver Art Museum and Rudi Gernreich at MOCA.

There's no shortage of ways for museums to stay relevant and exciting. Many run an extensive slate of films, concerts, lectures, and children's workshops. To improve accessibility, many museums stay open a few evenings a week and remain open the last 24 hours of the run of a show. For a while, the director of the Dallas Museum of Art led an 'Insomniac Tour' once a month at ten pm, and New York's Rubin Museum of Art hosted a series of 'Dream-Overs' where a psychologist interpreted the dreams of individuals who spent the night sleeping under specially-selected works of art. Meanwhile, social media platforms, like Facebook, Twitter, and Meetup.com alert art lovers to museum tours, lectures, and impromptu gatherings, and allow their users to converse online with others with similar interests. Do I hear a need for ArtMatch.com?

Museums are making big efforts to hang their permanent collections in more populist ways. It used to be *de rigueur* for art to be installed chronologically. This approach works for me because I think of art history like a football game in which one generation of artists passes the ball to the next, and so forth. But many museums, including The Getty Villa in Malibu, have installed parts of their collections by theme or subject. That way, visitors can observe differences in artists' approaches unencumbered by dates. Sounds good, but in 2013, Tate Britain did a new chronological hanging and got kudos from critics for switching back.

A GUIDE TO THE GUIDED TOUR

Education is an important mandate for most museums. Traditional gallery lectures and audio tours have been replaced or supplemented by newer technological tools, like dial-in gallery talks and iPhone apps, which enable visitors to connect to the art with a few well-placed clicks. The Cleveland Museum of Art spent ten million dollars on an iPad app called ArtLens. As visitors enter the museum, they encounter the "Collection Wall," a forty-foot interactive screen with images of works in the collection that can be swiped onto iPads, enabling them to custom build their own tour. They then can walk through the museum and listen to what the staff has to say — at their own pace.

Of course, human guides still exist, and some are so good, no recorded spiel can top them. They can put a show in historical, social, and artistic contexts in a way that makes even an average exhibition memorable.

Some museums are so determined to 'connect' the public with the art that they employ guides to interact with visitors on a one-to-one basis. If you're walking through at an exhibition, don't be surprised if a stranger approaches you and asks, "You seem puzzled. May I explain this painting to you?" I usually nod politely, even when I'm dying to shout, "Can't I just look at this painting in peace?" I don't want to break their rice bowl, but I do find it a bit creepy. Aren't we supposed to be quietly contemplating the works on view? Frankly, if you're having a problem understanding something, you might turn to the guards. They've been standing in front of the same paintings for weeks, months, or years, and they've heard it all. I've gotten lots of new ideas from them about how to look at and think about certain works, so you might, too.

HOUSE MUSEUMS AND OTHER LITTLE JEWELS

House museums like The Frick Collection in New York, The Isabella Stewart Gardner Museum in Boston, and Apsley House in London, are almost always worth a visit. The art is interesting, the settings are unique. They can feel so alive that you can imagine walking into a bedroom and seeing the owner's clothes hanging in a closet. In some, like the artist Rosa Bonheur's house museum near Fontainebleau, the clothes *still are*!

Not only do house museums offer an opportunity to see great works of art, but they're also a window into the taste of a certain time and a collector's quirky personality. Isabella Stewart Gardner's old masters, hand-picked by Bernard Berenson, who'd been her protégé when he was at Harvard, hang in a fantasy palace that could only have been conceived by a grande dame newly returned from the Grand Tour. And how peculiar that smack in the middle of his Beaux Arts jewel box stuffed with important paintings by every famous artist from Vermeer to Whistler, Frick plunked down a huge, hideous pipe organ. Imagine his weekly ritual of having an organist play while he sat on a Renaissance throne reading the *Saturday Evening Post*.

And whatever you do, don't miss the Huntington Library near Pasadena, California, built by railway baron

Henry Huntington and his wife Arabella, his uncle's widow. Surrounded by acres of the most extraordinary gardens (the succulent garden includes 5000 species), the Huntington has a stellar collection of paintings, including those two popular chestnuts of art history, Thomas Gainsborough's *The Blue Boy* and Thomas Lawrence's *Pinkie*. After a few turns around the galleries, you'll feel as if you're about to meet the characters from *Pride and Prejudice*.

After her first Huntington husband died, Arabella was guided by Duveen in collecting old masters. She married her husband's nephew, Henry (just think of all the monograms she didn't have to change), who favored British paintings. According to S.N. Behrman in his biography of Duveen, the Huntingtons sailed on the Lusitania to Europe in 1921, accompanied by Duveen. The couple stayed in the Gainsborough Suite, decorated with reproductions of Gainsboroughs, and, over dinner, Henry asked Duveen who painted the young boy in blue, who owned it, and could he buy the original. When Duveen got off the ship, he went straight to visit the owner, the Duke of Westminster, and bought *The Blue Boy* (ill. 12). Although Behrman's facts aren't accurate (Huntington had known the painting, and Duveen had been trying to acquire it for years), it's a breezy tale of *The Blue Boy* (c. 1770).

For a long time, the sitter was thought to be the son of a friend of the artist, a wealthy ironmonger in London.

Now it's believed he was Gainsborough Dupont, the nephew of the painter, who grew up to be an artist. He's dressed in a 17th-century costume, the rage during Gainsborough's time and looks as if he's stepped out of an Anthony van Dyck painting. That's no mistake, as Gainsborough revered Van Dyck's paintings. The artist's choice of blue for the costume was in purposeful defiance of his rival, the famous academician, Joshua Reynolds, who taught students that it was inappropriate to paint a composition dominated by a cool color, like blue.

The sale of this famous masterpiece to an American caused a public outcry in Britain. Ninety thousand people attended its farewell appearance at The National Gallery in London before it set sail to the US. The museum's director was so moved that he wrote, "Au revoir," on the back of the painting. From London, the painting was supposedly sent surreptitiously, for high drama - if not safety, to Paris before making the crossing to New York, where it was shown in Duveen's New York gallery to great fanfare. From there, Duveen accompanied it by train to the Huntingtons' home in Pasadena. It was an amazing PR stunt on Duveen's part, but the work was considered a masterpiece worth all the attention.

Lawrence's *Pinkie* (ill. 13), painted in 1794, twenty-five years after *The Blue Boy*, depicts eleven-year-old Sarah Barrett Moulton. Gainsborough would have been the artist of choice for Pinkie's family, but he'd died, and Lawrence was next best. The painting came to be called *Pinkie*, not because Sarah's wearing pink, but because she was tiny and Pinkie was her nickname. When the painting was commissioned, Pinkie's grandmother knew that Pinkie was gravely ill, and the little girl died of consumption shortly after the painting's completion. Had Pinkie survived, she would have been the aunt of poet Elizabeth Barrett Browning, the daughter of Pinkie's brother.

Attitudes toward *The Blue Boy* and *Pinkie* have dramatically changed over the past century. For a long time, the two were "destination paintings," the reason visitors flocked to the Huntington. My husband remembers being taken there by his mother when he was a little boy to see 'the most famous paintings in the world.' Today, they're hung with other great 18th-century British portraits, including the blockbuster *Sarah Siddons as the Tragic Muse*, and still many visitors skip them and head straight for the gardens.

How can artists and paintings that famous fall out of favor? Is it due to a change in taste? Style? Subject? Or something else? *The Blue Boy* and *Pinkie* may have become 'unfamous' because of the Huntington's policy against lending. They were cloistered in a community as near to Los Angeles as Newark is to New York but not easily accessible. Had the paintings been on view in other museums, in other major cities, from time to time, the excitement about them may have continued and generations would have grown up caring.

A tragic blow to house museums was the moving of the Barnes Foundation from its original location in

Lower Merion, a Philadelphia suburb, to a contemporary shell of a museum in Center City. When Albert Barnes died, he left instructions in his will that all his paintings and numerous other collections, including African sculpture and American Indian artifacts, were to remain where they were, in an idiosyncratic installation he devised. When the trust voted in 2002 to relocate, the case went to court. Based on the doctrine of *cy pres* (if change is necessary, "the nearest thing" to what was intended must be done), the judge allowed for the paintings to be moved, provided the rooms would be installed exactly as they'd been in Lower Merion. Unfortunately, the experience isn't the same. To enter the Barnes at its old location, you had to check in at a tiny guard gate and walk up a path through the arboretum (another extraordinary Barnes collection). It was an intimate experience that you don't have with the new building.

As most public museums can no longer afford to buy the best works on the market, collectors, richer and more nimble, snap them up. Especially because most collectors today focus on contemporary art, and many of the works are too big to be installed in a domestic setting, house museums have given way to renovated warehouse spaces and commissioned "private museums." These museums fill the gap and perform an important service, by enabling the public to see works absent from most public museums. Crystal Bridges Museum of American Art, started by Walmart heiress Alice Walton, is a terrific example. Walton hired Moshe Safdie, the architect of the Skirball Cultural Center in Los Angeles, to design a museum in Bentonville, Arkansas, for the American Art she's collecting. Walton's efforts have made it possible for major works of our country's past and present to be seen by inhabitants of a region of America who otherwise wouldn't have the opportunity. The list goes on. Mitch and Emily Rales have built Glenstone in Potomac, Maryland, for their private collection of 20th- and 21st-century art, with two museum buildings designed by Gwathmey Siegal & Associates and Thomas Phifer and Partners. Eugenio Lopez, the Jumex (fruit juice) heir, opened the David Chipperfield-designed Museo Jumex in Mexico City, and at least fifty Chinese have opened private museums. In America, owners take advantage of tax write-offs if their museums are open to the public some of the time. The Brant Foundation Art Study Center, opened by Peter Brant in Greenwich, Connecticut is an example. Eli and Edythe Broad, who commissioned Diller Scofidio + Renfro to build a museum across the street from MOCA, in Los Angeles, have taken a unique approach. Although the public will see the Broad Foundation as a museum, the Broad's also a lending library, making works available to museums all over the world.

I do worry what will happen to some of these private contemporary art museums fifty years down the line if there's no policy for buying and selling. If the cutting-edge artists shown fall out of fashion, these private fiefdoms may start looking like bizarre time capsules, rather than timeless wonders.

Donor museums shouldn't be criticized because they're egos trips of collectors. I think T.S. Eliot was mistaken when he wrote in *Murder in the Cathedral*, "The last temptation is the greatest treason: to do the right deed for the wrong reason." Many great accomplishments have been achieved by individuals acting for selfish reasons. The man who gives the $100 million wing to a hospital may do it to see his name in lights or to make sure that, if he gets ill, he'll get great care. It doesn't matter. He's providing a great service to the community. The same goes for collectors who create fine collections open to the public. They may do it for their own self-aggrandizement, but it benefits all of us. No one remembers Henry Clay Frick's business triumphs or his ruthless suppression of workers' strikes. We only know his name from the museum he founded.

TROUBLE IN PARADISE

With few exceptions, including the Getty, which has a seven billion dollar endowment, life for museums in the 21st century is more challenging than ever. As patronage and endowments fluctuate with the economy, it's been a roller-coaster ride, and not in a fun way. Many would-be donors have or are opening their own museums, and others have lost fortunes and reneged on large gifts. Corporations have failed to come up with promised funds and aren't running to support new shows. Even memberships have declined, as middle class museumgoers cut 'unnecessary' expenditures. On average, of the 61 million museum excursions made in 2014, visitors spent $8 on admission, shopping, and food, whereas the museums spent $53 on every person entering. That leaves many museums, old and new, beset with financial problems. Roanoke, as I described earlier, proudly raised the money for a new museum, but found itself without sufficient revenue for operating expenses. It became one of many public institutions in a program on cultural overbuilding at the Cultural Policy Center at the University of Chicago called *Set in Stone*, in which scholars examined what went wrong. One criticism of the study was that it's impossible to compute in dollars and cents the impact museums have on local pride and tourism. Meanwhile, Denver, with its awkward Daniel Libeskind-designed Denver Art Museum, in which paintings have to be hung from ceilings or on baseball bat-like projections off curved walls, and other museums have learned the painful lesson that donors may be willing to pay for buildings, but not light bulbs.

"Hey, wait a minute," I hear you saying, "If a museum is having trouble making ends meet, why not sell a couple of masterpieces?" No way. If it wants to remain a member in good standing of The American Alliance of Museums (i.e. eligible for loans from other institutions), it can only de-acquisition works to generate funds to buy other works. Selling art, even works museums never show, to pay the electric bill and guards' salaries, is forbidden. After the National Academy of Design (NAD) sold two American landscapes in 2008 to stay solvent, it was shunned for years by other museums (none would lend it art), and, in some quarters, it still hasn't been forgiven for going off the reservation.

MAKING IT WORK

Meanwhile, public museums aren't waving the white flag and giving up. They're employing creative new ways to stay in the game. Many are cutting back on full-time curators and are hiring independents on a show-by-show basis. They've also gone into the lending-for-dollars business. In 2004, the MFA in Boston sent twenty-one Monets to the gallery at the Bellagio in Las Vegas for which it was well paid. In 2007, while the Art Institute of Chicago was closed for renovation, it lent $92 million worth of paintings to the Kimbell, charging a purported $2 million and a percentage of sales on related goods in the gift shop.

Shows like those help, especially since blockbusters have become impossibly expensive, with the costs of insurance, shipping, and couriers spiking. As I mentioned, institutional lenders have become increasingly reluctant. If Museum A wants to borrow a Monet from Museum B, B may agree if it can borrow

A's best Van Gogh at A's expense for the duration of the Monet loan. So, museums have to be inventive in coming up with less-expensive, less difficult to mount crowd-pleasing shows. In 2011, The Met hauled its own Picassos out of storage for a Picasso retrospective. The public was none the wiser (it was the museum's fifth highest attended show to date). Cynical critics insinuated that the show was designed to point out the gaps in The Met's Picasso holdings, hoping donors would step forward to fill them with gifts of appropriate paintings. Leonard Lauder seemed to follow the script by promising his billion dollar collection of Cubism to the museum, including many landmark Picassos.

Some museums expand their boards as a way of increasing revenue. They're also breaking the unwritten rule not to exhibit trustees' collections. Maybe they like the works and hope such shows secure generous donations or, at least, cement relationships. Too often, that backfires, and the collectors *use* the museum. The "cred" of a museum show enhances the value of a collection, and once collectors get that, they sell the art, leaving the museum with egg on its face.

Museums have always commercialized themselves by peddled 'naming rights.' Jorge Perez, a Miami real estate developer and collector, came up with $40 million (half in cash, half in art) out of the $220 million the Miami Art Museum needed for its new building (including an operating endowment). What did he exact in return?

That the museum would change its name to the Perez Art Museum Miami (PAMM). Done! Moral of the story? Be the lead donor or the last one to come through at the right time with sorely-needed dollars.

Museums use a variety of other commercial drivers to raise money, including renting out their great halls for events. If the Vatican can rent out the Sistine Chapel, why can't The Met host a hot party at the Temple of Dendur? That's the kind of thing that led New York art dealer Richard Feigen to liken The Met to "a nice girl from a good family who just once in a while goes out and turns tricks for pocket money." Michael Gross in *Rogues' Gallery*, a 2009 behind-the-scenes look at The Met, put it another way: "As costs have escalated, she's grown promiscuous." What would Philippe de Montebello say about all of this? To help his beloved Met survive, would he sell works or allow his museum to become a wedding venue or three-ring circus filled with blinking video screens, dubious exhibitions, and shopping malls? I think he'd do what he always did — find a tasteful way to raise the funds that allow the museum to continue its role as a sanctuary for contemplating great art.

But not everyone is de Montebello, and not all museums are The Met. That's why MOCA's board reached over to the business side of the art world and hired Jeffrey Deitch, an experienced dealer, as its director. But Deitch didn't have it easy. As he walked me through a Lynda Benglis show, he expressed fear that the museum model was broken. "Who benefits from this show?" he asked. "Benglis and her dealer get valuable PR and make money on sales, the public gets to see the work, but the show's $250,000 cost is shouldered by the museum. At that rate," Deitch shrugged, "shows like this won't be possible forever." As I left, I wished him good luck, thinking that I wouldn't want his job. He left after three years.

ASK NOT WHAT THE MUSEUM CAN DO FOR YOU...

If you join a museum, you get invitations to fascinating programs, shows, and openings. If you write a slightly bigger check and become a member of a special interest group like the "Friends of Contemporary Art," you get to mix with well-heeled collectors and attend private high-level museum functions. And, if you ante up and join the board, you enter a whole new world of privilege. As one of our clients said, "To become a city father, I had two choices; I could have joined the opera board and sat through five hours of Wagner night after night, or the museum board, which required only a few weekends of perspicacious shopping." It was an easy decision, one that reminded me of Barbara Kruger's piece, *When I hear the word Culture, I take out my checkbook*. It's rumored that membership on The Met's board requires a commitment of five million dollars *per annum* plus an expected larger gift down the line. No wonder Richard Feigen called The Met's board "the most exclusive club in the world."

As a trustee, you'll learn in advance what shows are coming and what the curators are buying. Supporters on this level are not only allowed to buy works by artists the museum acquires, they're encouraged to do so. Do I hear you ask, 'Isn't that insider trading'? You bet. One enterprising London dealer, realizing that the Tate wanted a work by one of his hot, hard-to-get artists, ingeniously arranged for six trustees to buy one each, provided they chip in to buy a seventh for the museum. Everyone profited.

Is a trusteeship for you? Social and art market perks aside, a close connection with one of the country's great public collections can be deeply rewarding. You'll learn a lot, spend time in the presence of great art, and have the pleasure of supporting an institution that's important to your community. On the other hand, if it's not for you, don't fret. The art's still there, waiting for you to slip anonymously through the door and enjoy, with no responsibilities. And, who knows, you may have time for a trip to the gift shop.

WRITERS: ART CRITICS, ART JOURNALISTS, AND ART HISTORIANS

THREE DIFFERENT ANIMALS

Admit it: You're not entirely sure how art critics differ from art journalists or how either of them differ from art historians. Join the club. Since these professionals all write and speak about art, it's sometimes hard to understand the distinct roles they play and how you can utilize their wit and wisdom. Since all three can be useful when you're learning about art, scouting potential acquisitions, or deciding what or what not to buy, let's take a minute to get them straight.

ART CRITICS

Art critics attend exhibitions at museums and galleries and, using their 'eye' and experience, analyze what's on view and pass judgment on its quality and importance. Much of what they look at is hard to understand, and explaining or reacting to it in print isn't easy. As a result, every successful critic has developed his or her own purpose and methodology. As *New York Times* art critic Roberta Smith described her mission in an interview with Sarah Thornton (in *Seven Days in the Art World*), "You draw attention to artists and give people ways of thinking about them." Yes, and critics also tell thousands or millions of readers whether those artists are bad or good. That used to give art critics tremendous power as market makers. If they liked a show, collectors would rush out to buy. If they didn't, it would bomb. Today, their power has diminished. Big collectors and advisors buy out shows before the critics even get a chance to see them, let alone write a review. If enough collectors buy, everybody else jumps on the bandwagon, critics be damned. It's the same in the film business. A movie critic can pan a film, but if millions of Americans go see it opening weekend and love it, word of mouth will follow, and millions more will go after that. Still, art critics are worth listening to. Every major newspaper in the country, as well as a lot of magazines and websites, has one on staff, and the best, like Roberta Smith, are household names among those interested in art.

Art criticism isn't new; it can be traced back to 18th-century France. Much of it grew around the French Salons, the king- or government-sponsored yearly exhibitions. These were particularly important for artists, as commercial galleries, as we know them, didn't exist. Paintings of hundreds of artists were 'skied' (hung floor-to-ceiling, with every inch of space used), and lines of visitors filed through the rooms to see them. Self-styled critics wrote about what they saw in the gazettes of the day.

Since I have neither the space nor time to outline the history of art criticism, I'll mention just a couple of my favorite examples. One was a critique written by Etienne La Font de Saint-Yenne in 1746 accusing the artists of the Salon of being less conscientious than the old masters. He also railed that serious painting was disappearing from the walls of the rich in favor of mirrors and carved plaster. Mirrors, of course, remain an art dealer's enemy today. Another famous example is Emile Zola's defense of Edouard Manet's *Le Déjeuner sur l'herbe* (Luncheon on the Grass), shown in the 1863 Salon des Refusés. That year, over 3000 paintings were rejected by the official Salon, and the Emperor, Napoleon III, fearing repercussions from the public, allowed an official Salon de Refusés to be installed as an annex. This event led to the exhibition of the Impressionists in 1874. The moniker "Impressionism" came from a reference to Monet's painting *Impression: Soleil Levant* in a satirical article by another critic, Louis Leroy, entitled, "Exhibition of the Impressionists."

Numbers of critics took up the gauntlet in the 20th century, and they persisted in challenging the establishment or dumping on artists for being too imitative. In the mid-20th century, critics Clement Greenberg and Harold Rosenberg, fixtures on the art scene, had the art world riveted with their dueling views on Abstract Expressionism. Things became less riveting when Conceptual Art made its appearance some years later. Art writers found it more difficult to talk about works by Don Judd, Carl Andre, etc., and many turned to Marxism and French philosophers, like Jacques Derrida and Roland Barthes, for ideas and a new 'language' to describe the work, in itself "conceptual."

With exceptions, like Rene Ricard, who championed Schnabel and put Basquiat on the map with his famous 1981 *Artforum* essay, "Radiant Child," this has led to insufferable 'artspeak.' The following example is an excerpt from an interview with Shamim Momin, a curator of the 2008 Whitney Biennial:

I wrote about a nonlinear idea of time. This notion has been informed by both scientific developments over the course of the last century and then also reiterated in technological developments, literalizing this idea of fragmentation and dispersal. It's kind of a different way of conceptualizing space that changed static, Newtonian ideas of time. And it's not to say that the artists are using this as content, but that it's restructuring the way we think about the world, time, and history. It's a non-modern take, as opposed to postmodern or anti-modern.

Say again?

I thought I was alone in my confusion, until I read Eric Gibson's piece, "The Lost Art of Writing About Art," in *The Wall Street Journal*. Gibson lamented that the 2008 Biennial catalogue was "...incomprehensible drivel," that could inspire potential museumgoers to "walk away." Barry Gewen, in his article, "State of the Art," in *The New York Times Book Review* (2005) also thinks we have a problem: "We live at a moment when artists have been asking the kinds of questions children ask – What is art? What is it good for? – and critics for the most part have been giving answers not even an adult can understand." He mocks the situation with a fictional conversation between a mother and child:

'Mommy, why have we come all this way to see pictures of soup cans?'

'It's Andy Warhol, sweetheart, and he's wielding a sharp, insinuating heuristic chisel to pry at the fault lines and lay bare the sedimented faces of his surround.'

Well, she certainly cleared *that* up.

Why has artspeak become the *lingua franca* of the art world? Some commentators call it a case of the Emperor's New Clothes – suggesting that writers use indecipherable prose to cover up the fact that, when they look at today's art, there's nothing *there*. Hey, let's not blame the art for the sins of the people talking about it. Perhaps they write the way they do to protect their accountability, or because *they* have nothing to say. Or maybe they have a lot to say, and it'll just take me a long time to figure it out.

The public likes it when critics inspire a "conversation" about art, as Clement Greenberg and Harold Rosenberg did. Contrarian Jed Perl got people thinking when he had negative things to say about Richter's 2002 MoMA retrospective, dismissed Eli Broad's gift of a building to LACMA for not donating the art on view along with the building, and denounced Koons and Hirst. And I still miss Hilton Kramer with his ultra-conservative views. I didn't agree with most of what he said, but we have plenty of liberal critics, and no one's taking an opposing view, presenting it in a way that's relevant today. And remember Kenneth Clark? You've got to love a guy who, as a young man, announced his profession as an art critic before he'd written a word. Despite his upper class British accent and manners, Clark made the wonders of art real and exciting and used plain talk, like describing works as "revolting" or "disgusting."

Today's best art critics, like Roberta Smith, Jerry Saltz, and Peter Schjeldahl, write in a way that's easy to understand, and they can help you make an informed decision about what you see without worrying that you're having the 'wrong' reaction. Schjeldahl, who writes for *The New Yorker*, says that the most important thing he does is to help the general public enjoy art. Saltz, who's with *New York* magazine, is described in Sarah Thornton's book, *Seven Days in the Art World*, as being interested in context. "I'm looking for what the artist is trying to say," he's written, "... what the work reveals about society, and the timeless conditions of being alive."

For these reasons and more, critics will always be important and relied upon to impact our thinking and appreciation. Whether you're reading their criticisms in print or online, they'll open your eyes to new artists, art, and the politics of the industry. And often, their commentaries will make you want to hop on over to see a show. And when you do, you'll want to thank them for enriching your experience.

ART JOURNALISTS

Art journalists are a very different animal from critics. Like critics, they write for newspapers, magazines and web-based media, but, rather than evaluating an artist's work, their job is to report on the goings-on in the art world and the art business. They write before auctions (why someone is selling, what market expectations are) and/or after the fact (what sold, what didn't, and why). They write about art fairs (what dealers showed, what sold and what that says about the market), new museums (how wealthy patrons spend their money), and about anything and everything that goes on in the business. Like art critics, journalists are paid to express their opinions, but their opinions are supposed to be based on observations of fact, not personal or emotional reactions.

Insiders often complain that art journalists don't have the story exactly 'right,' and, sometimes, they don't. Perhaps that's because art journalists aren't just writing for insiders; they're simplifying things for the general public. Outsiders are fascinated by what art world insiders are thinking and doing, and they devour stories like "Russian businessman spends $100 million on Picasso painting and hangs it in Vladivostok brothel." Once upon a time, few publications had any interest in such stories. But, since the late 1980's, when the art world became hot and sexy, journals rushed to hire journalists to report on the huge sums of money changing hands and other spicy tidbits. As long as big-ticket art continues to be part of "The Lifestyles of the Rich and Famous," these scribes will have a lot to write about.

But there are art journalists and *art* journalists. Those like Judd Tully, who writes for *Blouin ArtInfo* (you can watch him on YouTube), are head and shoulders above the rest and should be on your reading list. They don't just give you the names of secret consignors or the results of the major sales, they draw on their vast experience and contacts to put events in context. All of this is grist for your mill.

ART HISTORIANS

Art historians are usually academics who write and speak about art history — even historicizing what happened yesterday. They also uncover new information that could change our perception about an artist or a period of art. Such discoveries can lead to turf wars in which academics battle over who gets to publish the latest sliver of knowledge about, let's say, Caravaggio's life of crime (Did he kill one or two people?) or Winslow Homer's Paris sojourn (Did he or didn't he go there?). Many art historians stake out a single artist and spend their whole life working on that artist's oeuvre. They'll write copious articles, and the culmination of their careers may be a book or many books that are meant to alter the world's perception of that artist forever — and provoke a lot of grouchy criticism from competing academics.

While critics and journalists publish in newspapers and magazines, art historians typically write books published by university presses and articles that appear in museum and gallery catalogues and academic journals. Today, they're also writing for popular magazines like *Vogue* and *Harper's Bazaar*.

Although art historians offer important insights on an artist that can affect generations of scholars, they're less central in most collectors' decision making. The most important place where the ivory tower and marketplace meet is the catalogue raisonné. Compiled according to the standards of the Catalogue Raisonné Scholars Association (who knew?), these volumes are undertaken by scholars who devote years or a lifetime to studying a particular artist. Along the way, they become the world's leading 'expert' on that artist and often become the last word on authenticating that artist's work. Compiling a CR is a long-term project requiring the compiler to identify and assemble dossiers on every work by the artist, travel to examine them, etc. No scholar can afford to take that on himself, so CRs are usually sponsored by foundations, universities, art dealers, or collectors. The CR for Rothko works on paper, for example, is being funded by the National Gallery. If a commercial gallery does the funding, the art historian remains above the commercial fray, but the dealer enjoys the financial fruits of the scholar's labor. He gets to know where all the works are, what's for sale, and becomes the clearinghouse for collectors who want to buy or sell works by that artist.

If you're considering a particular work, a discussion with an art historian who specializes in your artist can be a game-changer. He's likely so steeped in the lore of 'your' artist, and he can make 'your' painting come alive in ways you never knew possible. Unable to find a particular catalogue on Georges Braque in any New York library, I called John Richardson, a preeminent expert in Cubism, hoping he had a copy I could borrow. I asked Richardson how Quentin Laurens, the son of Henri Laurens, the sculptor, came to hold the *droit moral* for Braque — the power to authenticate Braque paintings. Richardson described a moment that changed art history. Henri Laurens was bicycling, fell off his bike, and crushed his testicles. Because he was unable to father a child, Braque stepped in, so that Quentin was actually Braque's son. I certainly got more information than I bargained for. Call on these scholars, offer to pay them for a consultation and enjoy.

Each of these art world commentators — critics, journalists, and historians — has useful, but very different kinds of information to impart. Look to critics for educated opinions on exhibitions and artists, journalists for reports on the market, and art historians for historical expertise. Then take a break and look at the art for yourself.

COLLECTORS & COLLECTIONS

THE ANATOMY OF A COLLECTOR

Once a work of art leaves the artist's studio, all roads lead to the collector. Without collectors, museums would be the principal art buyers, and although there'd be some random purchases by individuals, for home decoration, we wouldn't have the activity we call "collecting" or the excitement surrounding it.

Collectors make the wheels of the art world go around. And even those who don't, think they do. In exchange for supplying the capital that greases the wheels, collectors reap the greatest benefits of all. They get to own and live with beautiful objects, learn a fascinating field, and enjoy the excitement of the chase and the status that owning art confers. In addition, if they choose, they can move in a fast-paced social set and make significant profits when they sell — all on their own terms and timetable. In this chapter, we'll look at what makes collectors tick and some of the strategies they employ to build collections.

First, a definition. What makes someone "a collector"? Is it the amount he spends, the number of works he owns, how active he is, or some other more mysterious criterion that makes someone worthy of that designation? There's no one answer. A simple, serviceable definition of a collector is an individual who acquires several objects that share a common denominator yet exhibit differences. If, for example, you have a six-pack of Budweiser in the fridge, you're not a collector; but, if you've got a Bud, a Heineken, and a Coors, you are.

WHY DO PEOPLE COLLECT?

What drives individuals to collect is one of those mysteries that's been pondered by philosophers and scientists for ages. Some scientists find its roots in the ontological need to classify, and plenty of collectors, including those who create wish lists, exhibit that desire. Other collectors are fascinated by statistics. Michael Chow, the restaurateur, has total recall of art prices the way a baseball fanatic knows every player's batting average. Just ask him what any major post-war painting brought at auction, and he'll tell you where and when it came up and how much it brought.

Other scientists see collecting as a vestigial form of hunting and gathering. Certainly, everyone's born with an acquisitive nature, and if you like something, it's natural to want more. Children love to acquire miniature cars and stuffed animals. When you grow up, it's only *what* you acquire that changes, as dolls and building blocks are replaced by art and antiques.

The psychiatric community has weighed in on the 'why' of collecting, with Sigmund Freud leading the charge, radically proclaiming that collecting is a way for individuals to compensate for the loss of control experienced during toilet training. Since Freud, generations of psychiatrists and psychologists have pushed his ideas further. "Dr. X," who wrote a popular book on the subject, explained collecting as a way of offsetting any childhood loss. He could be right, although I've since learned from a friend, one of his patients, that "X" turned out to be a veterinarian. When my friend learned the truth, he stayed in therapy with "X," shrugging, "It's too late to change now."

William Davies King, in his bizarre but poignant memoir, *Collections of Nothing*, one of very few autobiographies by collectors on their collecting activities, bears out "Dr. X's" thesis. For him, collecting thousands of pieces of other people's detritus, like old chopstick wrappers and tin cans, is a way "to salve... a wound that many of us feel in our personal histories." No doubt we all have holes in our heart that could use some infill, but how big and deep must his be to keep all that junk around? And when does collecting turn into "hoarding disorder"?

The urge to collect can also arise from practical considerations. When twenty- or thirty-somethings outgrow the posters they had in their college dorm rooms, they want to get into "real" art. Couples in their forties or fifties who move into their dream home *need* art to fill blank walls. And empty nesters searching for a shared hobby are hard-pressed to find anything as satisfying as art collecting to fill their time and satisfy their intellectual curiosity. Then there are the lucky few who've had a wealth event, like selling a company or receiving a big bonus, that kick-starts them into collecting. And for those who inherit money, collecting art is a logical step in a life of shopping and spending. You can imagine their thinking: "We've got all the houses, cars, and yachts we could possibly use, and my wife has all the jewelry she'll ever want. What's left to do but buy art?"

A few people collect because it's a family tradition. Whereas many British aristocrats, guardians of collections formed centuries ago, have had to sell art to keep their estates intact, Lord (Jacob) Rothschild, as Patron of the Rothschild Foundation, has expended great effort and resources buying back treasures once owned by his ancestors and adding others to the collection at Waddesdon Manor, the late 19th century Renaissance-style chateau built by Baron Ferdinand de Rothschild. And as Nelson Rockefeller told Werner Muensterberger, in his book, *Collecting: An Unruly Passion*:

You see, in my position I must collect. My mother did it, and my grandfather did it. It is an obligation. After all, the Medicis did it too.

Today, many couples try to instill in their children a love of art and collecting, and encouraging them to amass Barbie dolls or miniature trucks can be good training. My brother-in-law, Russell, was eleven when the baseball card fad took hold of him. In those days, cards came free with Topps Bubble Gum. Now, Russ has a complete set of 1959 cards — and a mouthful of fillings to show for it. Unfortunately, when Russ collected, he discreetly marked his cards with his initial, a tiny "R," in the corner to tell his cards apart from those of his friends. Too bad. If the cards were in pristine condition, they'd be worth tens of thousands of dollars. Instead, they're worthless. Fortunately, that experience didn't sour Russ on collecting, and he went on, with my sister, to make a thoughtful collection of academic drawings. He doesn't put his initials on those.

A long-time client uses his growing collection of panoramic American landscapes as a geography lesson for his kids. Whenever he buys a new work, he takes the children to the spot where the artist painted it. I usually tag along, and thanks to him and his private plane, I've visited parts of the United States I never would have seen on my own — from Mt. Hood to Deer Isle. I can't wait to find him a Frederick Church painting of Cotopaxi.

UNCOVERING YOUR PASSION

You have to love what you buy. Elaine Wynn, cofounder of Wynn Resort, paid $142,405,000 for a Francis Bacon three-part portrait of Lucian Freud. Interest on that sum, at a modest 3.6 percent per year, is $5,126,580, or $14,045.43 daily. That means it costs Elaine $585.23 an hour for the pleasure of owning the painting — including the hours she sleeps! It's got to be love.

One of our clients loves his collection so much that he walks around the house before he goes to sleep every night and spends a few moments in front of each work. If his wife weren't around, he'd probably kiss them all good night. Moreover, he used to have such separation anxiety from one of his paintings, a small jewel of a Classical period Picasso, that he had a velvet-lined box made for it, and he takes it with him from one of his homes to another. Renaissance nobility carried portable altars with them, so why shouldn't he take his Picasso?

No one would dispute that there are certain qualities in works of art that emotionally grab certain individuals. But are there universal characteristics that attract, revile, or stir other passions in everyone who sees them? The conceptual artist John Baldessari poked fun at the art market's preferences in his 1966-68 word painting, *Tips For Artists Who Want To Sell* (ill. 14). To quote the painting:

"GENERALLY SPEAKING, PAINTINGS WITH LIGHT COLORS SELL MORE QUICKLY THAN PAINTINGS WITH DARK COLORS." "SUBJECTS THAT SELL WELL: MADONNA AND CHILD, LANDSCAPES, FLOWER PAINTINGS, STILL LIFES (FREE OF MORBID PROPS_ _ _ DEAD BIRDS, ETC.) NUDES, MARINE PICTURES, ABSTRACTS AND SURREALISM." And lastly, "SUBJECT MATTER IS IMPORTANT: IT HAS BEEN SAID THAT PAINTINGS WITH COWS AND HENS IN THEM COLLECT DUST_ _ _ WHILE THE SAME PAINTINGS WITH BULLS AND ROOSTERS SELL."

We can laugh, but many in the trade would say that Baldessari's probably right.

When a client asked us to bid on a hokey painting of a dog coming up at auction, I was stunned. I love dogs, but this was badly painted. You could say, the painting was "a dog" (OK, it was "a turkey"). But nothing I said dissuaded him. He'd had a Labrador like the one in the painting when he was a boy, and he simply had to have it. "Why confuse reality with the way I feel?" he asked. Passion ruled.

It's not uncommon for strong negative feelings about a particular subject matter to cause a visceral reaction in collectors. One day, I was in a gallery in New York with a San Diego-based client, and the dealer brought out a Pissarro snow scene for him to see. The would-be buyer turned up his nose. "I moved to Southern California from Boston to escape the snow, so why should I buy a painting of something I hate?" For me, it was a 'eureka' moment. In all the years I've been an advisor, I've only placed one snow scene in a Southern California collection. Now I know why.

TODAY'S COLLECTING ATMOSPHERE

The tide of art collecting has become a tsunami and, with it, the rules of the game have changed. Therefore, it's beneficial to examine how collectors approach their collecting activities, why they've become so powerful, and how they wield their power.

To begin, there are more collectors buying more high-priced works than ever. According to a 2007 study conducted by Clare McAndrew for The European Fine Art Foundation (TEFAF), *The International Art Market: A Survey of Europe in a Global Context*, sales in the European art market alone grew by 95% in value and 24% in numbers of transactions between 2002 and 2006. Instead of coming from the US and Europe, collectors now come from all over the world. Ten years ago, if a great work came on the market, everyone would have known the half-dozen potential buyers for it. Now, if a trophy work (the great iconic work) comes to auction, someone unknown is likely to walk in from Malaysia, China, or anywhere else, plunk down the 50 or 100 million dollars, and take the prize. According to Sotheby's, in Damien Hirst's 2008 two-day auction of his own works, 39% went to new collectors of contemporary art and 24% went to buyers new to Sotheby's. And in a recent London sale, according to *The Baer Faxt*, buyers came from 23 different countries. As the non-Western world continues to develop and the number of affluent individuals increases, the collecting base will continue to expand, adding thousands of South Americans, Indians, Chinese, and residents of Arab countries to an already rich mix. To them, art is today's reserve currency, the way many have held U.S. dollars. They hope that the value of the works increase, but their primary goal is to put money someplace safe, and the portability of art is a contributing factor.

The level of commitment for collectors has changed dramatically. Several works of art have sold for over a hundred million dollars, including Picasso's *Les Femmes D'Alger* for $179 million, a Cézanne for $250 million, and a Gauguin for $300 million. I'm often asked how a work can possibly be worth *that* much, and it's easy to understand. Think how unique and special a painting can be, and if many houses and apartments, which are a lot less special, sell for over a hundred million, why shouldn't a superb painting be worth more? Another way to understand it stems from our belief that artists are great inventors and innovators. Why shouldn't an important work by Picasso, for instance, be equal in value to the invention of the airplane by the Wright Brothers or the Salk vaccine? How much would they be worth?

Or, if Picasso is considered at the top of the cultural heap, why shouldn't anyone superrich who wanted to make an investment, buy something in permanent short supply that should at least keep its value? And can you put a value on being able to live a life with a great object?

A few years ago, a young hedge-funder from Chicago bluntly asked, "If I set aside 100 million dollars to build a contemporary art collection, is that enough?" If he meant world-class Rothkos, Warhols, and Twomblys, the answer, sadly, was "No." Our hedge fund client would have to set his sights on less important works by the majors, works by lesser-known artists, or works by hot emerging artists that can run into the millions and don't come with any guarantee that they'll retain their present value. And on that level, there's huge competition. Not since the Gilded Age have captains of industry fought over art riches this way. The difference is that the paintings collected then were old masters, and today it's post-war and contemporary art.

The pace of collecting has changed in recent years. Collectors used to build their collections slowly and deliberately over decades, and most would stop when the walls of their homes were filled. Today, they want instant gratification and collect with lightning speed, often in bulk. As we've discussed, they build additions onto their homes, free-standing 'galleries' on their property, renovate warehouses, or open museums of their own to accommodate their growing collections. It's not unusual for contemporary art collectors to have hundreds or thousands of works. David Roberts, a British real estate investor has approximately 2,000 works he shows in a former furniture factory in London's Camden Town, and Jose "Joe" Berardo, a Portuguese investor, owns 50,000 works, many of which have been shown in the Berardo Collection Museum in Lisbon. Some do it because they love what they buy, others are addicted to the activity, want to create a museum, or perhaps they're playing the odds and hope that if they buy a critical mass, a few of their artists are bound to make it big.

The mega-collecting trend has resulted in a surge in collector power. With museums unable to compete, influential collectors with deep pockets have become today's tastemakers. They buy emerging artists' work in numbers before critics get a chance to write about them. Then other collectors and dealers pile on. You see it clearly in Miami during fair time. Collectors go to the Rubell, de la Cruz, and Margulies collections, and leave thinking, "I want what they have," and they rush to the fair to buy it. According to Andrew Rice in *Bloomberg Businessweek*, these mega-collectors become, as Alberto Mugrabi describes his family, 'market makers.' The Mugrabis have the largest private holdings of Warhol, over a hundred Hirsts, scores of Basquiats, and everyone in the art business considers them dealers in collectors' clothes.

COLLECTING STRATEGIES

There's no "right way" to collect. In fact, there are probably as many ways to collect as there are collectors. Of course, having a ton of money doesn't hurt, but it's not everything. You can put together a great collection on a limited budget and have a lot of fun.

Herb and Dorothy Vogel, subjects of the 2008 documentary *Herb & Dorothy*, became legends for collecting on a shoestring. They lived in a one-bedroom, rent-controlled New York apartment on her modest income as a librarian and used his salary as a postal worker to buy art. From the 60s to the 80s, they were habitués of galleries and artists' studios and collected principally works on paper. Dealers and artists admired them and offered them long-term payment schedules and special discounts. In 1992, thirty years after they started, the Vogels donated their collection of almost 5,000 works, all kept in their apartment, to the National Gallery — in exchange for a small annuity. They then used the annuity to buy more art, which they also gave to the National Gallery.

It's useful to find a collecting area that differentiates your collection and you from the herd. When the strippers in *Gypsy* sing the lyrics, "You gotta have a gimmick," they could be talking about art collecting. In art circles, probably a better word than "gimmick" is "niche," and many collectors focus on a particular theme, culture, time period, geographical locale, or movement. They find it easier that way to develop a working knowledge of the field and intimate relationships with the dealers and collectors. As a result, they tend to make smarter aesthetic choices and deals. And once dealers know a collector's specific interests and goals, they'll generally try to help, as they did with the Vogels. They enjoy being a part of something special.

The best collections seem to be those which reflect the individuals putting them together — not a dealer, museum curator, or advisor. For example, it was no mistake that a client of ours with flaming red hair and a flair for creating high-drama interiors in her various homes responded to large-scale, often violent Baroque paintings. Her collection included a painting of Lucretia after she stabbed herself (she was raped by the Etruscan King's son) and another of Judith with the Head of Holofernes, blood dripping, which she hung in her bedroom. I always wondered if she was sending a message to her husband.

The late Dan Melnick, producer of *Roxanne*, *Altered States*, and *Footloose*, collected Ellsworth Kelly, Agnes Martin, and Don Judd. His reasons were clear. After a tumultuous day at the office, he needed to come home to a serene environment. No art conveyed that better than Minimalism.

Kathleen Kennedy, a film producer responsible for dozens of films, including *E.T.*, and *The Sixth Sense*, and her husband, Frank Marshall, who produced *The Bourne Identity* series, were casting around for an area to collect when I met them. I showed them American Social Realist works done between the wars. Probably because they saw themselves as storytellers with a deep sense of social responsibility, they related and loved the works. Today, they live surrounded by images of subway straphangers, sailors, and dockworkers by artists such as Thomas Hart Benton and Reginald Marsh, and they've collected prints and first edition books of the same period.

HOUSE DECORATORS

Not all collectors are interested in creating a cohesive collection or getting on any Top Hundred Collectors list. They just want a few works of art that look great in their homes. So, don't feel guilty if you're one of them. There's nothing wrong with wanting a painting to match your blue sofa. You don't even have to tell the artist or gallery why you happen to love the painting with the sapphire background.

Buying art to decorate your home and building a fine collection are not mutually exclusive. Liz Familian became one of the first collectors of contemporary art in LA in the 1970s at the insistence of her legendary interior designer, Michael Taylor. Rather than spend $25,000 for wallpaper, Taylor suggested that she paint her walls white and buy paintings by young artists. She bought several works, and her final pick was between a Ron Davis and a Cy Twombly. Unfortunately, she chose Davis, whose work fell into obscurity, while Twombly became world famous.

Ray Stark, the legendary Hollywood film producer (*Funny Girl*, *The Way We Were*), had a great collection — including a Monet Water Lilies painting, a 13-foot Giacometti *Standing Woman I*, and dozens of Aristide Maillols and Henry Moores. Yet, he described himself as 'a home decorator.' In a way, he was, because he never bought a work without knowing exactly where he'd put it. By the time I met Ray, he'd run out of space in his LA home, the market had passed him by, and he missed the action. He only had one empty space left, a long hallway at his Santa Ynez ranch. Did I have any ideas? I suggested that, rather than buy one or two large paintings, he collect *petit format* — works under 12 inches. He loved the idea and over the next several years bought over forty pint-sized works, ranging from an Albrecht Dürer woodcut to an 8-inch Warhol flower painting. He loved being back in action. When he died, he left one of the works to each of about forty friends. I have fond memories of Ray whenever I look at the tiny, but lyrical Kandinsky he was generous enough to leave me.

When a San Francisco couple approached me for help, they made it clear that they had no interest in getting caught up in the frenzy of the art world like so many of their friends. They'd just finished decorating a new home and simply wanted to find some nice things to finish it off. The first work they bought was an early Sam Francis watercolor that looked great in their entry. After that, they bought a gorgeous orange-on-red Mark Rothko on paper, which gave their quiet interior a pop of color. Works on paper by Willem de Kooning, Franz Kline, and Richard Diebenkorn followed. One day, they called from The Met where they'd wandered into an installation of Abstract Expressionist works on paper. They were amazed to realize that, artist for artist, everything they had at home was better. They'd started out as decorators but had become much more.

LIST MAKERS

Some collectors handle uncertainty well. They roll with the punches and buy whatever they fall in love with whenever it comes along, even if it doesn't fit perfectly into their collection. Others feel the need to be in control, either because that's who they are or because they have narrow interests or limited funds and can't afford to get off track. Such collectors establish parameters — artists to be included, years the collection will encompass, subject matter, and/or media — and they stay within those confines. Our clients who collect sculptors' drawings are like that. As owners of radio stations, they decided to create a "Top 40" list of artists whose drawings they wanted to collect which mimicked the "Top 40" songs on most radio music stations. They now have their 40 drawings, so whenever they find another one they want, rather than make it #41, they pass it up or sell one they have to make room.

They aren't alone; the art world seems to thrive on lists. Every art magazine has some version of "The Top Hundred Collectors," or "The 100 Most Powerful People in the Art World." I've been on some of these lists and am #53 on a recent one. I'm not sure how to take that. Should I be pleased, or eat my heart out that I'm not #52? Or, is it all BS? The British artist, Peter Davies, made lists the subjects of several paintings. *The Hot One Hundred*, (ill. 15) and *The Hip One Hundred*, may be send-ups on today's art world, but they're also a commentary on our deep-seated compulsion to taxonomize. In my opinion, it's good to make lists, but it's also important to be flexible, so if something wonderful comes along that isn't on your list, you'll grab it anyway.

SHOPPERS

When the public learned that Imelda Marcos owned more than a thousand pairs of shoes, she was assured a lifetime of infamy. Lucky for art collectors, no one is ever skewered for owning too many paintings or spending too much money on art. So, if you're in need of retail therapy, buying art is an acceptable alternative. It's especially easy these days, when art's the talked about investment, to spend guilt-free. The champion of shopper-collectors was Andy Warhol. In the '80s, when I knew him, he shopped several times a week for art and antiques. On Sundays, when the galleries were closed, a mutual friend and I would pick him up at church (he was a devout Catholic) and head for Manhattan's 26th Street flea market. All the regular vendors knew him, and he admired much of what they were selling. Andy seldom left the flea market empty-handed. High or low art, genius or kitsch, he didn't care. He had a child-like amazement and an ability to find beauty in almost everything he saw.

But Andy wasn't trolling the galleries and flea markets just for fun. He was on the hunt for inspiration for paintings, and he kept receipts for everything he bought, considering it all tax deductible. According to Anthony Haden-Guest, *The Last Supper*, Warhol's last series, came out of an idea a dealer, Alexander Iolas, cooked up for a commission for a Milanese bank. Perhaps it did, but think of all the plates, rugs, prints, and other items emblazoned with the image of *The Last Supper* Andy must have seen at the flea market all those Sundays. They had to have some impact.

I don't think anyone realized what a magpie Andy was until he died in 1987 and his estate came up at

Sotheby's. Perhaps he suffered "hoarding disorder," before it was identified as a medical problem. The sale took four days and included everything from priceless Art Deco furniture to cookie jars. It was the biggest single-owner auction to date.

Another shopaholic collector friend is always on the prowl for high-quality small sculptures and bibelots – scrimshaw, netsukes, etc. He puts them on his bedside table, preparing for the day when he's old, bedridden, and blind. He reckons that all he'll have to do is to extend his arm and there'll be something great to fondle. But his compulsive shopping habits extend to larger works as well. One day, I bumped into him outside Sotheby's where he was pacing the sidewalk. He'd just bought a $10,000 Renaissance chair and nervously admitted that he didn't have the money to pay for it. When I asked why he bought it, he shrugged, "Whose tush should sit on such a great chair, but mine?" When I asked how he planned on paying for it, he shot back, "I'll borrow the money." "From whom?" I asked. "How about you?" After a few laughing refusals on my part and heartfelt pleas on his, I reluctantly loaned him the money, exacting a promise that he'd never do anything like that again. I got repaid a few months later and shortly after that, I saw him at Christie's bidding on an 18th-century tapestry. The tapestry was 12-feet high, and his apartment only had eight-foot ceilings. I confronted him. His defense? "Yes, but isn't it gorgeous?"

It's not uncommon for collectors to collect in several areas simultaneously. Albert Barnes, renowned for his Impressionist and Post-Impressionist paintings, including 181 Renoirs and 69 Cézannes, pursued African art, Renaissance paintings, American Indian jewelry, and early American ironwork, in addition. You can see it all, installed cheek by jowl, at the new Barnes Foundation building in Philadelphia.

Some shoppers like buying in bulk. A prominent LA collector boasted that he bought five of every artist he collected, so he could leave one to each of his five children when he died. Many collectors, including British ad man Charles Saatchi and the Rubells, regularly buy out artists' studios. But that's not new. Roy Neuberger, whose gift of over a hundred works was the nucleus of the Neuberger Museum of Art in Purchase, New York, bought out artists' studios the way he bought stocks; when he felt there was growth potential, he'd commit in numbers. He owned a hundred Milton Averys, including 46 bought in a single year.

Mass buy-outs take place in galleries, too. One Christmas Eve early in the 20th century, a New York old master dealer was in a funk. He was worried that he couldn't make his January payroll, when a stranger came in, walked around the room, pointing, "I'll take that and that and that." At first, the dealer thought the guy was insane, but he turned out to be 'for real.' He was Charles Phelps Taft, a Cincinnati businessman and half-brother of President Taft. His family home, now the Taft Museum of Art, was gifted to Cincinnati along with the 690 works of art housed there, some of which were bought that Christmas Eve. Years later, a different man went into Spanierman Gallery, walked around, looked at all the paintings, and started taking down the wall labels, one after another. An assistant ran over and asked him to stop. "Don't worry," the man said, "I'm only taking down the labels of the paintings I'm buying."

Walter Chrysler, the son of the founder of the Chrysler Corporation, spent much of his life on the prowl for art, starting at age fourteen when he bought a small Renoir nude for $350. He took it back to his room at Hotchkiss, where the dorm master, considering the subject too risqué, destroyed it. Luckily, that experience only spurred Chrysler on, and, over the next 70 years, he bought over 10,000 works from a various periods, including 8000 pieces of glass. He donated many of these to the Norfolk Museum of Art and Sciences, which, not surprisingly, changed its name to the Chrysler Museum of Art. At one point, Chrysler, the archetypal *marchand d'amateur* (amateur dealer), stacked a storefront on the Upper East Side with paintings, more warehouse than shop. I loved going there, as you never knew what you'd find. He quietly bought and sold, and had many success stories in his collecting career, including the sale in the 1970s of a Picasso for $1.6 million that he'd bought earlier for $450. He was living proof of the saying, "Collectors make the best dealers."

HUNTERS AND GATHERERS

Collectors come in two distinct styles: hunters and gatherers. Gatherers are passive, like a Venus flytrap. They don't actively go after works of art, preferring to wait for things to be offered to them, or they might find something in an auction catalogue delivered to their door. Hunters, by contrast, are always on the quest. They've got dealers all over the world on speed dial whom they're constantly calling, reeling off the names of artists they're looking for. "Got any Christopher Wools?" "How about Basquiat?" They schmooze other collectors to shake works loose, and, like dealers, they make it their business to know when collectors are divorcing, dying, or suffering business reversals.

Arthur Altschul, a collector of Post-Impressionist paintings, took a unique approach to "hunting." He'd worked as a *New York Times* reporter as a young man, and he applied the skills he'd learned as an investigative journalist to collecting. While on a visit to Paris in the mid-1950s, Altschul wandered into an exhibition, "Seurat et Ses Amis" (Seurat and His Friends), and instantly became enchanted with Pointillist works that looked like Seurat but were a lot cheaper. A pair of ovals by one of these Pointillists, Albert Dubois-Pillet, came up at auction in New York not long after, and Altschul bought them for $1,200. After that, he sought out works by Seurat's *amis* with a vengeance. He tracked down descendants of the painters and bought works out of private collections listed in the literature on the movement. Within a few years, he built a collection that was one of the best of its kind. When John Rewald, *the* Impressionist and Post-Impressionist scholar, visited Altschul, he suggested, "Why not do the same for the friends of Gauguin?" Reflecting on Gauguin's difficult nature, Altschul shrugged, "I didn't know Gauguin had any friends." But Rewald was barely out the door before Arthur was hunting again, this time for works by artists who followed Gauguin to Pont Aven, including Maurice Denis and Paul Sérusier.

Altschul's two collections became the subject of an exhibition and a scholarly catalogue at Yale. For not much money, he had become quite the expert and added considerably to the body of knowledge in the field. Although Altschul had decades of fun with what he called his "look alike" collections, and his accomplishments were widely admired, I occasionally wonder what the outcome would have been if he'd hunted big game, Seurat and Gauguin, instead of rabbit.

What do hunters, like Altschul, do when they've acquired an object of desire? They move on to the next. Not that they don't love what they have; they just find the hunt as much fun as ownership. In the 1970s, I'd often bump into Christian Humann (that was his real name) in the galleries buying 19th-century European paintings (he also had a huge Asian collection). He'd pay for them but seldom picked them up. Apparently, living with the art didn't interest Mr. Humann as much as the conquest.

THE BEST OR BUST

Some collectors want the best and only the best — period. For that pleasure, they're prepared to pay a premium price. Wendell Cherry, the co-founder of Humana, a health insurance company, was a great proponent of this kind of collecting. He was open to buying works of any style, nationality, or period, provided they were textbook examples. He owned John Singer Sargent's famous *El Jaleo (The Spanish Dancer)*, Klimt's *Lady With a Fan*, and Picasso's self-portrait, *Yo, Picasso* (ill. 16) — all different, all iconic.

Victor and Sally Ganz were also best-of-the-best collectors. They made their money in costume jewelry, lived in a $250-a-month rent-controlled apartment in New York City, and simply took a chunk of what they made every year and put it into art — but not just any art. The Ganzes were drawn only to five artists they considered 'A plus' — Picasso, Jasper Johns, Robert Rauschenberg, Frank Stella, and Eva Hesse. They followed those artists' careers and bought their work in depth. At one time, they had the greatest collection of Picassos in America, including *Les Femme D'Alger*, which brought $32 million in their estate sale and $179 million at auction in 2015. They also owned the famous *Le Rêve, (The Dream)* (ill. 17), which they bought in 1941 for $7000, a real stretch for them. The erotic 1932 portrait of Picasso's then lover Marie-Thérèse Walter asleep in a chair was famous for many things, including the way the artist depicted the sitter's cheek in the shape of an erect penis. In the 1997 estate auction, the painting sold for the then astounding sum of $48.4 million to Austrian investor, Wolfgang Flottl who kept it crated in Geneva Freeport for several years, until he sold it for about $60 million to Steve Wynn. In 2006, Wynn sold it to Stevie Cohen for $139 million. Unfortunately, before the deal was consummated, Wynn put his elbow through the painting. Wynn sued the insurance company for his loss and settled for about $40 million dollars, leaving him owning *Le Rêve* for very little (in masterpiece terms). A supposed $90,000 worth of conservation and a lot of publicity later, Cohen bought the painting for a reported $155 million, more than he was willing to pay before it was damaged.

When it comes to buying best-of-the-best, who's leading the charge? In the past, if something great came onto the market, everyone knew the half dozen likely buyers. But today, buyers who may never have bought art before come out of nowhere and drop 50 or 100 million dollars on a painting at auction. In 2008, for example, Roman Abramovich, the Russian oligarch, surprised the art world with his buying spree of a $30 million Lucian Freud painting one night and an $86 million Francis Bacon the next, for a total of almost $120 million.

The spread between what you have to pay for an 'A plus' painting and an 'A' painting can be much greater than the difference between an 'A' and a 'B' painting. Although you may have to pay more going in, the financial upside over time may be greater. After Gregory Callimanopulos, a best-of-the-best collector, paid more than triple what he thought he'd have to pay for a work at auction, he reminded me of something Duveen said, "If you spend too much on a masterpiece, it's cheap."

The market isn't *always* a one-way street upwards for great things, however, and recessions aren't the only reason prices can drop. Market gyrations may pull sellers and buyers too far apart. Or, if the market is too top heavy in one area, there may not be sufficient supply to feed the demand. In old masters a single painting can plummet. When the newly-discovered Peter Paul Rubens' *Portrait of a Man as the God Mars* (ill. 18) came fresh onto the market in the 1980's, tremendous excitement caused it to make a high price, $13.2 million. When it came up again in 2000, it brought $8.2 million, and, subsequently, in 2002, it brought $6.8 million.

"A" WORKS BY "B" ARTISTS

Collectors who have the right kind of eye, or advisors who do, often look for 'A' pictures by 'B' artists. Paintings like that have the advantage of being museum-worthy, but they don't carry the price tag of an 'A' artist. Years ago, I was in a New York gallery and saw a ravishing painting by a minor league 19th-century American artist, Charles Sprague Pearce. Called *Lady with a Fan* (ill. 19), it was a breathtaking portrait of a beautiful woman painted in such a way that the golden threads in her kimono seemed to ignite. I called out-of-town clients who collected only "A plus" American Impressionists, described it, and asked them to fly in to see it. They thought I'd lost my mind. "You want us to get on a plane and fly all the way to New York to see the work of a second-rate bum?" I knew they'd love it if they saw it, so I shipped the painting to them. They bought it on the spot, and it now holds pride of place among Sargents, Chases, and other megawatt paintings. The purchase speaks volumes about them as collectors, demonstrating that they have the taste and confidence to buy a great object even if it isn't by a name brand.

OVERLOOKED AND UNDERVALUED

J. Paul Getty, the oilman, collected art the way he amassed oil interests — by acquiring overlooked and undervalued assets. He looked for fields that had fallen out of favor, the result of changing tastes. He felt that in areas where there was less competition, he could get masterpieces without spending a lot. His original focus was 18th-century French furniture and ancient antiquities, both unpopular fields when he started. He added English and Dutch paintings, and when he founded his museum in Malibu in 1954, he was urged by Bernard Berenson to add Italian Renaissance to the mix. Getty never felt that he was getting the most for his money when he bought paintings, but he needed them to broaden the appeal to the public, and he had to have *something* to hang over all those *bureau plats*. Actually, he was wrong, and old masters were undervalued when he was buying. Prices had peaked in the early 20th century when Duveen sold boatloads to American tycoons, but by the time Getty got involved, after World War II, the Rubenses, Raphaels, and Rembrandts were 'out,' and French Impressionism, Modern Art, and Abstract Expressionism were "in."

What's out of fashion can come back even more quickly than it falls from grace. The resurrection of French academic 19th-century painting expedited by Hoving at The Met in 1972 changed the market almost overnight.

Of course, works that fall out of favor can stay that way. In the 1980's, I found a copy of *Art Treasures of America* at a flea market. Published in 1879, it listed the major American collections of the day and what was in them. I noticed that apart from the William-Adolphe Bouguereaus, Jean-Léon Gérômes, Sir Lawrence Alma-Tademas, and other sugary academics, many collectors were long on works by the Barbizon school — Daubigny, Diaz, Rousseau, Miller, and Corot. These artists' leafy scenes of the Forest of Fontainebleau had been immensely popular among middle-class Parisians and others living in the sooty cities of the Industrial Revolution in Europe and the U.S. Only Corot and Miller, the powerhouses of the group, was beyond my budget. The rest, market leaders in those days, were a drug on the market in mine. For only a few thousand dollars, I could buy examples as good as those in any museum. Over the years, the value of the Barbizons crept up, particularly when Japanese buyers were after them, but never as much as the paintings of the next generation of Impressionists. I love them, nonetheless, and now that I spend my summers in a village not far from Barbizon, the paintings mean more to me than I ever imagined.

STATUS

Art brings its owners a cornucopia of benefits. According to a recent poll of art professionals done by Deloitte, 76% described collectors as seeing art as an investment, and almost as many felt that collectors buy art for the social scene and a boost in social status. If these things interest you, why not let art collecting help?

Collecting wasn't always the way to gain entry into high society. During the 1880s, when Mrs. Astor gave balls at her New York mansion for "The Four Hundred," supposedly named for the number of people her ballroom seated, you had to be born into society to get invited. It didn't matter how much money or art arrivistes like the Vanderbilts had; they were "in trade." Later, Mrs. Astor had to accept them because they had too much money to be excluded, and their art collections were evidence that they had *some* culture.

Things changed quickly. In the 1899 classic, *The Theory of the Leisure Class*, Thorstein Veblen coined the term, "conspicuous consumption," referring to the way the rich bought expensive items hoping to be admired and envied by their peers. Veblen observed that the more expensive the objects, the more desired they were. Art was one of those items. Over a hundred years later, there seems to be no difference. Antonio Rangel at California Institute of Technology (CIT) did a study about wine in which twenty subjects drank wine of all levels of cost. Rangel lied and told them that the cheapest was the most expensive. Surprise! That was the wine everyone liked best.

Today's masters of the universe go after the kind of "positional goods" described by Veblen and Rangel, including yachts, planes, and paintings. Neither author would have been shocked by David Kaplan's book, *Mine's Bigger*, chronicling Tom Perkins' quest to build the largest sailboat, or the race between art collectors for expensive works. Andrew Rice quotes Alberto Mugrabi,

"Demand for an artist's work tends to rise as prices do, because the more expensive it becomes, the more status it confers." Is there a difference between yachts, planes, and Picassos? Anyone with wealth can buy the first two, but it takes wealth *and* some sensitivity to buy a Picasso. It's that little extra which gives a collector the opportunity to publicly air his intelligence and aestheticism and gain status in return.

William Clay Frick, who made a fortune manufacturing coke (coal) and had the reputation of being "the most hated man in America" for his strikebreaking tactics, epitomized Veblen's 'conspicuous consumption.' He built a big mansion on Fifth Avenue and filled it with art as a way of outdoing his rivals, particularly his partner Andrew Carnegie. The genius who 'enabled' Frick and other robber barons was Duveen, the legendary, conniving dealer. He realized that Europe's impoverished aristocrats needed to sell their art, and that Americans had the money to buy it, along with a desire to elevate their social status. Duveen knew how to get the competitive juices flowing between titans. If he sold a Rembrandt to Frick, he knew that Carnegie and others would want one, too. Duveen's clients followed him the way collectors follow star dealers today. Whether they bought Rembrandts or Titians didn't matter; they were just happy buying "Duveens." In the end, the collections that Duveen built for many rich Americans morphed into the nuclei of some of the finest public museum collections and best house museums in the world. Duveen was right. He sold them not just paintings, but status and immortality.

Allow me to digress for a moment to extol one of Duveen's clients, Samuel Kress, founder of a "five and dime" store chain, for his largess to our country. Rather than open his own museum or give to a single institution, Kress gave away almost 800 paintings (150 or so bought from Duveen), mostly Italian Renaissance works, to regional museums in 18 cities across America, many where his stores made him a fortune. I wish other owners of billion dollar corporations would follow Kress' example. Or wouldn't it be great if Costco filled a double wide with paintings that crisscrossed America, pulled up in parking lots where they have businesses, and allowed the public to see art while they shopped?

Today, art is the *lingua franca* of a flourishing new "society." If there's a "new" Mrs. Astor, she's probably a big art collector, and being a collector can get you invited to her balls. At a recent dinner party, I overheard a Frenchman telling a German he'd never met, "You have a Mike Kelly? I have a Mike Kelly." This translated as, "You have a million dollars to spend on a work of art? So do I. You got to the head of the line? So did I. We can be friends." For people who have hundreds of millions, if all it takes to get into this elite club is buying a few million dollars of art now and then, it's cheap at twice the price.

For sure, buying works by record-breaking name artists can confer status. When Stevie Cohen bought two de Koonings owned by David Geffen in quick succession (the 1955 masterpiece, *Police Gazette* for $63.5 million, and *Woman III*, for $137.5 million) in 2006, he made news outside the business section of the papers. And when the name of the buyer of Munch's record-breaking *The Scream*, Leon Black, head of private equity firm Apollo Global Management, got leaked to the press, he became grist for journalists' mills the world over. Leon wasn't seeking publicity, but many collectors do. And have you noticed being a big collector gets some people a two-column obituary?

Lately, there's a twist on the kind of art that conveys status. Whereas everyone used to flock to the accessible and transportingly beautiful works, now it's the expensive, difficult, esoteric works that distinguish their owners from the herd. At the 2012 sale of Peter Norton's collection, the bidding for tough conceptual pieces by artists such as Charlie Ray and Paul McCarthy was far more heated than for the usual big name works that came up later that night. By owning a radical, strange, and extremely costly piece of art that few people understand, you bask in more than the aura of wealth. You broadcast the impression that you're on a different plane — you're one of the rare, brilliant and far-seeing intellectuals who "gets it." And maybe you do.

IN SEARCH OF A LIFE

You may already have a great life and not need collecting to enhance it, but who couldn't use a little extra zing? At very least, collecting gives you an additional topic to talk about at cocktail parties. Some collectors dine out on tales of their acquisitions: the troubles of shipping a piece of porcelain from Paris, or the one that got away. But that's the least of it. Because the art world doesn't follow the 9-5 business model and burns bright seven days a week, morning, noon, and night, it's like the film business, one of the few industries in which you can "take a meeting" 24/7. For that reason, it attracts a lot of people who otherwise don't have a 'real' life or decide to make it their life. When I asked a Warhol collector, "What attracted you to Warhol?" he shared a secret. He was an insomniac, and the only other night owl he could call at 2 am was a guy who dealt in Warhol. When he couldn't sleep, he'd call his dealer/friend, who'd show up at his apartment carrying an armful of Warhol paintings, and some time before dawn, he'd buy one or two.

A longtime woman friend in her fifties, married to a much older man, asked me to tea at her Fifth Avenue apartment. She'd never been interested in art before, so when she asked me to help her collect, I was surprised. "When I'm a little old widow," she sighed, "if I collect, museums will court me for my paintings. I'll get invited to the best parties, and I'll have a curator as an escort.

It'll be a great life." What a dopey plan, I thought, as I left her apartment and jumped into a cab. As we inched down Fifth Avenue in dinner hour traffic, I saw a smarmy British dealer coming out of a primo building pushing the wheelchair of an elderly woman, swathed in sable. She must have had some very valuable art he was after. Maybe my friend was onto something after all.

And then there's art world tourism. Plenty of people build their travel schedules around art fairs, auctions, trips offered by museum support groups, and so forth. Last fall, a divorced friend in her sixties reeled off a list of what she did over the summer, including visits to the Zabludowicz Collection in Finland, Documenta in Kassel, Art Basel in Switzerland, and a side trip to London to see some gallery shows. When she's not art-tripping all over the world, she's busy, in New York, going to art-related events. Oh, and in case I forgot to mention, she's not even a collector.

KEEPING THE HOME FIRES BURNING

Collecting often changes the dynamics of a marriage. Many couples whose kids are grown and are looking for a new activity to share, find that art collecting beats hiking, bridge, and lots of other 'together' activities. It combines intellectual stimulation, travel, and fun. And it has the potential for financial gain, something else couples can enjoy together.

Among my favorite collecting couples are Reba White Williams and Dave Williams, the print collectors I've already introduced you to. Both were MBAs and highly successful in the world of finance when they married. They got tired of friends teasing them that their pillow talk must be about debentures and derivatives, so they decided to find something they could share beyond monetary policy. They turned to collecting prints, and in over thirty years, created an extraordinary collection of American black and whites. Reba went back to school and got a Ph.D. in Art History and published several terrific crime novels, including *Restrike*, *Fatal Impressions*, and *Angels*, set in the world of print collecting. Dave wrote *Small Victories*, chronicling their adventures forming their collection, and made a film, *All About Prints*, which provides the clearest explanation of printing techniques I've ever seen. Collecting has been a joint activity that's enriched their already strong marriage.

Some argue that four eyes can't make a great collection, that it should be the vision of one person, not two. Reba and Dave would disagree, as would I. The couples I work with choose together. If a disagreement arises, which rarely happens, the negative prevails, i.e. the couple won't buy a work if one dislikes it. But of course, every couple has their own way of dealing. As John Liebes described the division of labor in his collaborative collecting with his wife, "My wife did the picking; I wrote the checks." That's one way of doing it.

ART AS INVESTMENT

Many of today's collectors want it all, and making a profit is high on their list. For some, sadly, it's the only reason they get involved. The majority buy what they love and, although they're not active traders, they expect their art to be an investment. Why not? Dealers tell them it is, the press regales them with stories about big winners, and they probably know someone firsthand who's made money buying and selling art. In 2015, Laurence Fink, chairman of BlackRock, the world's largest asset management firm, went on record saying that contemporary art, along with certain real estate, had usurped gold as a store of wealth. Although art isn't a foolproof investment (please tell me what is), if you choose wisely, it can leave you smiling all the way to the bank. Now that I have your attention, I'll explain some of the ways successful collectors have made it work.

First, a little history. During the Renaissance, the likes of the Medicis and the Sforzas commissioned painters to create religious works for private chapels and churches as a way of buying their way into heaven. They thought that a show of piety would make others forget the unscrupulous ways they made their fortunes. In case a viewer missed that point, some cunning donors had the artists paint their portraits in the altarpieces standing alongside saints and martyrs. Important artists were well paid. When one could comfortably live on 200 ducats a year, Leonardo was making 2000 a year, and Michelangelo got 3000 ducats to do the Sistine Chapel. But most of what was commissioned wasn't portable, so there was little resale market.

In 17th-century Holland, as I've mentioned, with the rise of a new middle class, a market flourished for small, non-religious landscapes, paintings to decorate homes and impress visitors. From 1630-1660, millions of such works were produced to satisfy avid buyers. Along with tulips (tulipmania peaked in the 1630s), there was speculation in high-end paintings to the point that a painting could cost as much as a house.

A century later, when British aristocrats made the grand tour, it was *de rigueur* to bring back souvenir *vedute* (views) of Venice, which announced to their peers at home that they were well-traveled, cultured intellectuals with money to burn. By the early 20th century, American robber barons collected to impress and make it into high society, *and*, like the leading Italian Renaissance families, to make others forget how they really made it up the ladder of success.

Throughout the first half of the 20th century, using the words 'art' and 'money' in the same sentence was considered as gauche as gossiping in front of the servants.

No one cornered their dealer with the urgent whisper, "Is this a safe investment?" or "What will this be worth in five years?" But by the 1970's and 80's, things changed. A rising tide of art prices, especially in contemporary art, brought a sea change in the way art buyers approached collecting. Buyers were no longer the idle rich. If they were spending a lot of money, they couldn't afford not to ask those questions.

So, is art a good investment? Today it seems a foregone conclusion that it is. But as recently as 1989, economists Bruno Frey and Walter Pommerehne, in their book *Muses and Markets: Explorations in the Economics of the Arts*, argued that investing in art is too risky. They pointed to art's illiquidity, and they're right. You can't call a dealer the way you can a stockbroker and have him convert your paintings to cash while you wait on the phone. Naysayers also observe that there's no price/earnings ratio to consult, and that there's tremendous opacity, irregular supply, and hidden transactional costs, such as commissions, and sales tax that can skew the profits, while risks, like damage or forgery, can gut them entirely. Lastly, they point to the fact that holding art generates no income. "Think of the money you're not making on those millions you've tied up in several square inches of painted canvas." "Buy securities," they urge, "and decorate your walls with reproductions."

All along, wealthy families understood that their paintings were good investments. If they didn't when they bought them, they certainly did when they needed cash. Lord Grantham in *Downton Abbey* may have said that he sold his Fra Angelico for reasons other than money, but he used it to finance a new housing development to ensure Downton's future.

The first hard proof that art is a good investment, however, didn't come until the 1990's, when the British Rail Pension Fund released the results of its investment in art. In the 1970's, this giant fund took about $70 million, roughly 2% of the total under management, and bought a diverse portfolio of more than 2500 objects from numerous cultures and time periods. In 1987, at the height of the Japanese-fueled market, it began selling and unloaded a number of Impressionist and Modern pictures at huge profits. By the 1990's, 1100 works had been sold for $115 million, producing a return of what would have been roughly 13% annually. Yes, the raging Japanese market had been a lucky break, but the profits were undeniably real and bankable. It confirmed what a lot of collectors already knew and made a lot of potential investors sit up and take notice.

It took the Mei Moses Art Index, which came out in 2000, however, to make Wall Street finally climb aboard and accept art as an asset class. This study, updated yearly, is designed to compare the performance of art with the equity market and evaluate its role in asset allocation. The authors, New York University professors Jianping Mei and Michael Moses, started by tracking 6000 sets of *repeat* auction results (when the same item came up twice) in a cross-section of categories — including Impressionism, 19th-century European art, old masters and American art created before 1950. They subtracted the prices the works brought when they first sold from their second selling prices. They averaged the results and calculated that, over the last fifty years or so, art generated a compound annual return surpassing the S&P for the same period. To keep the study up-to-date, they add 3000 pairs yearly. If you're someone who lives by stats, Moses and Mei's are convincing.

Moses observed that art is an "...asset class that in many ways works a hell of a lot like real estate." As real estate investors will tell you, your rent may barely cover your expenses, but it's the "equity build-up" that counts. Property investors know that real estate doesn't go up a set amount every year, and they don't expect it to. The conventional wisdom is that it takes five years to get your money back, ten years to double it. Art is much the same, with insiders noting that great art doubles every seven years. Warhol paintings, for example, are notorious for taking a quantum leap in price one year, plateauing, and taking another jump a few years later. Investor/collectors have to be patient, but, since they do get to live with art while waiting for the value to increase, perhaps "rental value" should be factored in. What would you pay per year to hang a great Picasso in your living room? It beats framing municipal bonds.

The Mei Moses study became the gold standard in the industry, because it overcame the argument that, since no two works are alike and variations in quality can create a huge range in value, quantifying prices is impossible. And it offered something Wall Street loves — graphs, lots and lots of graphs. Yet, it does have flaws. First of all, its data is drawn solely from auction sales. If the results from private sales had been included, the rate of return would likely have been higher. The study also suffers from the fact that data collection started so long ago that it's considered ancient history by today's investors. This point was brought home to me by Daniel Gross' observation in a 2006 *Slate* article that "...a J.M.W. Turner view of Venice which sold at Christie's in London on May 29, 1897 for $35,000 and then sold at Christie's in New York, in 2006, for $35.8 million — would have yielded an owner about a 6% annual return for 109 years." That may be true and interesting, but, unless you're Mel Brooks' 2000-year-old man, who cares about the rise in value over a hundred years?

Since Moses and Mei, there's been an avalanche of other art market indices produced by art funds and art lending institutions, many of which aren't reliable. They may choose a particularly ebullient time in the market and/or skew the stats in other ways to make you want to invest in their fund or borrow against your art from their institution. Or they poll from a ridiculously small number of people, if they actually poll at all.

Friends and new acquaintances often ask me, "How's the market?" as if there's *one* art market. That's no more the case than asking the same question in regard to the financial world. There are many sectors, and each behaves differently. Latin American art doesn't rise at the same rate as Indian art. European art doesn't move apace with Chinese art, and so on. At this moment, the auction sales for contemporary art are robust with buyers, while the auctions of Impressionist and Modern works are doing well, but the air is thin with fewer bidders. And the prospects for different fields aren't the same. Although prices for 19th- and early 20th-century American paintings rose considerably in recent decades, a big red light is flashing over that market sector right now. The supply of great things has dwindled, there's no international appeal, galleries who handle it are closing, and demand has lessened among younger collectors. There are still enough players to keep the market going, and isolated record-breaking sales, like that of a $44 million Georgia O'Keeffe, support the thinking that the pendulum will swing back. I hope so. But check out the state of your target market before you invest your hard-earned cash.

Financial analysts spend a lot of time trying to figure out how the art market correlates with the economy in general. They observe that in periods when the stock market is up and economic growth is strong, the art market is buoyant. Great works by great artists are sought after and prices go up. This causes a trickle-down effect, with the prices of works by less expensive artists rising to fill the void. Thus, when Rothkos sell for $60 million plus, and a great de Kooning tops $50 million, Gerhard Richter moves up into the $20-30 million range, Agnes Martin, $5 million, and Sean Scully, a million. This happy trend continues until there's a recession or market correction. When interest rates are low, the art world booms. Investors would rather put their money in art and take the risk that its rate of return will be higher than bonds or sending it to Switzerland, where they may have to *pay* Swiss banks to keep their money safe.

In recessions, art generally has been a lag indicator, i.e., the last to go and the last to come back. But in 2008, that wasn't the case. Art plummeted along with everything else, perhaps because the crash started at the top with the same financial guys who were the big art buyers. However, whereas stocks fell roughly 37% that year, the value of *great* contemporary art fell only 4 or 5%. I got many "shoulda" calls from clients who wished they'd bought the paintings I'd offered them in the months before (so they would have lost less money) — and after (when there were bargains) — the crash. Generally though, some wealthy collectors who didn't need to sell had the confidence to wait for the market to rebound. Others who were still rich but had lost vast sums on paper, felt poor and stopped buying. That caused a period of stagnation, which happens in every recession. Eventually, sellers 'gave' a little and buyers became hungry enough to 'bite.' That 'giving' and 'biting' happened quicker for art than for other investments. Until the market stabilized, there was less competition, more time to consider purchases, and a few rare, once-in-a-lifetime opportunities that arise when collectors in debt are forced to sell. The contemporary art auctions held that November 2008 were heavy with low-hanging fruit. Eli Broad picked off a 1990 Donald Judd (estimate $2-3 million) for just $1.1 million and *Desire* by Ed Ruscha (estimate $4-6 million) for $2.4 million.

One of the dangers of a prolonged recession is that, when the market rebounds, the next generation of buyers wants new and different things. That's what happened when the economy plummeted in 1990. Super-hot artists like Schnabel, Salle, and Fischl became cold over night. By the time the economy improved in the mid-90's, new young collectors didn't want the old stuff. Only prices for Basquiat, considered *the* artist of his generation, kept steadily increasing.

Some collectors in many countries buy expensive art as a way of avoiding the tax collector's reach. At the very least, they hope to pass wealth to the next generation, undetected. And many art buyers never take possession of the works in their home countries. Thousands of crated works of art, worth billions of dollars, are parked in 31 acres of climate-controlled warehouses in Geneva freeport alone, not to mention Luxembourg, Singapore, Delaware, and other tax-free havens. These freeports charge no import tax and impose no transactional tax should a work be sold while it's there. This may be legal for some, but illegal for others. If you're a US citizen, US taxes probably apply wherever you sell your art. So before you ship your prized works to Geneva freeport, please consult your tax advisor.

The summer I started my career as an advisor, a Mexican collector invited me to see his collection in Puerto Vallarta. In planning my flights, he asked if I minded routing myself home through Aspen to drop off the family's skis. Skis in summer? It didn't take a genius to figure out he'd planned a new spin on diamonds sewn into the hems of dresses. He was going to roll up millions of dollars worth of art into ski bags for me to smuggle out of Mexico into the United States. I begged off and spent the holiday in New York, sweaty but legal.

Art has been used in money laundering with greater frequency in the past several years. In 2007, a Basquiat painting, *Hannibal*, worth eight million dollars, was seized at Customs in New York when a courier from London tried to bring it in as an anonymous painting worth $100 (anything $200 or less can enter the country without a customs declaration). It turned out that it had been smuggled out of Brazil by Edemar Cid Ferreira, who'd embezzled money from the bank he headed and is now serving 21 years in jail. The Brazilian government, which considered the painting bought with illegal gains, was after it. It took 8 years, but the painting finally got sent back.

AND SO, TO THE TASK AT HAND

Individuals build their art portfolios based on their needs, expectations, and risk tolerance. So, let's take a look at some approaches collectors take.

DIVERSIFICATION

Because art has high volatility, low liquidity and performs differently from other financial instruments, many investors see it as a hedge. When Don Simpson, the film producing partner of Jerry Bruckheimer, became a client, he brought his brokerage statement to our first meeting. Pointing to his pie chart, he said, "I like the slices as they are. You're going to have to explain to me why I have to change them." Ultimately he created a diversified art collection, buying several works by several name artists. But diversification can mean something different to you. You can buy one painting and feel you've accomplished your mission, or you may want to spread your dollars and risk by buying works by many artists and many movements, time periods and/ or geographical locales. Recently, a successful investor asked me to create a diversified art portfolio that mimics his stock portfolio — some start-ups (emerging artists), mid-caps (mid-careerists), and blue chips (established stars).

BEACHFRONT PROPERTY

A client who buys and sells top-of-the-line properties on the beach in Malibu invests only in "A plus" works of art. Whenever I offer him a painting, he asks only one question, "Is it beachfront property?" If my answer is "Yes," he buys it. He's willing to hold for the long haul.

UNDERVALUED

Some investor/collectors buy works by fallen stars with proven artistic chops, betting that the market wheel will turn and prices of works that have grown cold today will heat up again tomorrow. In the 1960s, interest in works by 19th-century French academic artists like Bouguereau and Gérôme was at its nadir. No one wanted that old-fashioned stuff. I vaguely remember a weekly ad that appeared in *The New York Times* encouraging readers to buy John Canaday's *Metropolitan Seminars in Art*, and learn the difference between good and bad painting. The "good painting" illustrated was an Expressionist Kokoschka, and the "bad painting" was a meticulously painted Pierre Auguste Cot, *The Storm (La Tempête)* (ill. 20). The Cot, lambasted for its blatant sentimentality, had been gathering dust in the 'bad painting basement' at The Met for years. It depicted a young woman and man — running through a forest, clad only in the skimpiest, classical drapery made too diaphanous to be prudent by the rainstorm they're escaping. In 1972, Hoving took a look at the Cot, liked what he saw, and installed it, along with other works from the same period, in the museum's 19th-century galleries. Critics were horrified and demanded Hoving's resignation, insisting that he was mentally unstable. But Hoving wasn't cowed, and his actions sparked a resurgence in the fortunes of these painters of history, myth, and religion.

Allen Funt, of *Candid Camera* fame, had been buying paintings by the English Victorian, Alma-Tadema, who worked around the same time as Cot. By the early 70's, he owned thirty-five, for which he paid only a few thousand dollars apiece. In 1973, as a result of his accountant embezzling $1,200,000, his life savings, Funt was forced to auction off his beloved paintings which he replaced with life-size photos in elaborate frames. Luckily, the sale took place after Hoving's basement cleanout and the museum's exhibition of Funt's collection, *Victorians in Togas*. The paintings sold well, for a total of $570,000. The seven-foot wide masterpiece, *The Finding of Moses* (ill. 21), brought $72,801, a vast sum at the time. Since then, it resold at auction in 1995 for $2.7 million, and again, in 2010, for a whopping $35.9 million.

For years, journalists and dealers have been touting old masters as the next hot area. Headlines like "Russians

Fight Indian Billionaires for Old Master Records," in Bloomberg, make it sound that way. That story, however, chronicled the battle over a single painting in which a Russian beat out an Indian for a 9.2 million pound El Greco. In fact, according to the Moses and Mei Index, old masters gained a compounded annual rate of return of only 3.3 percent over a ten-year period ending in 2012. Old master collectors shake their heads in disbelief, especially when they hear that a Jeff Koons sells for five times more than an El Greco.

There are several reasons why old masters haven't had a breakout and become the next hot area. First off, most old masters subjects — portraits of aristocrats and religious and mythological scenes — aren't everyone's cup of tea. If you don't know a lot about history and don't have a firm grip on iconography and know how many Bellinis there were in Venice (no, not *that* kind of Bellini), you'll miss a lot of what you're looking at. Secondly, the décor of most collectors' homes today isn't conducive to the old master look. But, if you're willing to make the leap and study, and you think a good depiction of Saint Sebastian with his body riddled with arrows would look good in your house, I have some advice. Works by minor artists under $200,000 are considered decorative and are unlikely to jump in value. Buy them because you love them and not because you think they're an investment. The works that will increase the most are the kind collectors buy for bragging rights. Another caveat is that the pecking order of the artists seldom changes whenever a field does pick up. No minor artist is suddenly going to eclipse the famous names of the movement, although there may be a shift in interest in subjects and style. For example, because still life paintings by the 18th-century Spanish painter Luis Meléndez have a simplicity that appeals to our 21st-century eyes, they're more desirable than before, and their prices have risen dramatically.

Sometimes, a certain period of an artist's work thought to have been 'lesser than' can suddenly command new respect. Late Picassos, once a drug on the market, are now prized, and the same is true of de Kooning's late ribbon paintings of the 1980s. After being left out of many major de Kooning shows, they were considered the highlight of his 2012 MoMA retrospective. Even some paintings made when he had full-fledged dementia have sold for record prices.

A swing in popularity of an artist or a movement can result from a change in the taste for interior decor. After World War II, cultivated immigrants and veterans of the European theater brought stateside a taste for all things French, from fondue to French poodles. The wealthy decorated their homes with Louis XV and XVI furniture and Impressionist art. Another, avant-garde group went in a different direction and furnished their homes in mid-century blond furniture by Scandinavian or American designers and Modern paintings by Picasso, Léger, and the Abstract Expressionists. In the

1980s, tastes changed, and English country furniture and chintz fabric, along with English and French 19th-century academic paintings, became the rage among Park Avenue tastemakers. Today "Brown" furniture, as English country furniture is called, is out. And certainly, not a lot of thirty-somethings want the gold ormolu French 18th-century furniture and puddling silk damask curtains preferred by their grandparents' generation. They want to live in minimalist environments that make Impressionism's colorful, light-filled canvases in their ornate frames seem fussy and out of place. Early 20th-century and contemporary art works better with the mid-20th-century furniture that's popular, by designers like Jules Leleu.

Does that mean that buying good quality Impressionist works at their current prices is a workable investment strategy? Trophy paintings, like Monet's *Water Lilies*, always sell well, but will the average Impressionist scenes of 19th-century French villages by Pissarro and Sisley be relatable to hard-driving 21st-century folks living in big cities? I doubt it, but it's possible. So, if you're going to bet on the Impressionists, the usual caveats apply. Buy the best.

As the pendulum swings, so does the style of art. As I mentioned, Minimal Art of the late 60s and early 70s became a casualty when the expressive works of Schnabel, David Salle, and Eric Fischl turned the tide of collecting. Eventually, when they fell out, Conceptual and Minimal art came back as an historical movement, with prices of artists like Bruce Nauman and Don Judd soaring. Does that mean that the Schnabels, Salles, and Fischls are permanently 'dead' or will their works come back and bring higher prices than they did in their heyday? Many collectors are betting on it, stockpiling Schnabel's early plate paintings. Who knows. In the meantime, Schnabel's made some outstanding paintings and films and, of course, he's still...well...Julian.

THE BOTTOM FISHER

Bottom fishers only buy if they think they're paying bargain basement prices. They make unreasonably low offers and, if doors are slammed in their face, they move on to the next deal. The thrill of "stealing" a work at a fraction of its value is what motivates them more than the work itself. Many bottom fishers I've met remind me of a Hollywood director I know who crudely propositions almost every woman he meets. As he says, "I get slapped a lot, but every so often, I score."

A recent visit to the house of a card-carrying bottom fisher upset me tremendously. He boasted about the deals he got, not the art. A Lichtenstein was the result of a forced sale to pay inheritance taxes. A Rothko came from a divorce. A Twombly came from a Madoff victim. I braced myself, half expecting him to chuckle about buying a painting from parents who needed money for their child's operation. Thank heavens he didn't. It's one thing to take advantage of someone else's misfortune, quite another to crow about it.

A down market is great news for a bottom fisher. A wealthy friend, who didn't collect, kept promising, "When the market tanks, I'll be your biggest client." I thought he was blowing smoke, but after the 2008 crash, he called, looking for opportunities. When I told him about a collector who needed to sell a beautiful early de Kooning to cover a margin call, he made a low, 'take it or leave it' offer, sight unseen, which was accepted. When the Madoff scandal broke a few months later, the same guy called asking, "Anyone bleeding yet?" Only he had the nerve to ask.

Like deer hunting, there's a season for bottom fishing — August and December, before the galleries close for vacation. Bottom fishers find that most dealers can't resist doing one last deal before the holidays, even if it means taking a big haircut. The lure of getting a work off the premises, off their insurance policy, and off their books is often too great to resist. And, if they make enough to pay for their vacation, all the better.

At art fairs, bottom fishers go into high gear on closing day. Exhibitors realize that unsold works are perceived as being passed up by "the world." So, rather than go to the expense of shipping the work home and having it languish in the gallery's storage, they'll accept a bottom fisher's low offer.

At auction, bottom fishers target works that may not attract the level of bidding they should, either because they're over-estimated, dirty, poorly framed, placed in the wrong sale, badly hung in the viewing, or they come up at the end of a long sale when most bidders have already left the salesroom. Bottom fishers always stay to the bitter end. After the sale, BFs comb the unsold lots and make offers. One season, I called a bottom fisher I know when a terrific Vlaminck painting didn't sell. He was delighted we got it at a low price and even more thrilled a week later when the journalist Souren Melikian, in *Art + Auction*, wrote that the Vlaminck was a prize the market had foolishly overlooked.

Being a bottom fisher doesn't always work. Dealers catch on quickly and either stop offering them their best things or they double or triple their prices when a bottom fisher asks, knowing he'll offer outrageously low prices. Bottom fishers don't care.

SPECULATION

'Speculation' may be a dirty word to many art collectors; but others live by it. Of course, it takes different forms. Some collectors, knowledgeable in a field, do it for a quick turnover if they find a painting worth more than the seller's asking. Others think long-term. Sometimes speculators, for example, gamble on the potential economic growth of a developing country. If you'd bought Chinese antiquities or the right Contemporary Chinese art ten or fifteen years ago, waiting for "new Chinese money" to collect art, you'd have done very well. Be careful, though, because not all developing nations are the same, and you may invest in one that's developing in many ways, but not in respect to art.

By far, the most talked about area of art speculation is emerging artists. Identifying an artist with potential, buying his work early and cheaply, and watching his star and prices climb is the fantasy of everyone who collects emerging artists. But speculating is less about an "eye," and more about a nose or an ear. It requires knowing how the art world works or working with an advisor who does. Even with all that, you may need to buy works by a hundred artists to get one winner.

Sarah Thornton, in *Seven Days in the Art World*, observes that 'it takes a village' to make an art star rise — galleries, auctions, critics, museums and curators, and collectors. Some speculators band together and try to manipulate the entire system to advance the artist. Joel Mesler, the owner of Untitled Gallery in New York, described in *True Confessions of a Justified Art Dealer* how it happened to Parker Ito, an artist he respects. Ito sold 20-30 pieces to a few collectors each for 50-60 percent discount. The group formed an informal 'cartel', as it's called in the trade, and the members bought and sold among themselves.

I've actually heard one speculator describe it as "taking a position."

Typically, dealers involved strategically 'place' work by "hot" artists with other important collectors and museums, buzz builds, and a waitlist forms. When the time is right, someone in the cartel consigns work to auction and others in the cartel bid and push the prices up further. Outsiders, often frustrated that they can't get work from the artist's gallery, bid to buy. What does it matter to a hedge funder making hundreds of millions of dollars a year if he has to pay triple what a work costs in the gallery to get what he wants? Every time a new price level is set, the world sees a dramatic upward trajectory for the artist until either the artist becomes an accepted master or his star fades. Speculators don't care; they've already made their money and moved on to the next artist.

As evidence of how rapidly this all happens, look at the auction catalogues. If you're used to catalogue entries listing substantial provenance on works coming up, it's very disconcerting to see works coming up that have been painted only a year or two earlier with little or no provenance. In a November sale in New York, a Damien Hirst spin painting came up dated that same year. It's hard to imagine, even if the painting was painted January 1, how it got from Hirst's studio in the English countryside, to London, to one of his dealers, then on to a client who managed to send it to the auction house in time to meet the August deadline for the November sale. Whoever did it — a speculator, one of artist's dealers, or the artist himself — was like a heat-seeking missile.

For serious galleries and artists, "flipping" like that is a major "no-no." They're fearful that if new work sells too soon at inflated prices, it'll disrupt their careful 'placement' of the work and methodical escalation of prices. So, they blackball collector/flippers. Ito certainly wasn't happy at the outcome of his encounter with the cartel, as per his website post : "For a full list of collectors who have sold my work at auction plz write shitlist@parkerito.com."

In 2014, Jonas Lund, a Swedish artist, showed paintings in his Flip Series at Steve Turner Gallery in LA. Lund studied the Phillips catalogues and combined elements from works by young artists which sold above estimate to make generic-looking abstractions. He attached a GPS to the stretchers, which gives the zipcode (not the exact address) of their whereabouts (ill. 22). That allows anyone to follow a painting's change of hands on www. flip-city.net. I checked and was amused to learn that one painting had already moved 6 times.

Papers filed in a lawsuit by Craig Robins, a Miami collector, against the dealer David Zwirner gives us insight into the problem. Robins, who owned over twenty works by the South African-born Marlene Dumas, sold one of her paintings through David Zwirner, not her primary dealer. Since the artist refused to deal with collectors who flipped her work, Robins made Zwirner promise he wouldn't tell Dumas. Later, when Zwirner became Dumas' principal dealer, he told her. Robins sued Zwirner for breach of confidentiality and first choice of her next show, which he said he was promised. The suit was dismissed for lack of written documents.

To better control the market and make additional profits on resales, some dealers insert a clause in their invoice giving them the right of first refusal at market value should the buyer want to sell within five years. When an Alex Israel painting sold by his European dealer, Almine Rech, turned up at auction, Rech had a fit. She claimed she had such a contract with the buyer and that he'd whited out the clause and colluded with his buyer to consign it to auction to pump up Israel's prices. Israel may have been completely innocent, but he's given interviews in which he seems to be a willing participant in creating a market frenzy.

Even if dealers have no such clause, they feel they deserve the right to resell works. A major dealer recently went into a fury when he saw everything a salesperson sold to a client that year in an auction catalogue. He fired off an email to his sales staff specifying that, if any of them sold work to a client who betrayed them that way, they'd have to return their commission to the gallery. This may have made the dealer feel better, but realistically, how could a salesperson prevent a buyer from re-selling without a contract?

Flipping has become an epidemic. In January 2011, Adam Lindemann, in his *New York Observer* column, responded to the rash of flipsters in his list of New Year's resolutions for collectors with his "radical" suggestion, "Buy and hold." In a subsequent column, February 11, 2013, Adam further condemned market manipulation. "When the shiny new stuff hits the resale market, it'll sell like used cars." A painting by Anselm Reyle, at the artist's peak in 2007, brought over $600,000, and by 2013, the most one brought was $130,000. In the past, if word got out that the artist wasn't as promising as everyone thought, the auctions would be flooded by works from collectors who "pumped and dumped." That still happens, but there's also a lot of collectors who "pump and move on." The obvious takeaway is to avoid hitching your wagon to an artist whose works rise only by market manipulation.

Cartels have formed around established artists, such as Warhol and Basquiat. A journalist reported a 2009 conversation in which Alberto Mugrabi, the dealer/collector whose family owns the largest private collection of Warhols, told Larry Gagosian that an auction house expert had implied that two Warhols coming up didn't have any interest at the level of the reserve. Because Gagosian and Mugrabi concluded that the reserve was unrealistically high, Mugrabi called the expert and told him that if he could get the consignor to lower his reserves, his family might buy them just to support the prices.

One reason for all the market manipulation these days is that it's relatively easy to do. Whereas the auctions used to charge *all* sellers and *all* buyers premiums, today's powerful consignors negotiate a zero seller's premium, and, on high priced material, they can even get an 'enhanced hammer' (lingo for part of the buyer's premium, usually on a non-guaranteed lot). That means that the cost of transaction for cartels is low. When Peter Brant sold his prized Koons *Balloon Dog*, he said he paid no seller's premium, received a third-party guarantee, and an "enhanced hammer" which didn't oblige him to give the house a share of the buyer's premium until the price exceeded a certain number (it could have been as high as 110 or 111 percent). His *Balloon Dog* sold for $58,400,000, including the buyer's premium, and there's speculation that either Brant made a deal with the buyer to share the buyer's premium, so that the sale record would be higher than otherwise, or that Brant bought his own piece back.

Sure, everyone would like to find a winner. If you're interested in collecting emerging artists but aren't sure that speculation is for you, turn to my chapter, *Collecting Emerging Artists*. It details other pleasures you can expect. Then, you can decide which approach best suits you.

MAKING MONEY IN ART WITHOUT SELLING IT

Buying and selling art isn't the only way to make money in the art world. Years ago, I was on the phone with a client discussing that night's Sotheby's sale, which I thought would bomb. The client, a financial guy, didn't tell me until afterwards, but, based on our conversation, he shorted Sotheby's stock. The sale went badly, and he made a small fortune.

Another opportunity to make money is by being a third-party guarantor. Since auction houses are reluctant to put up their own money, they ask outsiders (usually collectors and dealers with an interest in that particular artist) to place irrevocable bids. So, if you're a big Warhol collector, you may be asked to guarantee a Warhol at, let's say, $15 million. To entice you, the house tells you as much as they can about the work and the deal, which is as close as it comes to inside trading. You make the decision that at that number, you're willing to buy it, knowing that if it doesn't reach $15 million during the bidding, you have to pay that sum anyway. If the bidding goes above the $15M, you can let someone else buy it and receive a pre-arranged share of the overage or you can continue bidding. If this sounds interesting, but you don't have the connections at the auction houses or don't want to guarantee *one* expensive painting, there are funds that pool investors' money to supply third-party guarantees to sellers who can't get a guarantee through the auction houses. In those situations, the seller pays a fee to the fund.

BACKING A GALLERIST

If you're a player, there will come a time when a dealer may ask you to back his gallery. It may sound glamorous, and the dealer may offer you first crack at everything he gets in at a discount, but don't do it. You need to pay a gallery's overhead like you need an extra head. If the relationship deteriorates, you could end up auditing the dealer's books and learn that he's been living like a pasha on your money.

A more limited role which makes better sense is to partner with the dealer on specific works. But if a dealer approaches you with this offer, make sure he has a stellar reputation and structure a deal that makes sense. Some dealers may ask you to put up 100% of the purchase price for half of the profits. Avoid that scenario like the plague. If the dealer has no skin in the game, he could put a high mark-up on the work and wait for a sale. On the other hand, if he puts in some of his own money, he'll work harder to make a sale. If a dealer asks you to "go in" half-shares on a painting, ask to see the invoice. You don't want to learn that he's charged you more for your half-share than the entire work cost him.

Buying works with a dealer is usually straightforward, but there's always the danger you might fall prey to a ponzi scheme or other scam. In the thirty-five years I've been in business, I've only heard of a handful at most, but you can't let your guard down. In 2010, dealer Larry Salander went to jail for bilking clients and friends out of $120 million. In at least one instance, he sold up to 350% shares in a single work.

A friend's unhappy saga with a dealer began when he put up $1,000,000 for a half share of a fabulous small Warhol. Within a month, the dealer sold it, and my friend made a $500,000 profit. So far, so good. The dealer then convinced him that, if they rolled over the $3,000,000 they got for the Warhol and added another $500,000 each, they could buy a great Rothko on paper. A month later, the dealer reported a profit on the Rothko, and, this time, he asked my friend to add another million, so they could buy a Giacometti sculpture. The only problem was that although the Warhol was real and the profit was legit, there was no Rothko or Giacometti. When my friend found out, he realized that turning the dealer into the police wouldn't have gotten him his money back. Instead, he had lawyers draw up a two-year payback schedule. It was upsetting, but eventually he got his money back, and he still earned more than he would have parking his money in a Treasury Bond.

ART FUNDS AND LENDING INSTITUTIONS

Dealers and auction houses aren't the only games in town; you can also invest in an art fund. Like other investment funds, your money gets pooled with that of other investors. Some have a menu of funds — a general fund, a fund of funds, and special sector funds, focusing on Western art, Chinese art, etc. Despite lots of talk, most have failed. They've been criticized for overhead and transaction fees, but I think the reason most haven't taken off is that art investors prefer making their own decisions, using an advisor they know and trust, staying in control, and having the joy of living with the art. The "funds" that do work seem to be those started by small groups of like-minded friends who hire an art advisor to look for opportunities. The participants put up their money on an ad hoc basis and keep the works in their homes.

Many collectors see their collections as giant ATM machines, an easy way to borrow for other business opportunities or to buy more art. This way, would-be sellers don't have to part with works they love, fight against a time clock to sell, or be perceived as needing money, which might happen when word gets out they're selling expensive works. When interest rates are low, collectors who borrow against their art to buy more art are betting that they can buy something that will increase in value more than interest rates. Major banks, like

UBS, Citibank, and Bank of America, do a brisk business lending on art in recourse loans, in which lenders pledge their art and also give a personal guarantee against other assets. Specialized private lending institutions have cropped up to service high-risk dealers and collectors. These private lenders, which you can invest in, function like 'pawnshops' in the 'loan to own' business. By charging a whopping 30-60% rate of interest annually, they hope that the borrower defaults. It can get nasty. In 2009, Art Capital Group lent photographer Annie Leibovitz $24 million against her negatives, at an annual interest rate of 44%. She defaulted, and it appeared likely she'd lose ownership of her entire body of work. A public outpouring of support induced Art Capital not to foreclose, and another lender stepped in and bailed her out.

It's not surprising that the number of people investing in art has soared. I can't think of another 'commodity' that provides substantial profits while simultaneously enriching its investors' lives. But the devil is in the details. There are no guarantees and no short cuts to a winning game. Whether you choose to buy one work, a painting in shares with a dealer, or join a fund, you can hit a home run or strike out. Your success depends on experience, information, intellect, and good judgment. As I've said before, the better educated you are about art and the art market and the better advice you get, the less you'll have to rely on luck.

COLLECTING EMERGING ARTISTS

Not all collectors involved in emerging artists are speculators. Of course, they'd love to find the next art world star. Who wouldn't? At very least they'd love to find artists who develop respected careers, if for no other reason than to validate their eye. But market manipulation is not their thing. If this approach appeals to you, you're going to have to do a lot of looking. But what do you look for, and where do you look? As Steve Jobs quoted Wayne Gretsky, the famed hockey player, "I skate where the puck is going to be, not where it's been." That's fine for Wayne Gretsky and Steve Jobs, but how does that apply to you? How can you know where the art puck's headed?

There are millions of emerging artists all over the world, and any of them could be 'the one.' Even collectors who know where to look and have spent years training their 'eye,' scan the field and fail to find Waldo. I'll spare you the 'needle in the haystack' analogy, but I can't spare you the grim reality. If the spoils are huge, the task is daunting. Finding an emerging artist who becomes the next art world star is like going to the racetrack without a tip sheet, making a wild guess, and putting your money down. Only it's worse; instead of choosing from a field of twelve, there are thousands of horses in the race. In this section, I'll explore the ways to balance risk with reward and explain what art world insiders do to find emerging artists with promise. Who knows, you might just shift the odds in your favor.

Let's begin by being clear about what we're looking for: what exactly is an 'emerging artist'? It turns out that the term is both ambiguous and controversial. The blogosphere is filled with indignant partisans who'd like to ban its use. To them, the term suggests an artist who springs forth as a fully-formed genius, rather than one who develops slowly over time, as most artists generally do. Artists over forty also hate the term: they feel it's synonymous with "young" which leaves them out of the running. I wish I could come up with a better moniker, but since I can't, I'll stick with it for now.

In going after emerging artists, you eliminate the zillions of artists who haven't had any success, as well as those who've had their fifteen minutes of fame and have either gone on to stardom or have failed to endure. Your quarry is in that sweet spot between total obscurity and fulfilled promise, artists who may have had some notice by the art establishment, but haven't realized their full potential. If you're willing to invest in their future, they'll take you along for the ride. You...and plenty of others. "Emerging art" is the fastest growing sector of the art market, with new collectors pouring in daily.

WHAT'S THE ATTRACTION?

What is it about collecting emerging artists that's so alluring? Just about *everything*. It offers the perks other fields offer – on steroids. If you collect Renaissance bronzes, you might go to Maastricht and, if you're lucky, find one or two sculptures to consider. You'll attend the occasional museum show and auction, read the odd article published on the subject, keep in touch with the few galleries in the world that handle the material, and correspond with a handful of like-minded collectors and scholars. At a cocktail party, if you try discussing Renaissance bronzes, most people will smile and edge away even before you get to 'patina,' let alone 'iconography.'

By contrast, if you collect emerging artists, you'll find people who share your passion almost everywhere in the world, day or night. You can attend art fairs, biennials, auctions, museum and gallery shows, and openings. You'll meet tons of interesting people who, like yourself, are looking for works that hit them over the head like a ton of bricks or words of wisdom from the cognoscenti that will lead them to the right artist. You'll meet sympathetic dealers who welcome you into their orbit and share their knowledge. They'll invite you to parties with other interesting clients and artists. And when you walk into their galleries or booths at a fair, they'll greet you with palms and salaams, depending on how much you spend. And if you follow the right drums, you'll find yourself at the center of every discussion, with everyone else listening intently to what you have to say.

Another reason the field is so attractive is that it requires a relatively small investment to participate. Most collectors can't afford big name artists, but many can afford to stay active collecting emerging artists. And since the art was made yesterday, or maybe last year, there's no due diligence to do. Verifying authenticity, condition, and title isn't necessary. There's no literature or exhibition history to check, and you don't have to investigate the appropriateness of the price. It's also a field that requires less knowledge to get started. If you're considering a 19th-century painting by Thomas Moran of the Grand Canyon, you really need to understand Manifest Destiny to fully appreciate it. And if you're purchasing a Picasso portrait of Maria Thérèse, it's good to know who she was and what was going on in the artist's life and in their relationship when he painted it. But with emerging artists, since 'innovation' and 'concept' are the watchwords, you only need a general idea of what happened in the past and a working familiarity of the contemporary scene, mass culture, and technology to get you going. But make no mistake, getting going is one thing, and making it to the finish line is another. Understanding what makes for truly innovative work and picking the right artists out of a huge, diverse field of contenders requires years of experience.

WHAT MAKES ONE WORK STAND OUT FROM THE REST?

For years after World War II, the art scene was dominated by one movement after another. In the 50s, it was Abstract Expressionism. Everyone knew who the artists were, and it wasn't hard to prioritize them. Pop Art rose in the early 60s with its handful of protagonists, Minimalism and Conceptual Art in the late 60s and 70s, and Neo-Expressionism and graffiti art in the 80s. This seamless hand-off from one to another gave collectors a clear path and roster of players to choose from.

That pattern has now shattered like a glass dish on a stone floor. There's no dominant 'school' whose concerns, subject, media choices, or focus defines what art should look like or what constitutes a desirable work. There are no rules, no guidelines, no universal 'goals' informing the work being made. In fact, it's rare to find two artists who share a similar style. Some want to make memorable objects, while others aren't concerned with the physicality of the work. Some are interested in reinterpreting the past, while others want nothing to do with what's gone before.

As for media, artists are also all over the place. Many make work that is photo-based or digital, or some combination with video, computer-generated images, and installations. And yet, plenty of artists paint on canvas or make sculpture using traditional techniques. And whereas some say it's the idea that counts and shun "craft" as unimportant, others embrace tools and materials. To complicate matters further, an artist can be interested in so many different issues, materials, and techniques that no two of his works look like they're from the same hand. A one-man show can look like a group exhibition.

In short, these days you can expect to stand in a gallery of 'important,' recently created works by different artists and find it difficult to identify what's best or even what's "good" — if the concept of "good and bad" still applies. The only constant is that every artist there is trying to be an innovator and do work that's 'seminal.' 'Derivative' is the worst epithet you can hurl at him. Artists who create a new language, force us out of our comfort zone, and encourage us to think about art and the world in new ways have a better chance of succeeding than others.

These things can drive collectors crazy. Some collectors are so desperate for a hook that the minute there's the slightest suggestion that a group of artists shares an ideology or aesthetic, they're ready to proclaim it the 'next big thing.' That's exactly what happened several years ago when a number of young realist painters in Leipzig circled around Neo Rauch. 'The New Leipzig School,' as it was called, including Tim Eitel, Matthias Weischer, and Martin Kobe, took off, and collectors loaded up on their works. But have you heard anything about the New Leipzig School recently? Neo Rauch, yes (Remember how cream rises?); the rest, not so much.

New collectors may say they want works that are fresh and hip but are often startled by what they see. Even the most sophisticated collectors might be perplexed by Susan Philipsz's *Lowlands*, which won the 2010 Turner Prize, as there were no visuals at all. The piece was comprised of Philipsz singing a Scottish lament in a room in which visitors sat on benches listening. The work challenged the barrier between music and art and evoked Scotland as strongly as any 19th-century realist painting. But did it move the needle or not?

What criteria, if any, can you use to decide what is good, better, or best? How do you pick an artist who will get on everyone's "artists to watch" list? I'd love to make things easy for you, like the family friend in *The Graduate* who whispers the word "plastics" into Benjamin's ear. But there are no secrets, no tips to bank on. It's not even easy to get a consensus from the experts. When, in 2010, the *Baer Faxt* did an end-of-the-year poll asking subscribers, most of whom are professionals or collectors, to vote for the best emerging artist of the year, over a hundred people responded, and no two voted for the same artist.

I recently polled a random sampling of art world colleagues to ask what *they* look for in works by emerging artists. Surprisingly, few had even thought about formulating a workable checklist. What started out as a series of casual phone calls and lunches wound up, like the quest for the Holy Grail, elusive, to say the least. I began with a well-known, articulate artist who blustered, "If they copy you, you're good." "But," I asked, "how do I know you'll be copied in the future, when you've just made the piece?" No answer. I next asked a renowned critic. "If it stands the test of time, it's good," he intoned. How could I possibly know the longevity of a newly-minted work especially if, as the cognoscenti say, it takes twenty years to know? I felt I was getting warmer when a dealer said, "If the work upsets me, and I walk out of the studio clutching my stomach, I know I've seen something good." And I had to admire the collector who gruffly cut to the chase by saying, "Hon, if it sells, it's good." His point? The marketplace dictates approval.

When I asked Irving Blum, the first dealer to show Andy Warhol's soup cans, how he managed that feat, he shrugged, "You have to have an 'eye.'" He went on to explain that before leaving Los Angeles for the trip to New York on which he found Warhol, he called friends for a list of artists to visit. Several mentioned Warhol. At this point in the story, it sounded as if Irving had an ear, not an eye. But when Irving got to Warhol's studio, his 'eye' kicked in and he saw what no other dealer had seen. Irving plunged when others didn't, and the rest, as they say, is "history."

A thoughtful, if not discouraging view came from a careful collector. He said the ordinary person couldn't tell good emerging art from bad. He said it takes a thorough background in art history to understand the seminal changes an artist makes from what's come before and to judge whether the artist has made those changes effectively. He analogized it to wine connoisseurship. A beginner can't tell the difference between bad, good, and great wine. It takes studying and tasting to tell a superb Chateau Margaux from an off-the-shelf Cabernet. "If you can't tell great wine from plonk, why would you think you could tell a really great emerging artist from the rest of the herd?"

Ed Ruscha, the famous artist, offered the most cogent explanation I heard. He said he looks for art that's interesting in a new way or that approaches art-making differently from anything he's seen. He cautioned that not all works meeting those requirements become bestsellers and make their creators rich and famous. But some do. Those become 'must haves' for collectors and touchstones of their era — objects that future generations will appreciate with fresh eyes and artists will continue to plumb for ideas. In Ruscha's experience, art that lacked that 'difference' and 'newness' and just did what others did, maybe a little better, won't go far.

The best I can do is to suggest some questions you can ask of any work you're considering which may help you find the next "plastics" or at least decide whether to give the work serious consideration or walk away. Let's begin with the supposition that every time an artist creates a work of art he's addressing a problem. It's your job to figure out what the problem is and whether he's solved it satisfactorily. It might be about the formalist issues of making art (composition, scale, style, etc.), subject matter, the way the artist uses new media, or something else entirely. The problem doesn't have to be new; great artists have been painting portraits and still life or dealing with angst, alienation, politics, etc., for centuries. It's whether they push the envelope that counts. If you think the work is a game-changer, is it being done in a way the market will find acceptable and embrace? For example, when John Currin paints figurative paintings, in which the figures seem part of a strange, slightly sinister narrative that the spectator can't quite understand but can't look away from, has he completed a successful pass from the old masters and changed the figurative art game forever? So far, the market says, "Yes."

Don't be discouraged if at first, these 'game-changers' don't grab you. It may take time for your eye to 'adjust.' To help spot the diamond in a sea of zirconia, here are some questions:

1. *Is the work 'unforgettable?' Does it grow on you as you look at it, and does it amaze you every time you return for another look?*

2. *Is the work easily identifiable? Many collectors have ADD when it comes to art, so instant recognition makes them more comfortable and makes the work easier to sell.*

3. *Does the artist create a new language in the way he constructs his work and does it fit his ideas? Or does he go for a shocking new look simply because it's shocking?*

4. *Does the technical skill and level of craftsmanship match the ideas?*

5. *If you've seen the artist's earlier work, has the new work changed in positive ways?*

6. *Do you see the work being important thirty years from now?*

And then, of course, there are questions not having to do with the work itself. Does the artist have a good dealer? Has the dealer placed works in important museums, museum shows, and private collections? Have important critics written enthusiastically about the work?

An artist's output may also be relevant. Rarity was always thought to be a desirable trait, but not so much any more. If the artist works too slowly and produces too little, his work may not sustain an orderly market. Conversely, if the artist is too prolific, he may flood the market with work. The ideal is a large and steady supply and demand.

If you're buying strictly for fun and don't care if the works you buy are good investments, you needn't worry about any of the above questions. You can decide what's "mad money" to you, and, if a work costs less than that and you love it, you can buy and enjoy it without second thoughts. But shouldn't you be able to find artists whose works you like, that don't cost the earth, and fit all the criteria we've set out?

THE ROLE OF THE ARTIST

Although many artists recede into the background and let their creations speak for them, others are out there 'branding' themselves, hoping it will help them sell their work and join the immortals. It worked for Picasso, a master of self-promotion. He dropped all his baptized names — Pablo, Diego, José, Francisco de Paula, Juan Nepomuceno, Maria de los Remedios, Cipriano de la Santisima — and his father's name, Ruiz, and became one of those celebrities known by one name. He allowed photographers to be a constant presence, documenting his family, his studio, methods of working, and adding to the myth. He understood how to manage the supply of work so that he didn't swamp the market. And he was driven to change his style constantly, which satisfied consumers who wanted something "new," like car models, to add to their collections of Picassos.

Damien Hirst took a page from Picasso's playbook. His reputation as a risk-taker and general 'bad boy' didn't hurt him or his bottom line, and Jeff Koons' talk of "market share" and his marriage to an Italian porn star, whose voluptuous image appeared in many of his works, made an indelible mark on everyone in the art community and beyond. In recent seasons, many of the under-35 hot artists have been attractive macho-looking guys with "five o'clock shadows." Coincidence? I think not.

Of course, we mustn't confuse 'branding,' personality, and looks with...talent. While Warhol, Salvador Dali, and Picasso all had outsize 'public' personas, their works have stood the test of time. But so have the works of Ellsworth Kelly, Wayne Thiebaud and a host of other artists who've led very private lives. Nonetheless, since we know that being recognizable and articulate adds to salability, should it make a buyer favor young artists they read about on *Page Six* as opposed to someone who's not on anyone's radar? Is that wrong? That may also be true of attendance at a good college or grad school or the receipt of a prestigious prize. But not all artists who go to Ivy League schools or win accolades turn out to be the Next Big Thing. In fact, the art world has a soft spot for autodidacts, like Basquiat, who gained notoriety doing graffiti on the streets.

There's no 'right' answer in this debate. You shouldn't buy a work of art just because the artist won a Guggenheim or is in the gossip columns, but if you're wowed by the work, the fact that its creator happens to be articulate and fascinating just might tip the scales for you. As my grandmother would have said, "It couldn't hurt."

HE WHO HESITATES IS LOST

Where do you find works by emerging artists with potential and how do you get them? A couple of decades ago, you could walk into a gallery and, if you loved a work, you could buy it and leave with it under your arm. If you weren't sure how you felt about the work, you had the luxury of "following" the artist and waiting for his next show to see how the work developed before committing. Today, competition among collectors is so keen that, while you hesitate, others jump in, prices spike, waitlists form, and the window of opportunity to buy a great work for loose change closes. So, even if you're seeing the work for the first time, you have to be ready to pull the trigger. If you don't, it may only be a matter of months until that striking $10,000 work sells for hundreds of thousands.

As I've mentioned, if the heat builds around an artist, he'll likely leave his 'starter' gallery and move 'up' the food chain to a more powerful dealer. This happens in Hollywood all the time. When an actor gets hot, he leaves the poor agent who found him in summer stock and moves to a big agency. In the art world, once the artist moves up, and the more demand there may be, the more difficult it is to get hold of his work. Collectors go to great lengths to distinguish themselves so that the dealer "places" work with them (an upscale word for "sell"). They buy into the dealer's entire program of artists, engage well-respected art advisors whom dealers want to be in business with, and even build private museums to assure dealers of their seriousness. Some try to impress with their "connections," like letting it drop that their sister is married to a Silicon Valley tycoon. The dealer is the artist's gatekeeper to the world, and it's his job to place the work where it's best for the artist — with serious collectors, museums, and in certain communities.

How much can you expect to pay for an emerging artist, and how much time do you have before he emerges and it's too late to buy? It varies. Julie Belcove's 2011 article in *The New Yorker* chronicled the meteoric rise of Jacob Kassay, with his elegant silver-dipped-solution paintings. Kassay was unknown, and yet before his first show, in 2009, at Eleven Rivington, a small downtown gallery, every painting sold in advance for about $10,000 each, most to important collectors and the cartel. It's easy to understand why the enthusiasm built for Kassay's work. His paintings, made by applying white flat acrylic onto the canvas and then outsourcing them to a chemist to dip in an electrified silver solution, were conceptual enough to appeal to the hardcore and beautiful enough to attract those looking for "pretty." Less than a year after the show, a work by Kassay came up at Phillips and sold for $86,500. Six months after that, another painting brought $290,500 at auction, and a year and a half later, one brought $317,000 (not the quantum leap you might expect). Early birds got the worm, and others, late to the table, had to pay five or six figures for a work. Kassay's prices at auction have not continued to rise, and although he's been the subject of fascination and the object of speculation, whether his work stands the test of time is in serious question. Before, the artist had a chance to develop in a serious way and artists who were talked about weren't always the artists making all the money. Today, they're one and the same. This kind of fast hyper-evaluating of artists, one after another, can be extremely destructive to the market. And the buyers/speculators, desperate to go down in the history books as "discoverers," are unstoppable.

A website, ArtRank.com, offers a shortcut for collectors. It claims to use algorithms to come up with lists of artists to buy, hold, and sell. If you subscribe, you get the intel 21 days ahead of everyone else. That an artist's fortunes can change within a month is shocking.

Some collectors prefer not to buy emerging artists at low prices. They'd rather wait until the artist has been bought by good collectors and museums, has hung in museum shows, and has representation by stellar galleries in various cities. At that point, collectors figure that if so much of the art establishment is behind the artist, he's too big to fail. They'd rather pay more as 'insurance.' They're also aware that early isn't always better. You might buy an early work, only to find years later that the work "collected" by important collectors and museums is later work, and yours isn't what anyone wants.

THE BEST HUNTING GROUNDS

You could be busy every day going to museum and gallery shows and visiting artists' studios looking for "the one," and still not scratch the surface. Many people's first, and sometimes only choice of hunting grounds are fairs which focus on new talent. They feel that they're seeing the best works dealers have vetted, and that there's more than ample material to choose from. According to a *New York Times* article by Carol Vogel, the Rubells saw a booth of sold-out Oscar Murillo paintings at an art fair, called the artist, and made an appointment to go to his studio, even though Murillo told them he had nothing available. When they arrived, the artist looked like he'd been up all night...and he had... creating work for them. The Rubells bought everything in the studio, invited him for a residency at their Miami foundation and showed the artist's work there during Art Basel. That had everyone talking about and buying Murillo. Within a couple of years, Murillo went from working his way through art school in London to being an art world star whose works were bringing mid-six figures.

A number of galleries specializing in emerging artists are found off the beaten track in the outer boroughs of New York, like Williamsburg and elsewhere in Brooklyn, and downtown and Eagle Rock, and Los Feliz in northeast Los Angeles. There, inexpensive storefront spaces and warehouses make it possible for young, idealistic dealers to show the works of artists/friends they believe in. These dealers may be relatively new to the business, but they're highly professional and wired into the scene. They know how to get to the right collectors to buy and how to push their artists into the big time.

Collectors and dealers also scour non-profit spaces and grad student shows the way sports teams scout promising young ballplayers. Another source is pop-up exhibitions which independent dealers and curators hold in clubs, galleries, or other spaces they rent or wrangle for free. These independents feel that without being encumbered by running galleries, they can be more agile in their choices, especially in representing performance artists.

Collecting emerging artists is a game of numbers. Many collectors own hundreds or even thousands of works. No matter how bulletproof your eye is, and how much homework you do, you will buy works you fall out of love with. What do you do then? When I asked an experienced collector of emerging artists, "What tips can you give a novice?" he counseled, "Get a warehouse."

Collectors may store works they don't want or try to give works to museums, hospitals, and schools. When my friend Beth Dozoretz was head of the State Department's Art in Embassies program, she was regularly approached by collectors who hoped to find a life for their works in US embassies abroad. If the works are saleable, collectors can put them in auction day sales and online auctions.

In 2015, Paddle8 held a widely publicized sale of works owned by Swiss collector Bibi Gritti. Was she selling because she was downsizing, as she was quoted, or was she getting rid of what she no longer wanted?

If collecting emerging artists appeals to you, realize that uncertainty is part of the game. It's one of the reasons why so many collectors find this sector appealing. If you combine the difficulty of getting what you want and the element of gambling, it's easy to see why Type A's are attracted. They love a challenge. There's nothing like the adrenalin rush of stepping into a gallery or artist's studio, seeing the work of a new young artist and taking a chance. Maybe you'll win, and maybe you won't. But the ride will be exciting.

AN ALTERNATE UNIVERSE: WORKS ON PAPER AND NEW MEDIA

Generally, when I've referred to 'paintings,' what I've said applies to all fine arts. Now, I'll discuss the unique qualities of other media so you can understand what draws collectors to them.

WORKS ON PAPER

Until recently, works on paper were considered inferior to oils. If you bought one of these poor relations — a drawing, gouache, pastel, print or photo — you'd have hung it in your bathroom or hall. But over the sofa or mantel? *Jamais*. The marketplace agreed. As late as the 1960s, London auction houses offered string-tied bundles of old master drawings as forlorn 'box' lots, and most beginning collectors had no interest in looking at works under glass. "I want *real* paintings," they'd sniff.

We've come a long way since then. The old 'hierarchy by medium' is out the window. When Leon Black paid $119.9 million for a pastel version of Munch's *The Scream*, no one said, "Are you nuts? That thing's on paper!!!" It's an iconic work, regardless of the medium. In fact, works on paper can outpace paintings by the same artists (a great Prendergast watercolor can bring more than an oil by the artist). Generally, however, since the prices of an artist's work on paper are lower than his paintings, you can buy a major name at a more affordable price point.

Works on paper come in two distinct types — unique works and multiples. Drawings, watercolors, gouaches, and pastels (definitions are coming) are 'unique'; i.e., no two are alike, and all are made directly by the hand of the artist onto a sheet of paper. Prints and photographs, by contrast, are 'multiples' created in editions. The exception is the monotype, which is a single unique print.

One-offs are no better or more valuable than editions. Editioned works, from Rembrandt prints to Cindy Sherman photographs, can command higher prices than drawings and watercolors by hundreds of "listed" American and European artists.

ONE-OFFS: DRAWINGS, WATERCOLORS, PASTELS, ETC.

"Drawings" generally refer to works on paper executed in graphite (pencil), colored pencil, gouache, crayon, charcoal, or ink. They're either created in a single color — often black, brown, red-orange, sepia, or grey — or they're multi-colored. Watercolors are made by brushing watercolor (pigment suspended in water) onto paper, usually in many colors. When artists limit their palette to shades of grey, the result is called "grisaille." And should it ever come up, a monochrome in brown is called "bruneille," and in green, "verdaille." The same titles, by the way, apply to monochrome oil paintings.

A gouache (pronounced "gwash"), is made with pigment dissolved in water mixed with gum Arabic and chalk. This makes the paint more opaque than watercolor, more like poster paint. If you hold up a work to the light and you can't see 'through' the paint to the paper, you're probably looking at a gouache.

The term 'pastel' refers to both a category and to the 'tool' the artist uses to make it. To create a 'pastel,' the artist uses 'pastels' — sticks made with powdered pigments suspended in resin or gum. The next time you're in Paris, please visit La Maison du Pastel, a small shop in the Marais. It's run by the family who started it two hundred years ago. I went, because I couldn't believe that it's possible to buy pastels where Degas bought his. Once there, I couldn't resist buying a few sticks (they're not cheap), and I don't even make art! The shop sells over 600 colors, which can be bought individually or in various-sized kits (available online). It's only open a few hours a week, and it's in an easy-to-miss alley, so check before you go.

Until the latter part of the 19th century, most drawings done by European and American artists were intended to be exercises or studies for paintings. Only occasionally did artists make stand-alone 'presentation' drawings, designed to show off their sense of composition and craftsmanship. Rarely, drawings were made *after* a painting, *pour memoire*, to be kept as a permanent reminder of a painting that would be sold. Today, many artists continue the tradition of drawing in preparation for works in other media, while others, attracted by the spontaneity and challenges that only working on paper affords, work on paper either exclusively or as one of their principal media.

Because corrections and changes remain visible in drawings, they offer more intimacy and more of a sense of what the artist is thinking than a painting might. The unfinished quality of many drawings appeals to our modern way of thinking: it's why we respond to fragments of antiquities or sculptures by Rodin and Maillols, purposely created without heads or arms. As opposed to finished works, where everything is given to us on a silver platter, works that are unfinished force us to engage, interact, and complete the images in our brains. Perhaps it's the same reason we like E.E. Cummings with his lack of punctuation and capitalization.

If you're spending serious money on a drawing, it makes sense to have a conservator who specializes in works on paper examine it before you buy. Tack holes, from where the paper was pinned to a board, may be readily visible, but they're a fact of life and shouldn't be worrisome. Of greater concern is whether there's foxing (brownish spots which result from mold) or tears, or if the work is 'light-struck' (faded) or has been re-colored, any of which can decrease its value. You could probably notice these things if the seller takes the work out of the frame. For example, look at the margins: If they're very small or uneven, the work may have been cut down (not good). If the area that's been covered by the matte is lighter than the rest, you can surmise it's been light-struck (also not good). If you turn the paper over and hold it up to the light, its back to you, most tears and repairs will show through. But as with paintings, remember that you're an amateur, and it takes a conservator to assess the problems and tell you what, if anything, can be done to improve the work.

PRINTS

Before you run off and buy a lot of drawings and watercolors, consider the equally enticing possibilities of multiples, including prints, photographs, videos, and new media.

If you want the best but have limited resources, multiples may be the way to go. You may never be able to afford a Rembrandt painting or drawing, but you could get a Rembrandt etching for under $10,000 and get the same bragging rights as someone who owns a Rembrandt painting. Big name, small price. And if you're willing to spend a million dollars, you might be able to get one of the greatest works Rembrandt ever created, an etching, *The Three Crosses*, dating from 1653, one of only 80 extant. The same goes for other great artists known for their contribution to printmaking, including Picasso, Johns, and Warhol. A set of Warhol's ten silkscreens of Mao has brought over $2,500,000, but an *Electric Chair* can be had for just over $10,000. So, if you've set aside a set sum to invest in art a year, rather than buying one expensive painting and hanging back the rest of the year, you can focus on prints and be continuously active.

Prints may be for you, particularly if you like knowing your net worth at any given time. Since prints come in editions, other prints like yours are likely to turn up for sale periodically, and when they do, you won't have to sell yours to know what it's worth and whether to celebrate or cry yourself to sleep.

Prices realized at auction may be misleading because you have no idea of condition, and, as you know, condition means a lot. Provenance can also affect price. The day after a Johns print sold for a record price in writer Michael Crichton's 2010 Christie's estate sale, a client who owns the same print called, thrilled. Sadly, I had to bring him back to earth by reminding him that the high price was due to the Crichton hype, and that he'd have to wait for a less publicized sale of the print to get a better gauge.

Before you buy 'print one,' it's best to know exactly what you're buying, since printmaking techniques can be confusing. The definitions in Dave Williams' book *Small Victories: One Couple's Surprising Adventures Collecting American Prints* are extremely clear, or you can watch Williams' film on printmaking or other demonstrations on YouTube. Spending time with a master printer at a print workshop, like Gemimi G.E.L. in Los Angeles, is eye-opening, especially if there's an artist in residence, because you'll see how artists and printers collaborate. Meanwhile, here are some basics to get you started.

To create a print, an artist doesn't draw or paint directly on a sheet of paper. Instead, he 'pulls' the work from a master 'vehicle' he's created. That is, he makes an image on wood, metal, stone, fabric, or computer. He can pull as many prints as he wants from the same vehicle, and each one will be the same as every other – hence the term 'multiple.' Traditional printmaking techniques vary, but all require the artist to cut, etch, or otherwise shape the vehicle so that only the negative or positive spaces of the composition will 'take' the ink or paint. When one of these substances is introduced onto the vehicle and pressure is applied to transfer it onto the paper, the result should be what the artist intended.

Essentially, there are four kinds of prints. The first, a 'relief' print (woodcut or linocut), is made by an artist cutting away the parts of the wooden or linoleum block he *doesn't* want to print. Once only the shapes he wants to print are left standing out in relief, he inks or paints the vehicle, and that's what appears in the finished product. It's like the old joke, "How do you carve an elephant? Carve away everything that doesn't look like an elephant."

Intaglio prints, etchings, and engravings are the opposite. Here, the artist carves or etches his image into a metal plate. The rest of the plate is covered by an ink-resistant medium, and ink is applied to fill only the recessed lines. When the plate is pressed onto the paper, the image that appears on the paper will be composed solely of those lines. In this kind of print, you may see a gently indented 'plate mark' around the image where the plate pressed into the paper. Traditionally, in aquatints, powder resin would be brushed onto the plate, and the acid bite would "take" on the areas around the granules, making graduated tones possible.

The third kind is a planar print, or lithograph, created on a flat surface — no carving, no etching. In years past, the artist drew the image he wanted on a stone with a greasy crayon to which ink would adhere. These days, a zinc or aluminum plate is used. Either way, the resulting composition is made up of only the 'greasy' ink retaining areas.

Rounding out this quartet is the silkscreen. To make one, the artist prepares a mesh screen covered in specific areas with an impermeable material. When ink or paint is introduced and pushed through the screen onto paper, it will appear only where the artist left 'open' spaces. Since each color requires a separate screening process, you can imagine the nightmare of getting the registration perfect when several colors are used.

Each plate, stone, block, or screen can be used an unlimited number of times, but artists typically control the number of prints by numbering an 'edition.' After that, they 'retire' the print by X-ing out or destroying the plate. Warhol often did runs of 200, but most runs over 100 are considered too commercial. If the edition size is an odd number, like "29," the artist may have followed the tradition of limiting himself to the number of prints he could pull in a day. Or he may have pulled a greater number, but only 29 met his standards.

Prints are usually numbered in pencil on the front bottom left. If the designation is '10/40,' it means that the artist created 40 prints total, and this one has been assigned number 10. Some people think a print numbered 10/40 is the tenth printed and that it's better and sharper than one that's 30/40. Not necessarily so. Artists sometimes number the edition backward starting with the last one pulled, so it's impossible to know where yours fits in sequence. Other designations you may see in pencil on the bottom of a print are "A.P." for artist's proof and "P.P." for printer's proof, each with a low number, as a handful or so were made for the artist and for the printer, often in exchange for payment. Those signed and numbered H.C. for *hors de commerce* were given to the publisher. If a print has "BAT" for *bon à tirer* written at the bottom, it means 'good to pull.' Although those prints aren't in the edition, they're considered superior examples, since they were the first images that met the artist's exacting specifications. In the past, it was thought that proofs were the most valuable, as they were where one saw the artist addressing problems, like working drawings, but today with new techniques, no distinctions are made.

Artists may make serial changes, producing different 'states' of the same print. Rembrandt was known for doing this, and Picasso did it in his famed *Minotauromachy* etching. Since certain "states" are more desirable and valuable than others, collectors should find out which is which before laying out cash. This is particularly true of old master prints, where it's necessary to know a wealth of arcane information to avoid buying the wrong print at the wrong price. Every antique shop in Rome sells Giovanni Panini "prints" of Rome, for example, and unless you can tell when they were made, you can get stung.

Watch out for posthumous prints. If the printmaking "vehicle" isn't destroyed or disabled, and a print becomes sought after following the death of the artist, there's every temptation for the artist's heirs, or total strangers, to pull posthumous editions and pass them off as originals. Since the artist had nothing to do with these prints, they have little or no value. The absence of a signature can be a giveaway, but even if there is a signature, you can't be sure what you've got. Some artists simply commissioned printmakers to copy their famous paintings and had no personal involvement. Dali famously signed some 350,000 blank sheets of lithographic paper at the rate of 1,800 signatures an hour. Prints were then produced, and the market was flooded with thousands of 'signed' Dali 'originals' that Dali had nothing to do with. Cruise ships, charity auctions, and commercial galleries in tourist towns like Honolulu are notorious for selling these, diluting the value of the artist's real prints, and making the Dali print market a dicey business.

As a result, some collectors look down their noses at prints and consider them nothing more than 'repros' of paintings made by artists to maximize their bottom line. They're very wrong. Many serious artists consider printmaking vital to their practice because it offers unique ways to try out new ideas and resolve different artistic problems than they're dealing with in other media. The prints you want to buy are by those artists, including Hockney, Picasso, and Johns. Hockney travelled for years with his printmaker, Maurice Payne, collaborating all the while. Picasso was so consumed by printmaking late in life that his printers, the Crommelynck brothers, opened a workshop near his home in the south of France and often worked through the night to keep up with the artist's daily output. During the last ten years of his life, along with thousands of paintings and pottery objects, Picasso produced 700 different prints — a staggering achievement. Johns' prints are so well thought of that they hung alongside his paintings in The Met show, *Jasper Johns: Gray*. The artist is known in printmaking circles for taking aquatint to a whole new level. Called 'sugar lift,' it enables the artist's brushwork to be preserved by permitting broad areas of color to be printed instead of only flat lines.

If you think prints are for you, you can attend print fairs where you can see thousands of examples and meet dealers, talk to curators, invest in some books, and study print auction catalogues. And, if you're interested in contemporary prints, you can keep your eye on the print workshops to find out what new editions are being made. The closer you buy a work to its release date, the less expensive. Prices go up as works in the edition sell.

When you can tell a silkscreen from an etching at forty paces, you're ready to rock.

PHOTOGRAPHY

Photography has had its own uphill battle for art world acceptance. Well into the 20th century, it wasn't just considered *less* important than painting, it wasn't considered art at all. It was thought of as a purely mechanical process appropriate for reportage in newspapers and magazines. It wasn't on most collectors' radar.

Gradually, attitudes toward photography changed, and, by the 1970s, an active market developed for 'vintage' 19th-century photography and 'art' and 'documentary' photographs made during the first half of the 20th century by geniuses, such as Alfred Steiglitz, Edward Steichen, Paul Strand, Ansel Adams, and Andre Kertesz. Photography galleries and specialty museums opened, and auction houses began holding photography sales. Nonetheless, photography remained 'quarantined' outside the mainstream art world. Collectors who bought photos didn't buy paintings and vice versa.

Whereas black-and-white photos by name photographers were in high demand, colored photos were still distrusted as being too commercial. Today, the art establishment makes no distinction between black and white and color and between photography and other media. And gallerists represent artists whose medium is photography along with artists working in other mediums. With the younger generations of artists and collectors brought up on the internet, photography has the edge in terms of accessibility, making it, as LA photography dealer Peter Fetterman says, "... the medium of our time."

While a history of the medium is beyond the scope of this book, here's some useful information to get you pointed in the right direction. Early in the 20th century, there were basically two opposing schools — "take" vs. "make," as some call them, or "point and shoot" vs.

"manipulation." The two greatest photographers of the day represented these opposing views. Stieglitz would sit for hours waiting for the right moment. Once that moment came, and he took the photo, it was set in stone. Steichen, by contrast, would take the image, then doctor it up in the darkroom. An exhibition at The Met in 2012, *Faking it: Manipulated Photography Before Photoshop*, showed just how ingenious early photographers were at changing images in the darkroom. My favorite photo was of a zeppelin moored at the top of the Empire State Building, convincingly "documenting" an event that never happened.

Today, new technological advances, from Photoshop to Instagram, have made it possible to alter "reality" in new ways. Andreas Gursky's photo, *Kuwait Stock Exchange II* (ill. 23), is a tour de force in contrast between the Arab world and an American stereotpye. At first, it looks like a straightforward scene shot from above, but if you look carefully, you realize that the only way Gursky could have captured all those dozens of figures with equal clarity was through digital manipulation.

Beginning photography collectors have a steep learning curve, especially if they're collecting historical photos. They must learn to distinguish 'vintage' prints (printed within five years of the creation of the original negative), from 'lifetime' prints (printed any time after that, but during the artist's lifetime), and 'modern' prints (posthumously printed from the original negative).

Vintage prints are the most desirable and valuable. Lifetime prints are less valuable but still desirable in most cases; and modern prints are considerably less valuable and likely won't appreciate, as will their earlier brethren. It's difficult to differentiate one from another, and you should ask the seller which he's hawking and check with your advisor or an expert. You don't want to pay for a vintage photo and find out it's a posthumous pretender. A useful hint: to determine if a print was made after 1950, pass a black light over it. After that date, photographic paper came with added 'brightener' to make the whites pop, which causes the image to fluoresce under UV light.

Contemporary photography isn't a whole lot easier to conquer. Artists are constantly using new materials and techniques, and you need to understand them. For example, generations after Man Ray created his rayographs (by placing objects on light sensitive paper, no camera required), Thomas Ruff, a German artist, achieved similar effects using virtual objects in virtual spaces. Techniques involving digitization are often bundled under the rubric of "C-prints," so if you're considering one, ask your seller to explain how the work was made and when.

Photography has something for everyone in terms of subject, price, and availability. For an exhibition of 1930s Hollywood glamour photos at the Santa Barbara Museum of Art, the curator bought many of the photos on eBay for a song. And in recent years, a number of collectors and even some museums, including The Met and MoMA, have been collecting Polaroids and candid photos by amateurs. Called "vernacular" or "anonymous" photos, these were taken by "nobodies" like your parents and mine. Several museums have asked members of their communities to contribute whatever they have at home. Although these 'found' photos were obviously not made as "art," collectors are drawn to them for their extraordinary points of view, subject, focus, or lack of focus. If this sounds interesting to you, flea markets, garage sales, thrift shops, and eBay are all good sources. I suppose, collecting selfies is next.

Of course, prices of some photos have sky rocketed. Works by Gursky, Thomas Struth, Cindy Sherman, Richard Prince, and others regularly trade for over a million dollars. With all that's happening around photography, you may find that collecting in this area is a way to feel part of something "bigger" and see the world and the creative process in ways that stir your imagination.

NEW MEDIA

These days, not only is there no discrimination when it comes to photographs, there's no discrimination by medium at all. Galleries are 'media neutral,' offering works on paper, videos, and other media alongside of paintings. Collectors buy works in all media and install them all together without thinking twice about it. In fact, for galleries and collectors, it's probably easier to find innovative artists who work in any medium *but* paint. Making art with video, digital technology, ink-jets, iPhones and other popular technology is as natural for today's artists as oil on canvas was for their fathers and grandfathers. Artists are always a few steps ahead of the rest of us, and they adopt new media as quickly and seamlessly as they're invented, without being the least bit self-conscious. Hockney was the poster child for this. When Polaroids were invented, he created works that were compilations of small Polaroid photos. After fax machines came out, he made fax drawings, including a piece in which an audience sat by a fax machine as parts of a multi-piece composition were faxed through to be assembled on the receiving end. And iPad drawings? Hockney worked with those before most of us had iPads. His approach now seems archaic though, as compared to an artist like Cory Arcangel. Arcangel uses videogames, software, Photoshop, YouTube and so forth in ever-innovative ways. For example, he recreated a 1909 work by Arnold Schoenberg by downloading videos on YouTube of cats playing the piano and piecing them together. And although he's represented by galleries, he sticks to his source culture and makes things available to the public through social media.

Whereas artists are quick to embrace new media, collectors haven't always been as quick to accept them. For a long time, works like Nam June Paik's videos and robot-like assemblages of TVs were too much for most collectors. But over the years, collectors have caught up, and increasing numbers, including the Kramlichs in Napa and the Stones in San Francisco, are making video art the focus of their collections.

Some collectors are even more adventurous. Francesca (Chessie) von Habsburg, daughter of Thyssen-Bornemisza, through her foundation Thyssen-Bornemisza Art Contemporary (TBA21), supports artists who create unconventional works, particularly those which can't be shown in traditional museum settings. For example, von Hapsburg is the force behind Matthew Ritchie's *The Morning Line* (2008). Ritchie collaborated with the architectural firm ArandaLasch to create an open-air sonic temple, involving mathematics, cosmology, science, and art with the goal of visualizing all the structures we use to understand the universe at once. In the 8-meter-high public structure they built, made of 20 tons of coated aluminum, forty speakers played sonic music all day long. Working with artists like Ritchie, von Hapsburg gives new meaning to the term "collector." Perhaps philanthropist/patron is a better way of looking at her and others like her.

Many museums have opened "new media" departments to show, study, buy, and preserve works that are time-, motion-, or sound-based. These include video, film, performance art... and beyond. An example is The Guggenheim's commitment to Tino Sehgal's "staged situation" (using his words), called *This Progress*, "shown," if that's the right term, in 2010. To begin, the artist emptied the museum of all paintings. Visitors encountered a couple embracing (played by dancers) on the entry level, and as they mounted the ramp, they were stopped by trained interlocutors. The first, a child, approached with, "May I ask you a question? What is progress?" The further you went up the ramp, the older the interrogator. After the initial "lines" were delivered, what transpired between the interlocutors and visitors was extemporaneous, all considered part of the work. Most people who went to see the work found the experience quite moving.

In 2011, artist Marni Kotak's "work" was giving birth in a Brooklyn art gallery, which she'd transformed into a carpet-lined birthing room equipped with rocking chair, bed and birthing pool. And whoever bought Andrea Fraser's *Untitled* (2003), got the right to have sex with the artist and a video recording of the event, but not the right to lend it. When I told my husband about the work, he quipped, "Maybe I have to reconsider my narrow views on performance art." He probably thinks I should have given it to him for Christmas.

The rise of new media may have moved the needle on what defines art, how the public interacts, and the role of galleries and museums, but it's created a huge conservation issue for its owners. How do you repair works that aren't really "there" or aren't meant to be repaired? What happens when the delivery system, whether it's a video machine, screen, or other mechanical part, is no longer available? Will the work still have the same value or any value at all if it's transferred onto the next generation of transmission, like cassettes to DVDs? Be sure to discuss these issues with the artist, the seller, or your advisor before you buy.

DUE DILIGENCE

IN "ACT ONE" OF THIS BOOK, you were introduced to the art world and its cast of characters, in "Act Two," collectors and their collecting strategies. Now, in "Act Three," the final plot point, whether or not you wind up with the painting of your dreams, hinges on the results of your due diligence. Let's say you've found a painting at a reputable gallery or auction house, and everything seems to be in order. Before you start writing a check with lots of zeros, take the advice of someone who's been there and done that many times. You have to do your homework and try to ascertain, if warranted, that the work you're considering is:

- in good condition
- being sold by a reliable seller
- a good example of its kind
- fairly priced

And those are just for starters.

Authenticity, provenance, literature and exhibition history, often listed on the seller's fact sheet, might also come under scrutiny.

Wall Street guys live and breathe due diligence, but in their world, it's always done by someone else...

lawyers, accountants, or faceless legions of grey-suited baby bankers. In the art world, the seller's 'doc sheet' isn't the end; it's just the beginning. You need to try to verify everything on it, and if you can't, you have to piece together what information you can gather to make an informed decision. Is this something you can do all by yourself? Perhaps. But, especially if it's complicated, you probably can't do it as successfully, efficiently, or as quickly as an art advisor. If there is an issue of authenticity, that may require consultations with specialized experts, conservators, etc. But let's go over what must be done, and you be the judge.

Start by realizing that vendors, if they're dealers or auction houses, are busy handling hundreds or thousands of works a year and don't have the time to give every item proper attention. Besides, they're not eager to find problems that may exist, since they're either the owner or are working for the owner. By contrast, you only have one work to worry about. So get out your loupe, power up your black light, and get ready to follow the trail. Does all that sound intriguing? It is. Discovering the truth about a work of art can have all the drama of a detective novel. No wonder best-selling author Daniel Silva's popular hero, Gabriel Allon, a secret agent by night, is an art conservator by day.

AUTHENTICITY: PROVENANCE, LITERATURE, AND EXHIBITION HISTORY

A painting, firstly, needs to be authentic. If a painting's not "right," there's no need to go any further. There are only two situations in which you needn't bother checking. The first is if the work you're considering is so cheap you don't care, and the second is if it comes directly from the artist's studio or from the gallery that represents the artist.

In art insider terms, an authentic work is 'right' — and not 'wrong' — a fake or forgery. The two words, "fake" and "forgery," are used interchangeably, but they actually mean two different things. A "fake" is something that's been misrepresented. That would include "forgeries" (paintings specifically created to deceive), and real paintings done by artists with no intent to deceive, but which have been tampered with (e.g., the signature removed and/or a bogus signature added), and passed off by a crooked seller as the work of a more famous artist. So, if a dealer tries to fob off an anonymous 17th-century painting as a Vermeer, he's selling a fake. But if he sells a work deliberately painted to be sold as a Vermeer, he's flogging a forgery.

Forgeries come in several different flavors: They can be stroke-by-stroke copies, pastiches combining elements taken from several compositions of the artist, or unique works created 'in the manner' of the master. All are minefields for the inexperienced and experienced alike. As Theodore Rousseau, Jr. a former curator of European Art at The Met said, "We should all realize that we can only talk about the bad forgeries. The good ones are still hanging on the walls."

Hoving once estimated that of the 50,000 works of art he examined in his life, 40% were fakes or forgeries. Even if you halve that number to compensate for Hoving's braggadocio and the fact that a great many of those works were antiquities, a field rife with a fakes, it's still a whopping number.

Fakes and forgeries have been around forever. As far back as ancient Rome, when there weren't enough Greek sculptures to satisfy the Romans' demand for them, Roman craftsmen jumped in and filled the void with forgeries. In the Renaissance, when antique Greek and Roman sculptures were highly prized, forgers enjoyed another field day. By the 18th century, con artists in Italy were churning out enough forgeries of Italian Renaissance drawings and Canalettos of Venice to satisfy British upper-class travelers on the Grand Tour.

Generally, whatever type of art is in the greatest demand is the forger/faker's favorite target. Barbizon paintings may be out of fashion now, but in the late 19th century when they were the rage, they were forged by the score, and fakers took paintings by lesser hands and signed them with the names of artists whose works brought the most money, especially Corot. Corot compounded the problem through his own generosity. He'd often sign his name on works of his less talented students so they could sell for more money. Right signature, wrong painting: ouch! By 1940, a *Newsweek* article quipped: "Of the 2,500 paintings Corot did in his lifetime, 7,800 are to be found in America."

At the beginning of the 20th century, when Easterners were dazzled by stories of the Wild West, the prices for California views by the painter William Keith soared. Once again, forgers and fakers filled the void. Today, there's not much of a market for Keith. Yet, if you want one, you have to be suspicious. Almost any 'Keith' you're offered may look old and likely is, but unfortunately, that doesn't guarantee that it's right. It could have been forged in 1910.

Traditional American still life paintings aren't immune either. Alfred Frankenstein, in preparing the second edition of his landmark study, *After The Hunt*, came across a body of work by A. Bianchi, an artist he hadn't known before. Frankenstein soon realized that A. Bianchi was a made-up name and that the paintings were done by a plagiarist who'd cleverly raided the first edition of his book. 'Bianchi' combined elements from the two most famous still life painters of the late 19th century, William Harnett and John Peto, to create a new body of work. In his new introduction, Frankenstein playfully begged 'Bianchi' to come forward and introduce himself, pointing out how rare it is for an art historian to impact the course of art history. But 'Bianchi' remained in the shadows — no fool he.

On occasion, master forgers have become as famous as the artists whose works they 'created.' Elmyr de Hory, responsible for countless 'Modiglianis', 'Matisses,' and 'Vlamincks,' was the protagonist of Orson Welles' documentary, *F for Fake*, and Clifford Irving's book, *Fake! The Story of Elmyr de Hory, The Greatest Forger of Our Time*. Han van Meegeren, who passed off several of his works as authentic Vermeers, has been lionized in countless books, including Edward Dolnick's *The Forger's Spell*. In 2010, the Museum Boijmans Van Beuningen in Rotterdam, the first museum duped by van Meegeren, bravely mounted a show of his forgeries. It had record attendance. Van Meegeren's, *The Men at Emmaus*, (ill. 24) bought by the museum in 1937 as a Vermeer, remains one of its star attractions.

The story of *The Men at Emmaus* is a fascinating chapter in the history of forgeries. Like many forgers, van Meegeren was a failed painter. But unlike most forgers of Dutch 17th-century paintings, he wasn't content to 'create' run-of-the-mill paintings by minor hands for which there was a brisk market. Instead, van Meegeren was determined to go for the gold and forge a Vermeer, the rarest and priciest of Dutch painters. Van Meegeren's first attempts to paint mature Vermeers (there are only

35 originals) failed miserably, because he couldn't achieve the master's unique sense of light and contour. Then he hit on the brilliant idea of forging an early Vermeer. Since no early Vermeers existed, he reasoned, comparison would be impossible. Using the two things he knew about Vermeer — that he was Catholic and that his early work is thought to have been influenced by Caravaggio — he created a religious painting, *The Men at Emmaus*, in a Caravaggesque style with Vermeer-like colors. He painted it on a 17th-century canvas with the kind of badger brushes used in the period, then rolled it over a tube to create craquelure (a pattern of cracks). To darken the cracks, he smeared ink over the surface and wiped it away, allowing some to sink into the cracks. Then, to give the painting the hard surface unique to 17th-century Dutch paintings, he finished it off with a coat of Bakelite, a 20th-century synthetic resin. Voila! An 'early' Vermeer was born.

Through an intermediary, van Meegeren contacted Abraham Bredius, the leading Vermeer scholar of the day. Bredius was close to retirement and so desperate to cap off his career by discovering a Vermeer that he didn't need much convincing to pronounce *The Men at Emmaus* a great early Vermeer. In 1938, he successfully urged the Boijmans to acquire it for 530,000 guiders, about $6.4 million in today's dollars. Van Meegeren went on to paint other early 'Vermeers' that weren't as good, including *Christ and the Adulteress*, for which Hermann Göring traded nearly 200 paintings. Göring considered his "Vermeer" the crown jewel in the collection he housed at Carinhall, named after his first wife. He was sure that if Nazi Germany fell, he'd be able to trade his Vermeer for his freedom. It didn't work.

After the war, van Meegeren was tried by the Netherlands for treason — selling a Vermeer, a national treasure, to the Nazis. When he testified that he'd painted this 'national treasure,' no one believed him — certainly not the judge. Under the surveillance of art historians and journalists, he painted another 'Vermeer' as proof — *Christ and the Scribes in the Temple*. Ultimately, he was cleared of treason but was sentenced to prison for forgery and fraud. He died while waiting for his prison sentence to begin.

For a 2014 show, "Intent to Deceive: Fakes and Forgeries in the Art World," originating at the Springfield Museums in Massachusetts, the Boijmans lent their van Meegeren, *Head of Christ*, bought by the museum in 1941 for 475,000 guilders ($4.4 million) as a study for *The Men at Emmaus*. Ironically, the cost for insurance and security the Boijmans requested was $31,000, only slightly less than the $32,000 selling price of *Christ and the Scribes* when it sold at auction as a van Meegeren in 1999.

One night, I was awakened after midnight by a call from a longtime client. He was in a panic. He'd just read *Provenance* by Laney Salisbury, the non-fiction account of British con man John Drewe and his forger accomplice

John Myatt. He begged me to 'call in the forensics' to make sure all of his purchases were genuine. I calmed him down and assured him that he needn't worry. What Drewe did, however, could cause anyone to be alarmed. He not only had Myatt forge drawings by various masters, but he phonied catalogue sheets, provenance, and other documents and smuggled them *into* the Tate Library, inserting them in gallery records and artists' notebooks. It was an almost foolproof scam. For a long time, whenever any expert got suspicious about a work, the supporting 'documentation' in the archives would assure them that the work was 'right.' Ultimately, Drewe's ex-wife turned him into the police, and Drewe and Myatt were arrested. Myatt now runs a business called Legitimate Fakes, successful enough to enable him to live in a beautiful farmhouse in the English countryside. Still, I shudder to think how many Drewe/Myatt forgeries are still in circulation.

Drewe and Myatt were successful because they chose artists whose works were relatively easy to 'make,' and, because they sold for only a few hundred thousand dollars rather than millions, they flew under the radar and were less apt to be noticed. The same is true of forged works of lesser-known artists. It's natural to think that no one would bother forging a minor artist work worth 50,000 pounds, right? Rizvan Rahman, a British art teacher turned forger, set up a posh-sounding business, Haslam and Purdey, through which he sold at least thirty forgeries of little-known post-war British artists, like

Mary Fedden, David Hockney's teacher. He ultimately got caught trying to sell a forgery of a work by a minor Cornish artist, Jack Pender, when, by hazard, a friend of the artist, probably the only expert on his work, got wind of it. When the police raided Rahman's gallery, they found copies of *The Art Forger's Handbook* and *Confessions of a Master Forger*. Evidently, Rahman was learning on the job.

Works by James E. Buttersworth, a 19th-century British marine artist, consistently sell for about $30,000. For years, Ken Perenyi made a career forging Buttersworths and eventually wrote a book about it, *Caveat Emptor: The Secret Life of An American Forger*. In 2014, The Mariners' Museum in Virginia mounted an exhibition of 35 paintings by Buttersworth, including one forgery. The public, prompted by clues on how to identify a forgery, was asked to vote on which it was. I presume the forgery was by Perenyi, but the museum didn't say.

Buying a forgery is a legitimate worry, but it seldom happens. I've heard about big cons like the one pulled over on oilman, Algur Meadows. Of the 58 paintings he bought, 38 were forgeries, and I never thought I'd encounter anything like those first-hand — until recently. For years, a friend kept telling me about one of his gym buddies who had a great collection of French Impressionism and Modern art. I was desperate to see it and nagged my friend for months to wrangle entrée for me. He did, and when we got to the house, the collector and his curator greeted us at the door. They walked us through the collection, pointing out Picassos, Sisleys, etc. I started getting a queasy feeling when I asked the collector if his Modigliani was in "Ceroni," the Modigliani catalogue raisonné, named after its compiler. Every collector or curator who knows anything about Modigliani knows that if a painting isn't in "Ceroni," it's not accepted as correct. They looked at me like I was a Martian. I then asked if they'd shown an image of it to Marc Restellini, a scholar working on the artist. Again, I got a blank look on both of their parts. Had they cared, wouldn't they have asked me for his contact info?

The friend who took me to see the collection and knows nothing about art, smiled and nodded throughout. Soon, I squeezed his hand and apologized to the collector, "I'm afraid we have to leave." When we got to the car, I explained that every painting was 'wrong,' and that both the collector and his curator had to know. Was the owner's MO impressing friends who wouldn't know a Modigliani from a painting on velvet? Or was it a scam, in which the collector borrowed at the bank against the fake art at "real art" values? If so, why would he let me into the house? Was it a test to see if they could get away with it? Looking back, I wish I'd had the guts the late dealer Frank Perls had when he walked into a party, looked around, and asked the hostess, "So, who painted your Matisse?" I guess some people really like going faux.

To confirm authenticity, an expert on the artist might begin by scrutinizing the 'doc sheet' given by the seller, which lists provenance, literature and exhibition history. Buyers often presume that dealers do the necessary research, and some do. Others, to save time, simply pass along the information they received from the prior owner. Wildenstein Gallery used to present their information in a beautiful folder tied with a ribbon, metaphorically suggesting that everything was neatly wrapped up with no loose ends. In all likelihood, they did a great job, but fact sheets aren't gospel. Remember John Drewe, who doctored the books in the archives?

The expert may look under "literature" on the fact sheet to see if the painting you're considering is in the artist's catalogue raisonné (if there is one). They'd measure the painting and check that the measurements are the same. They'd then take a loupe and compare the photo of the work in the CR and a photo of the work the seller has provided. Just because the doc sheet says the painting is in the CR or other books doesn't mean it's the same. Some fakes are easy to spot, others not so easy. As Jacques Dupin, the expert on Miró, said, "When a fake is good, my job is interesting." While they have the CR handy, they'd compare the artist's signature, if there is one, and see if it matches the signature on other works done by the artist at the same time. That can be confidence building, but don't forget that a forger could have studied the same entries as well as books on artists' signatures and practiced signing the artist's name.

Some CR's are the last word. If a Jackson Pollock isn't in the CR, forget it. Even if there's a chance it's right, no one will touch it. With Modigliani, as we've already discussed, if the work isn't in Ceroni, no one will accept it. The cognoscenti know there are mistakes in Ceroni — fakes included and real works omitted. But so far as the trade is concerned, Ceroni is cast in stone. Marc Restellini, a Modigliani scholar, who thought to update the CR, said he would accept another 70-80 paintings to Ceroni's oeuvre. Sadly, Restellini abandoned work on a CR for Modigliani works on paper after receiving death threats from owners whose works Restellini intended to exclude. If a new CR ever does come out, we'll have to see if the marketplace accepts it. In the meantime, what's one to think when the President of the Modigliani Institute in Rome, Christian Parisot, a man empowered by the artist's own daughter to authenticate paintings, was arrested for selling fake Modiglianis?

And not all CRs are bulletproof. For example, a known De Chirico forger, Renato Peretti, insisted that the De Chirico CR includes numerous works he forged. It's conjectured that they were included because Claudio Bruni, a dealer who compiled the CR, authenticated many paintings by looking at photographs rather than the actual works.

Sometimes there's more than one CR for the artist, and typically, older CRs are revised by younger scholars who have uncovered new documents or attributed new paintings. A new CR of Tintoretto has recently been compiled by Frederick Ilchman, Curator at the MFA, Boston, and Robert Echols, an independent scholar.

They demoted 148 out of 468 paintings formerly thought to be by the master, assigning 47 of them to the designation "Studio of" and 101 to "Circle of Tintoretto."

If there's a CR on your artist, but the painting you're considering isn't in it, that doesn't automatically mean it's a fake. It may have surfaced after the CR was published. If the compiler is still working, or there's a new reigning scholar for the artist, one might send him a photo and details and ask his opinion. He may know the work, but if he doesn't and has to see it, the seller will likely agree to fly the work to the expert or pay for the expert to come to the work. If the expert opines favorably, he'll write a letter saying that it'll be included in his forthcoming CR, or its addendum. If a seller has already done this, make sure he has the *original* letter and that you get it if you make a deal. Martin Kemp, *the* Leonardo expert, notes that con men forge his signature on letters authenticating forged Leonardos all the time. In fact, lots of forged letters of authenticity exist for almost every artist, famous or not. So, don't be too shy to ask. If the expert opines that the work is wrong, you've saved a lot of time and money. And, if it's right, the expert will probably tell you some fascinating things about the work you didn't know.

Who are these "experts" who can make life and death judgments? In addition to the scholar who did the CR, they could be the artist's descendants, or authenticating committees. Their mandate (called *le droit moral* in Europe) and the weight of their opinions vary. Even when the artist is in control, problems can occur. Yoshitomo Nara, a Japanese artist who paints cartoon-like children against monochrome backgrounds (at first glance, they're innocent-looking, but looked at closely, they're often sinister), vetted his own 2-volume CR. Yet, according to Dan Duray (*GalleristNY*, January 2012), Nara included two works on paper he didn't do. The opposite can also be true. Balthus, who had the last word on his own paintings while alive, was so furious with one of his ex-wives, he refused to accept one of his paintings she'd gotten in their divorce.

If you have doubts, and there's an authentication committee, you can ask the seller to send the work to its next meeting and offer to pay promptly if the committee opines favorably. No committee was more feisty and aggressive than the Andy Warhol Art Authentication Board, which, until it closed, brashly stamped "Denied" in bold letters on the back of any work that didn't pass. In one case, it "denied" a Warhol self-portrait owned by Joe Simon, even though another painting from the same series of ten was on the cover of the Warhol CR, on which Warhol collaborated. Authenticating bodies usually won't give reasons for rejection, as they don't want to tip off forgers who would correct their mistakes, but it came out during Simon's six-year lawsuit that the work was rejected because it was made by someone Andy gave the screen to *outside* the studio. Richard Dorment, an art historian and journalist, has documented Simon's struggle, and I urge you to google any of his articles to read brilliant detective work and a compelling art historical argument. Ultimately, Simon ran out of money, and the committee won the war of attrition. But, along with the authenticating bodies for Basquiat, Keith Haring, Roy Lichtenstein, and Robert Motherwell, the Warhol authentication board disbanded for fear that legal fees could bleed it dry.

In an article I wrote, "Exit The Deciders," for the *New York Observer*, I discuss the fallout from shuttering the committees. While some believe business will go on as usual, I think that closures will affect the marketplace. Works that have certificates of authenticity from committees will sell at a premium, and those without will be less desirable, unless airtight provenance can be demonstrated.

Various remedies have been suggested to allow committees to continue their work and limit financial risks. The New York Senate passed a bill, due to go before the Assembly, protecting authenticators and authors of catalogue raisonnés against frivolous lawsuits. It provides for compensation of legal fees and allows only valid claims to go forward to court.

Art scholars, committees, and other authenticating bodies aren't the only ones who make mistakes and get sued. It happens to lawyers, doctors, architects, and engineers all the time, when they're accused of giving faulty opinions or advice. And scholars and committees aren't necessarily liable just because a jury thinks their opinion is wrong. If their opinion is wrong but issued in good faith after exhibiting due care, there should be no liability. The College Art Association is trying to make it possible for authenticators to continue their work by offering liability insurance at affordable rates. Another workable solution may be to charge everyone seeking opinions fees large enough to cover insurance and structure an appeals process for works a committee rejects. Perhaps an arbitration panel could decide, with fees and costs paid by the losing party. Nonetheless, the committees continue to close, one after another.

It's one thing if the artist died in 1987, like Warhol, but what if your artist died in 1587? Many old masters are not signed or documented, and time, wear, and repeated restorations can make the work hard to "read." For these reasons, ascertaining authenticity is difficult, and discoveries, attributions, and re-attributions are made all the time. For forty years, the Rembrandt Research Project, a group of Rembrandt scholars, re-evaluated all works called Rembrandt. While it functioned, the RRP ruthlessly demoted nearly 150 works thought to have been by the master...47 to the "Studio" of Rembrandt and 101 to his "Circle." The poor Statens Museum for Kunst in Denmark had ten Rembrandts when the Project started, and all were eliminated along the way. Rembrandt scholar Seymour Slive once quipped, "If the Rembrandt Committee meets one more time, Rembrandt will cease to exist as an artist." Recently, the committee finished its work and announced its closure. One of the last members has rehabilitated a few paintings, including two at the Statens Museum. The art world has seen this before; when scholars are young, they're ruthless about disallowing works, and, as they age, they mellow and become more accepting.

To determine authenticity, today's experts can augment their trained eyes with sophisticated technical help, including x-rays, infrared reflectography (which reveals underdrawing), fingerprint analysis, dendrochronology (tree ring dating — useful if the work is on a wood panel), thread count, and pigment and medium analysis. Computer experts are now taking it one step farther and programming patterns found in accepted paintings by an artist, such as the pressure of his brush, the orientation of his strokes, or how often he used one color next to another and comparing that with works in question. They think that all they have to do is run the program and compare. A Dutch researcher Igor Berezhnoy, created a system called "Authentic," in which he uses digital analysis to identify color patterns in Van Goghs. Critics of the system suggest that it has no greater accuracy than formulas used in attempts to identify the true author of Shakespeare's plays, like comparing the number of times a particular phrase appears in the Shakespeare canon versus writings by other candidates.

An owner of a would-be Van Gogh, *Still Life with Peonies*, claimed to have found a strand of red hair imbedded in the painting, and since Van Gogh had red hair, he planned to have a DNA test done against an heir of the artist to determine the painting's authenticity. Already several experts have disputed his claim, and if it doesn't pan out, I can picture the headlines now: "Hair of heir leaves cupboard bare."

You'd think that technology could provide conclusive evidence, but often scientists reach opposing conclusions to scholars and others in the art trade. A huge controversy arose when Alex Matter, the son of an artist friend of Jackson Pollock, claimed to have found a cache of Pollock's paintings in a storage locker that belonged to his late father. Conservators at Harvard analyzed a few of the works and found pigments and binders (the vehicle the pigment is suspended in) that weren't in common use until after Pollock's death. Pollock partisans countered by saying that paint companies often gave artists like Pollock new materials in advance of marketing them to the public. A physicist, Richard Taylor, who examined the works using fractal image analysis (whatever that is), concluded that they were by the artist. Another team of physicists concluded that fractal analysis wasn't useful at all. Getting confused? And don't forget, if it's not in the Pollock CR, no one will accept it as right anyway. Would we pay Pollock prices for these paintings? Of course not. Although there's increased reliance on scientific testing, tests tend to be more useful in telling us who didn't do something, rather than who *did*.

Don't get the wrong idea. Not all authenticity checks end in disaster. Most of the time, you'll be satisfied that the work is right. There may be minor problems with the fact sheet, such as a typo or a mistaken year, but those things can be easily rectified. A few years before Cy Twombly died, I was offered a painting by him that was listed in the CR as being signed, but it wasn't. Since the painting looked right and everything else was in perfect order, I didn't want to walk away. To play it safe, I contacted Twombly's studio and asked if Twombly would sign it. Twombly agreed. He was due in New York that week, so his studio assistant suggested that I have the painting waiting in a truck parked outside his hotel on a particular morning. Whenever he left the hotel, he'd look at the painting and sign it. And that's what happened. On the appointed day, Twombly sauntered out of his hotel at eleven a.m. and walked over to the truck. The guys unloaded the painting, and the great artist signed it right there, on the Manhattan sidewalk.

PROVENANCE, LITERATURE, AND EXHIBITION HISTORY

The first thing every novice collector learns is that he's supposed to verify provenance, as it speaks to the authenticity of the work. It can be a fascinating exercise, and you may learn who owned the work you're considering in the 1990s, sometimes in the 1890s, and sometimes even in the 1590s. The individual might have been famous (good), or a Nazi officer (bad), or just ordinary folks who left the work to their nephew in Phoenix or Cincinnati. But too often, there's no way of checking. Even if you tracked down the descendants of a supposed owner, it's unlikely they'd remember what their long-deceased Uncle John had hanging in his living room. As Thomas Hoving once said, "Provenance is a laugh...the fact that it came from so and so, and so and so gave it to the prince of so and so. Fuck off, that can be all faked up."

Dealers typically leave off the name of the private owner they've gotten the work from, instead listing, "Private Collection." Auction houses do the same when they're not touting the seller, and may list works as "The property of a gentleman," or some other generic designation. This may sound bogus, but it doesn't mean that the painting is wrong. Sellers do it to protect their source, who may have other material to sell or who wants anonymity, or both. Many people in the trade will tell you that they omit names of dealers and auctions because they're only temporary custodians, not owners. That would mean that, if the work has gone through several private owners and/or several dealers and auctions, the provenance may read as a string of "Private Collections." Of course, you can't check that kind of provenance.

Provenance does more than speak to a work's authenticity. It can do for a painting what a bloodline does for a horse. If the work's been owned by someone special, it adds status and value, and its owner can bathe in reflected glory. The same phenomenon exists in real estate. A Beverly Hills mansion once owned by Brad Pitt will probably fetch more than one owned by an accountant.

Collectors love seeing famous names as prior owners. "Can you imagine," a collector once beamed, "I own a drawing owned by the Duke of Devonshire." It was as if that made him an aristocrat by association. And when David Rockefeller sold what became "the Rockefeller Rothko," *Yellow, Pink, and Lavender on Rose*, at auction in 2007, the price was pushed to a record $72.8 million by a raft of bidders who were anxious not only to acquire a vetted masterpiece, but one that belonged to American royalty. I'm surprised that nobody's made a business of provenance — selling paintings to celebrities short-term and buying them back at a small profit before selling them again.

Marketing genius Lynda Resnick cleverly maximized provenance when she and her husband, Stewart, bought Jackie O's signature triple-strand of fake pearls at the Sotheby's 1996 Jacqueline Onassis's estate sale. The Resnicks, who owned the Franklin Mint at the time, paid $211,000 for the pearls, which Jackie had bought at Bergdorf's in the 1950s for about $35. The Resnicks made and sold 130,000 copies at $200 a set. That's $26 million in gross sales. Characteristically, the Resnicks gave their profit to charity.

Sometimes the back of a painting can provide valuable information as to its past. The Brazilian artist Vik Muniz did a series of works recreating the backs of famous paintings in The Guggenheim, Art Institute of Chicago, and MoMA, all of which participated (ill. 25). He had craftsmen replicate the backs down to the most minute details. To Muniz, the backs of paintings show something museumgoers never get to experience. It's like a foreign language that only those knowledgeable in such things understand. A collection stamp can signify a famous collection the work was in, and chalk number, drawn or stenciled, can denote that the work came through an auction or was in the hands of the Nazis. According to Muniz, whereas the front of a painting is supposed to stay the same forever, the back changes over time, with labels added as the painting is loaned to museums and galleries. Muniz's finished works were shown leaning against the wall, and everyone who saw the exhibition could barely resist turning the paintings around. But there were no "fronts," only cardboard.

If a work is in the CR and the list of references and exhibition history is a mile long, give a silent cheer! The more a work has appeared in the literature and has been on public display, the more scholars and experts have had a chance to study it, and the less likely there is to be any problems. On the other hand, if there's no literature or exhibition history, you mustn't jump to the conclusion that something's wrong. The answer could be as simple as prior owners' not wanting to alert the taxman, or they didn't want to part with it long enough for it to be in a museum exhibition.

Reading the entries listed under "Literature" and "Exhibition history," as they appear on the seller's fact sheet, is informative. But it's especially important to compare images of the work in any texts with a photo of the work you're considering. I was once offered a Dubuffet, the kind that's painted with red, blue, and white spaghetti-like strokes. The doc sheet noted that the painting was on the cover of a book on the artist that we had in our library. Using a loupe, I compared the cover picture with the image supplied by my seller. It appeared to be the same, except for an extra stroke in the top right corner of the photo that wasn't on the book's cover. At first, I thought it was due to the way the photo was cropped, but it wasn't, and it bothered me enough not to offer the painting to any of our clients. Years later, I learned it was a forgery. The original was owned by the Florida couple listed on the provenance. Whenever they sent a work to be reframed, the framer forged a copy, and using the correct provenance, sent it to an unsuspecting private dealer in New York to sell. It wasn't until one of the forgeries appeared in an auction catalogue, and the owners noticed it, that the scam was exposed.

TITLE

The seller should warrant that he can convey clear title. Most often it's not a problem, but we all know how issues of title have plagued the field of antiquities. When Lord Elgin brought to England marble sculptures which had adorned buildings on the Parthenon, and Napoleon brought treasures from Egypt to France, the party line was that they were doing it to expose the general public to the Classics. Later, what they did was criticized as a form of cultural imperialism and crass looting. Since then, grave robbing and illegal exportation have been a constant problem, and the last thing you want is to find yourself embroiled in an international scandal.

A 1972 UNESCO ruling obliged collectors to prove that the antiquity they've bought was out of the country of origin before 1972 or that they have legal export and import papers. Even after that, smuggling was winked at. No one, and no country, much cared. Sharon Waxman in her 2008 book *Loot: The Battle Over the Stolen Treasures of the Ancient World*, cited a 2006 telephone call with Hoving in which he described the antics of smuggling small objects out of Italy: "My favorite story to get something out of Italy was to bring the children in a station wagon, put a mattress in the back on the hottest day of August and leave with this stuff under the mattress. Just before going through customs, you'd give the kids ice cream cones. And the custom officials in their dress whites, you can't imagine how fast they put you through." Hoving further boasted, "...I had a rolodex of the best smugglers to get stuff into Switzerland. I knew their names. I talked to them. I had dinner with them. I met them in London..."

Dealers of antiquities typically used to assure clients that a Swiss collector owned the work in the 1920s. Maybe so, but now the only way you can move forward with a purchase is to ask the dealer for records or photos from the period showing the work in the collector's house or installed in a gallery or museum exhibition. Needless to say, the market in antiquities has slowed to a trickle.

Similar issues have plagued collectors of Central American, African, and Oceanic art. In 2014, the Denver Museum of Natural History volitionally returned 30 totems owned by a Kenyan village when it came to the conclusion that, because they were taken or sold without the permission of the community, they were stolen goods. A similar event happened when I was in grad school. A Cameroon sculpture came on the market in New York and brought $60,000, a fortune in those days. It had been stolen from a community shrine, and a bunch of grad students led a successful fundraising drive to buy the object from its new owner and return it to its tribe. When the tribe's elders met and realized the piece was worth $60,000, they voted to send it back to auction in New York.

If the work you're after was created before World War II, the provenance during the years of Nazi occupation may be sketchy. Ask the seller if they've done a check with the databank at Art Loss Register. Between 1933 and 1945, the Nazis plundered millions of works of art, mostly from Jewish families. As with antiquities, it's only been in the past couple of decades that serious attention has been paid to the situation. In fact, it wasn't long ago that one of the major auction houses was accused of helping consignors fill-in-the-blanks when there was no provenance for those crucial years, so that no questions would be asked. They probably had good intentions, assuming that, had there been a valid claim, it would have been made long before. That's changed with rising prices which have led heirs to be more litigious in pursuing works that belonged to deceased relatives. The success of Maria Altmann's legal campaign against the Austrian government for possession of several Klimts which had belonged to her aunt, Adele Bloch-Bauer, has spurred many heirs to come forward and fight.

You don't want to buy something and discover that someone else says it's theirs. That's what happened to Marilynn Alsdorf, a Chicago collector. Alsdorf bought a classical 1922 Picasso, *Femme en Blanc*, from a dealer in 1975, a time when no one thought about restitution. Many years later, the grandson of Carlotta Landsberg, a former owner, claimed the work. Landsberg had bought the painting in 1926, and after Kristallnacht in November, 1938, sent it to a Jewish art dealer in Paris for safekeeping. In 1940, when the Nazis took Paris, they seized the dealer's property, and the painting 'disappeared.' Ultimately, it fell into the hands of a high-ranking Nazi, and after the war, it was sold repeatedly. Landsberg's grandson argued that, since the property was originally stolen, none of the buyers ever obtained good title. After spending hundreds of thousands of dollars in legal fees, enduring terrible publicity, and paying the Landsberg heir $6.5 million in a settlement, Mrs. Alsdorf got to keep the painting, which she abruptly sold.

When the provenance of a Léger I wanted for a client listed Maeght Gallery as provenance in the 1930s and 40s, I thought to check with the Maeght Foundation in the south of France. It was July and the Foundation was on skeleton staff, but after much pleading on my part, the registrar kindly went into the archives and confirmed the provenance. I was lucky; such checks don't always pan out.

Title can be a problem even if it's not a historical or cultural issue. There may be a lien against a work you're considering, or someone else may claim ownership. A Uniformed Commercial Code (UCC) search may yield some information, but that's impractical to do, as it must be done on a state-by-state basis. Years ago, a gallery offered me a terrific Monet, perfect for one of my clients. Since I wasn't familiar with the dealer, I asked him to tell me the name of the owner/seller. He refused and would only say that the painting was coming from a Palm Beach patrician going through a divorce. I googled the few society families I knew by name in the area and, sure enough, I found an article in a local paper chronicling the divorce of an elderly real estate scion and noted art collector. So far, so good. But alas, in the second paragraph, the reporter mentioned that the man's estranged wife was claiming the very Monet we were discussing. I had to walk away until the couple settled, and then my client got the painting.

Just to make sure you're covered, you'll want the following language at the bottom of the seller's invoice or sales agreement:

Seller represents and warrants that Seller is conveying to Buyer good, valid, and marketable title to, and right of exclusive and unrestricted possession, of the Work (title, date), free and clear of all liens, claims, encumbrances, and restrictions.

You might also consider buying title insurance. For a one-time fee, usually between 1.5 - 4% of the work's appraised value (on the high side of the range if the work might have Nazi restitution problems), you can insure a work up to the face value of the policy plus the cost of any legal fight against adverse claims. That allows you to buy a work with an incomplete provenance or unresolved past and still sleep nights.

CONDITION COUNTS

I can't impress upon you enough the importance of evaluating the "condition" of the work's physical structure — canvas and stretcher, paper, wood, metal, panel, stone, etc., and the paint, varnish, or other media that have been applied atop that support. Of course, if the painting you're considering is new and comes directly from the artist or the gallery that represents the artist, you don't need to check condition. But if the work's on the secondary market, even if it was painted a year ago, you should. If you're lucky, the painting is in pristine state, but that seldom happens. As with people, paintings are subjected to varying degrees of wear and tear with age. Bumps and abrasions go with the territory, and a certain amount is acceptable. More serious injuries, like tears, flaking, and bad restoration are of greater concern. Worst-case scenario, your painting has suffered all of the above. Does any of this matter if the painting looks good to you? You bet, because even if it doesn't affect *your* enjoyment, it may hamper others' appreciation, and it certainly may impact the work's value and your ability to re-sell it.

Think of a painting like a classic car. A shiny red 1964 Corvette may look good, but before you buy it, don't you want to know what's going on under the hood? What's all that shiny paint covering? Everyone knows that a car that's been extensively restored, no matter how beautiful it looks, is worth less than one in its original state even with some 'age' showing. It's the same with paintings. To the naked eye, a painting may look to be in fine condition, but it can be a totally wreck under the varnish. On the other hand, it may have a couple of scratches but otherwise be in excellent condition. Since what you see isn't always what you get, you have to be aware of the state of your painting and what that means. In this chapter, I'll describe the most common problems you'll encounter and how to identify them. But please know that there's no substitute for getting a professional conservator to examine a work for you.

Assessing condition requires a working knowledge of the way paintings are constructed. So, here's an abbreviated rundown. If an artist uses traditional materials and techniques, he starts with a piece of canvas or linen stretched over a wooden frame (a "stretcher"). He applies a coat of primer, usually gesso (chalk, glue, etc.), as a base for the paint. Stretching and priming a canvas takes time, and although many artists do it or have assistants who do it, off-the-rack canvases have been available for over a century. Impressionists used them, which probably accounts for the fact that many Impressionist paintings seem to "come" in two sizes, designated at the time as either "A" and "B," or "3 passage" and "5 figure."

Paint is composed of dry pigment, like face powder, suspended in a liquid medium. Oil paint is pigment suspended in linseed or chestnut oil. Tempera is pigment suspended in egg yolk, and watercolor is pigment suspended in water. If the artist uses oil, he may apply a coat of varnish (resin suspended in oil) over the painting to protect the surface and bring out certain darker colors. Varnish was so popular in the 19th century that yearly Royal Academy exhibitions in London had 'varnishing day,' before the opening, when all the artists would come and varnish their works or make last-minute touch ups while their paintings were hanging.

As paintings age, problems start occurring, often small nuisances at first, like dirt and dust accumulating on the surface. Over time, varnish discolors, like old floor wax, and can turn gray or yellow, obscuring the true colors underneath and the viewer's ability to "read" the composition clearly. These problems can often be easily remedied by having a conservator "clean" the work. To do this, he uses a solvent, similar to nail polish remover, to remove the old varnish. He applies a new coat, good to go for another thirty or forty years. Warning: don't try this yourself!

Not long ago, an elderly couple living on Park Avenue called to sell a Pissarro they'd bought on their honeymoon in Paris a half century earlier. On the phone, the husband described the painting as a brilliant, blue-skied landscape. When I arrived at their apartment, they were sitting on the living room sofa, puffing away on cigarettes. The painting hanging on the opposite wall was indeed a Pissarro, but fifty years of smoke had yellowed the varnish, and yellow over blue (of the sky) had turned the painting a depressing, muddy green.

I had the painting moved to a local conservator and followed up with a visit to discuss possible treatment. While I was there, the conservator took a cotton ball dipped in solvent and gently rubbed a small area at the top of the canvas, opening a 'window' as it's called in the trade. The dirty varnish melted away, revealing a bright blue sky. After every pass of a cotton ball, he carefully examined it to make sure he wasn't removing any pigment along with varnish, an error frequently made by inept conservators. Satisfied that he could clean the painting, I left it for him to finish. When I went back a week later, it shone, enabling me to get the owners a better price than they would have received if they sold the painting dirty.

Old master dealers face dark and dingy paintings all the time. They imagine what they'll look like after they're cleaned and gamble that they won't find hideous problems beneath the dirty varnish. That's what London dealer Derek Johns did on an otherwise disappointing trip to Milan. He went to see a painting in a warehouse that turned out to be a bust. On his way out, however, he noticed a huge, almost pitch-black painting leaning against a wall. He could barely make out an image of Christ on the Cross through the grime and thought it might date from the late 15th century. He tracked down the owner, bought the work, and sold it to LACMA, still filthy. The conservators at LACMA had the foresight to understand what it would look like cleaned and wanted to do the conservation themselves. Today, with its profusion of luscious, bright colors, the painting sparkles and could double as a Grumbacher paint chart! The work, identified as being by the Master of the Fiesole Epiphany (ill. 26, ill. 27), dominates the gallery in which it hangs. (If an artist's name is unknown, the artist can be identified by the work or the city in which he worked, as "Master of...")

In addition to dirt and discolored varnish, paintings show age by developing craquelure. Such cracks appear in a linear or bull's eye pattern, and they become more numerous and intricate as the paint ages and becomes more brittle (ill. 28, ill. 29). Those knowledgeable in such matters can identify a painting's age at a glance, reading webs of cracks like a dendrochronologist can tell the age of a tree by counting tree rings.

Craquelure shouldn't necessarily be cause for alarm. A certain amount is normal, even beautiful, like the lines in an older person's face. Cameron, an LA mystical artist from the 60's, thought that craquelure was so attractive she tried to get the effect by bending one of her paintings, which she later sold to my husband, over her knee. Trouble starts, however, if the painting dries out and cracks widen or deepen. In paintings that have been hanging over working chimneys for years, the cracks may look like alligator skin.

An impact crack is different. That's either a single pronounced crack or web of cracks in one localized area of a painting which occurs when something pokes into the painting from the back, not enough to cause a hole, but enough to cause an unsightly problem. Whether you should buy a painting that has cracking, caused by age or impact, depends on its period, style, amount of cracking, location, and how much it bothers you. Conservators and advisors can help you sort this out.

Another fairly common set of problems includes lifting of paint, flaking, and paint loss, which occurs when the top layer of paint pulls away from a lower layer or the support. A conservator can 'consolidate' lifting paint by injecting special glue that reconnects the paint and stabilizes the area. If paint has already fallen off, he can fill in the losses, called "inpainting." That may work, but over time, the new paint may discolor and stand out from its surroundings. In that case, a conservator may need to remove old inpainting and apply new.

Sometimes, to keep the paint layer stable, prevent lifting and cracking from worsening, and repair any holes and rips, a painting needs to be 'relined.' A conservator does this by placing it face down on a special table. He covers the back with heat-sensitive glue, paste, or synthetic adhesive, then lays down a new layer of canvas. Under heat and pressure, the glue passes through the original canvas and primer and adheres the new canvas to the original paint layer. After that, if necessary, the conservator weaves and fills in losses from holes and tears and consolidates any flaking. Obviously, the marketplace prefers paintings that aren't relined, but if the object of your affection is, that shouldn't necessarily deter you from buying it. You have to learn why it was done and whether the underlying problem will continue to cause losses. A prior bad relining job can cause its own problems, too. For example, a clumsy conservator may allow the glue to pass through the primer *and* the paint layer, creating an unfortunate 'waxy' look from the front. Or, if too much pressure has been applied during the process, the painting can lose some of its impasto and appear flat. You may walk away from purchasing a work when either happens.

Occasionally, a painting may have *pentimenti* (Italian for "repentance"), which occur when an artist makes changes while he's working and covers up the old with new paint. Years later, the original images may appear like ghosts through the overpaint, and those are called *pentimenti*. Most of the time, *pentimenti* aren't bothersome. In fact, old master aficionados are thrilled to find some, as they're evidence that the painting is the artist's first version, in which he's trying out ideas, not a rote copy he or a copyist did to satisfy a later customer. *Pentimenti* played an important role in the recent discovery of a Leonardo painting, *Salvator Mundi (Savior of the World)* (ill. 30, ill. 31), as experts agreed that the changes in the position of Christ's thumb on his blessing hand is consistent with Leonardo's working method.

Pentimenti can, however, produce weird results that have a negative impact on the viewer's appreciation. I once saw a Colonial American portrait of a woman with three arms. Obviously, the artist had moved the position of one and painted it out. But, over the years, as the top layer became more transparent, the phantom arm reappeared, and now the poor dear has three.

But not all changes have been made by the artist. Portraits are notorious for being repainted, most often by conservators in subsequent generations to update fashions or hairstyles. Portraits of England's King Richard III, were repainted for different reasons - political. Richard, head of the House of York, had been killed in battle by Henry VII, a Tudor. Since the Tudors had a weak claim to the throne and wanted to discredit Richard, they had his portraits doctored to give him a hump, which he didn't have. (Scoliosis yes, kyphosis no.) Almost humorously, some portraits show the hump on Richard's left side, others on his right. That reminds me of Mel Brooks' film *Young Frankenstein*, in which Marty Feldman's massive 'hump' moves from one shoulder to another in a subsequent scene. When asked about this, Feldman's character replies, "What hump?"

Often a work is altered to enhance its salability, which was the case with many so-called 'Shakespeare' portraits. Portraits of anyone and everyone's Uncle Fergus were made to look like the Bard. No one would pay much for poor Fergus, but a portrait of Shakespeare could bring good money.

How much alteration and repair is acceptable? It varies from artist to artist. Antiquities routinely excavated in countless broken pieces have been put back together and no one seems to care. At a cocktail party at Debbie and Leon Black's home, my husband and I were standing next to a table on which a beautiful Tang pottery horse was placed. Bert tends to speak with his hands, so I gently moved him out of arm's range of the sculpture. The man who took his place, unfortunately, did what I feared Bert would do. Gesturing to make a point, he sent the horse crashing to the floor, where it broke into a dozen pieces. In a magnificent display of graciousness, Debbie bent over to collect the shards, and with calming words, intoned, "Don't worry, it's been in hundreds of pieces for centuries."

For paintings, a general rule of thumb is that the closer a painting is to the artist's original intention, the more desirable and valuable it is. If a painting is in 'pristine' or 'excellent' condition, what conservators call 'a lovely state,' you can expect to pay a premium. Paintings in 'good' condition may have some minor damage, and paintings in 'fair' or 'poor' condition have sustained significant damage and/or bad restoration.

Generally, the older or rarer the work, the more forgiving you can be. You wouldn't blow off the *Mona Lisa*, even though it's been heavily revarnished and some of the colors have changed, would you? For 19th-century paintings, conservation over 5% of the surface is generally the maximum acceptable. The location of the problems or repairs in a painting can matter more than the amount. If you're considering buying a portrait, a repaired tear in the face might be a deterrent, whereas the same tear in the background might not faze you. And, of course, you have to ask yourself if you could find another, would it likely be in better condition?" For newer works, especially those which are about pristine surfaces, like Ellsworth Kelly, tolerance for problems is less.

What do you do about the conservation of works by artists who've left paint and canvas behind and work in non-traditional techniques and 'materials' like straw, lard, and heaven knows what else? Those works can present greater conservation nightmares than a severely damaged old master. Damien Hirst's embalmed shark, called *The Physical Impossibility of Death in the Mind of Someone Living* (ill. 6), is the poster child for this kind of problem. The shark was originally cmbalmcd in formaldchydc, not the correct long-term solution. When it started to disintegrate, Hirst replaced it. This prompted a public debate as to whether the work was still authentic and, if so, was it worth less? Hirst didn't consider it a problem, nor did The Met, which took the sculpture on loan from its owner, Stevie Cohen, for a few years. That gave the work credibility, but, then again, the museum may have been doing its own angling — to cement its relationship with Cohen.

The shark isn't the only tricky Hirst: other works by him have met a similar fate. Not long ago, I visited a collection in the midwest with a transporting Hirst sculpture of a dove floating in a huge vitrine, as if in flight. From there, I went to a warehouse where I mentioned to the manager how impressed I was at the condition of the dove. He laughed and, pointing to a box on a shelf, said, "Ah, the old dove's over there."

Turner Prize winner Chris Ofili, whose work speaks to issues of racial and sexual stereotypes, "paints" with glitter and other collage materials and has often applied balls of elephant dung to the surface or varnished them and used them as "foot rests" on which the paintings lean. Conservators at the Tate, which owns his work, in advance of any problems, enlisted the help of an elephant expert from the Whipsnade, the UK's biggest zoo, to secure and analyze samples of dung so they could get ready to make future repairs when necessary.

Sometimes, conservation problems arise when artists use new fabrication techniques or media without being aware or caring about long-term consequences. Michael Wilson, co-producer of the James Bond films and an avid photography collector, warned that C-prints from the early 90s by artists like Gursky have suffered chemical fading, especially certain shades of "blue," and he questions whether the works, if reprinted, should be considered authentic. Gursky enthusiasts counter that they see no evidence of fading in such works that have been kept under optimum conditions.

Chemical fading isn't new. Dye transfers are notorious for becoming paler over time. A few years ago, we were offered a beautiful one by Rauschenberg. I compared a photo of it with a photo from an old catalogue. What had started out an overall bright turquoise had turned a pale green. Had it been light-struck, one part would have faded more than the rest, but the evenness of the fading pointed to a chemical reaction. When I brought this up to the dealer selling it, he shrugged, "Fading happens all the time. Take Ed Ruscha. All the spinach and other vegetable materials he used have faded, but we sell those as fast as we get them, so why not Rauschenberg?" I thanked him, but passed. If Rauschenberg had turquoise in mind, I didn't want pale green.

You can imagine the problems of conserving a work that was created using a technology that no longer exists, and I'm not talking about one from the distant past. Some digital-based works from the 1990s were made with hardware, software, and other materials no longer used or made. Should owners of Nam June Paik's video sculptures constructed of numerous TV sets and Dan Flavin's neon pieces be stockpiling television parts and neon bulbs before it's too late? Should museums and collectors who own them keep them as is when they break, or translate the work onto newer digital media, only to have to update it in a few years when today's materials become obsolete? Or do they do both? According to Melena Ryzik, in a *New York Times* article, the Whitney tries to both preserve and change works. Conservators have had to become cutting-edge wizards employing new materials and new technology, and I can see teams of forensic computer engineers becoming the next generation's conservators.

Another problem arises when an artist uses materials that he knows will disintegrate, called "inherent vice." Again, the Whitney's ahead of the pack; it instituted a Replication Committee which decides on the extent of conservation to be undertaken, keeping the artist's intentions in mind. Sometimes, the dissolution of a piece is part of the artist's philosophy. When Richard Long uses wooden pieces in an outdoor sculpture, he anticipates that they will be eaten by bugs over decades. And what about artists like Dan Colen, who works in swathes of chewing gum instead of paint — a conservation nightmare waiting to happen. Perhaps artists who don't want you to repair their works should safeguard their intentions by attaching a directive to their invoices, "Do not resuscitate."

Since you're not the Whitney, your best bet is to ask the gallery or artist to provide a written explanation of the materials and adhesives used, how the work was made, and how much one should or shouldn't do to preserve it. That way, when the time comes, a conservator will know if and how to proceed, and, if you want to sell the work, the buyer won't sue you for peddling damaged goods.

So, now that we've gone through a short list of condition problems, it's helpful to learn how to recognize the most obvious ones yourself. That doesn't obviate the need to call in a conservator or advisor, but it's a way to become more observant and comfortable around art. To start, ask the seller if he'll take the work to a window so you can look at it in daylight. And when I say, "look," I mean *carefully* examine it. Step to one side and then the other, running your eyes from top to bottom, to see if anything pops out at you in raking light. If a painting's been damaged and repainted years earlier, the new paint may have changed color, something which may catch your attention. Next, ask to see the work under a black light (ill. 32, ill. 33) in a darkened room. Repairs, changes, 'new' signatures, and anything else added after the artist varnishes a work will fluoresce a lurid purple under UV. If you're lucky, nothing will show, but, because there are "no show" varnishes that mask conservation, you can't jump to the conclusion that all is well. The opposite is also true. If you see a big blob of purple under the black light, that doesn't necessarily mean you should run for the hills. Titanium white, for instance, a type of paint many artists use, fluoresces naturally.

Another easy-to-make observation which may signal, "problem ahead," is a shiny new coat of varnish. It may simply be a previous owner's preference, but since thick varnish isn't the style today, not even for old masters, it may have been applied to mask a condition problem, such as degraded pigments. If the varnish is removed, such paintings have no "life." Your conservator can tell you why it's there and whether the shine can be removed or reduced.

Next, turn the painting over and look at the back for other clues. You can snap an iPhone photo of the labels and markings to refer to later when you're checking provenance and exhibition history. But for the moment, you're looking for other things. If the work has a cardboard backing, ask the seller to take it off. It may have been put there to protect the painting. If so, when it's removed, you may find something wonderful, like the artist's signature. But, the backing may be there to hide a relining. Recognizing an *old* relining isn't always easy, but a *new* relining on an old painting is generally discernible — from the back it looks new, from the front the surface feels taut to the touch, and the tacking margins may show old and new canvas.

Years ago, conservators routinely relined paintings prophylactically to strengthen the support, especially if the paint was thickly applied. If that's not the reason a work was relined, was there a tear? And has the conservation been done well or did it go wrong? I already mentioned looking for signs — if the tops of the thick layers of paint have been flattened or the glue used in the relining has come through to the surface giving it a waxy look. While you're examining the work closely, you may notice passages where the paint looks thin and the canvas shows through, which may point to some clumsy conservator "skinning" (overcleaning) the work. Obviously, when you're starting out, you'll miss a lot, but the more paintings you study, the more you'll be able to observe.

If the painting you're considering is valuable, you'll want a conservator to examine it and suggest a course of action, if necessary. A conservator is a professional whose job is conserving objects when necessary, with an eye for the future. Such professionals used to be called restorers, and much of what they did was to apply stopgap measures to problems that occurred. Conservators today take a much more holistic approach.

A conservator will examine the painting the way you did — in daylight with a magnifying lens and then in a darkened space with a black light. He'll turn the painting around and look at its back. But he'll see things you didn't see, and possibly interpret what you saw very differently. He'll advise you on what can be done to remedy problems. It may be useful to talk to him, as reports are often hard to understand. A report conservators provide may document every wart and blemish to the point that you're sure that you're going to have to walk away. And then, miraculously, it ends with, "In conclusion, the painting is in fine condition." Wow!

Art advisors are also useful in checking condition and overseeing conservation. They'll examine the work as soon as you decide to pursue it and make certain preliminary decisions, such as the best conservator for the job. You wouldn't use a hand surgeon to operate on your brain, would you? Certain conservators specialize in a particular time period or paintings with special problems. After the conservator examines the painting, your advisor will explain to you the state of "your" painting, what the problems are, whether they will worsen, whether the work is stable, and how all of that affects price. If, for example, a condition report says that the Joan Mitchell you're considering has paint loss and cracks in many places which need consolidation, your inclination may be to run for the hills. An advisor who's studied many Mitchells before will assure you that a certain amount is normal, that it will continue to happen, but it's nothing to keep you from buying it and won't impact the value now or in the future.

One last thing....a trip to a conservation lab can be a fascinating experience. Museums realize that, and many, like the Uffizi in Florence, are putting their labs behind glass so that visitors can observe the process. Ask your conservator if you can come by and observe your painting being treated. You'll be utterly amazed.

THE "IT" FACTOR

Once you're satisfied with authenticity, provenance, literature, and exhibition history, checked out the condition, and you think you're ready to pull the trigger, think again. You need to consider one more factor, perhaps less tangible than the rest, but just as important. Does the work you're considering have the "It" factor?

The "It" factor is that elusive something that elevates one work of art above others of its kind — a compelling specialness. Finding a work like that isn't important to collectors who only care about having "names." But if you're interested in building a significant, respected collection and/or intend to resell the work later for a profit, you want to buy works that have "It."

It's impossible to put into words, but we know that some people have the connoisseurship required to discern "It." They have a "good eye," while others don't. Those who do can walk into an exhibition of a dozen old master drawings and make a beeline for the finest. If you don't have that kind of eye or an advisor who does, you'll probably end up with a perfectly 'fine' collection, but not one that's extraordinary.

To some extent, a good eye can be developed. But there's no shortcut to this particular nirvana. It takes a lot of looking at a lot of art over a long period of time. If this sounds like a chore, it shouldn't. You'll have *fun* doing it, I promise. You'll build an armature with the basic information and start to make visual and historical connections. You'll learn and discern, start to recognize quality, reject the second rate, and buy correctly.

Cynics will tell you that all you need to have an eye is a lot of money. Of course, with cash in hand, you can buy the cover lots on every auction catalogue, but that's no guarantee. Lots of collectors with unlimited budgets are blind like moles and repeatedly choose dreadful things time and time again, while some collectors with less money have "bulletproof eyes" and consistently buy the best.

The Met director Thomas Hoving was famous for his eye. When the Getty was considering buying a Greek kouros, an early life-size sculpture of a male youth, Hoving was called in to look at it. After a few minutes, he said, "If you haven't bought it, don't, and, if you have, don't pay for it." Why did he think it was a forgery? He revealed his secret in Edward Dolnick's book, *The Forger's Spell*. "If I'm going to see a Vermeer..." he explained, "what I do is spend three solid days with all the Vermeers I can get my hands on...you saturate yourself. And then you have it brought in. Then bang! You look at it, and you look away, and you record that first, split-second impression." That sounds a lot like Malcolm Gladwell's thesis of his book, *Blink*, that our best decisions are instinctive responses based on a lifetime of experience.

No one takes greater pride in having a good eye than old master dealers. They have to have one; that's how they make a living. Typically, they buy works that are dirty and unattributed which they recognize as having something special. If they're lucky, they figure out who painted it and make a discovery. No one did that more successfully than dealer Ira Spanierman who paid $325 for a grimy 'Italian School' portrait of a nobleman at a sale at Parke-Bernet in New York. It was hung so high on the wall that Spanierman had to climb a ladder to see it. When he did, his 'eye' kicked in. He had no idea who the painter was, but he was so taken by the enormous detail in the fur of the sitter's coat, he felt that it had to be by "somebody." And it was. That "somebody" turned out to be Raphael, and the sitter Lorenzo de Medici, Duke of Urbino (ill. 34). Years later, Spanierman sold his $325 find for $35 million.

In his day, Bernard Berenson considered himself to be the last word on authenticity, a 'committee' of one. He said that his ability to recognize the hand of the artist was a 'sixth sense.' "When I see a picture," he said in 1933, "in most cases I recognize it at once as being or not being by the master it is ascribed to; the rest is merely a question of how to try to fish out the evidence that will make the conviction as plain to others as it is to me." It's estimated that only a sixth of the paintings Berenson pronounced right were wrong, a fantastic track record considering that scholarship in his day was in its infancy and little technology was available. Without much to draw from, he relied on old-fashioned connoisseurship.

It's not surprising that old master dealers feel superior to other dealers. Some believe that the skill required in attributing paintings is tantamount to painting them. Years ago, I was with a group of OM dealers having dinner in a Chinese restaurant after a sale. Suddenly, ex-President Reagan and his wife, Nancy, walked in and were seated at the next table. The whole place dropped its collective chopsticks — except the guys at my table. They kept on talking shop. After all, *they* were talking about what *really* mattered.

If you use a reliable art advisor, you'll likely hit the bullseye from the get-go. But, if you're going it alone, here are some questions you can ask yourself about the work you're considering:

1. *What was the artist trying to do and did he achieve his goal?* Was it something new? Does it have to do with subject, composition, formal aspects of painting like line, color, texture, or something else altogether? Has the artist successfully pushed the limits and gone farther than anyone else?

2. *Are the subject, image, style and technique in keeping with what the artist is known for?* If an artist is famous for his landscapes, the lone still life he did in his student years may be attractive and interesting, but it's not usually what the market wants.

3. *Is the piece satisfying?* Do the composition, colors, the relationship of the background to the foreground, the scale, work together? Or does something stick out as disjointed?

4. *Is the work rare and the best of its type?* A look at the catalogue raisonné will tell you whether the artist created many works of this type or only a few, and whether others are in museums or private collections.

Needless to say, it's not always possible to buy works that have all the qualities you're looking for — life isn't like that. Works in pristine condition, that are the best of their kind, and that have been in the same family since the day they were painted are few and far between. So, if a work falls short in one area but has other things going for it, and it transports you, buy it. Consider John Baldessari's "word painting," *Clement Greenberg*, named after the famous art critic, which states, "...you can no more choose whether or not to like a work of art than you can choose to have sugar taste sweet or lemons sour."

PRICE AND NEGOTIATION

PRICING A WORK

Dealers give great attention to pricing a primary artist's work. Generally, works are priced by the square inch, and the price is the price, with some room for negotiation. But, if the work you're considering is on the secondary market, the situation changes. Suddenly, quality counts, and a smaller gem can be worth more than a larger work by the same artist. In fact, a work too large for most domestic settings can be a problem to sell. But there are still other factors to consider that affect the asking price and what you ultimately pay.

Let's say that you've been eyeing a Warhol painting of flowers in a gallery. You love it, you know where you're going to hang it, and you've done your due diligence. The work has a certificate of authenticity from the Andy Warhol Art Authentication Board. A conservator has checked it out, and the condition's fine. It's been in the same family since the year it was painted, and it's been loaned to many Warhol shows. The color combination of the flowers against the background is superb and the registration, resulting from different applications of paint in the screening process, is clean and clear. You've seen enough flower paintings to know that it's got the "It" factor. And you have no doubt that Warhol is one of the most important artists of the 20th century. All in all, it's a winner. What more do you need to know before writing the check?

Figuring out the right price to pay is the last piece of the puzzle. You must determine if the dealer's asking price is fair, close to fair, or, if it isn't, what is? You are about to enter the world of 'comps' – not 'comps' as in free stuff in Vegas – but 'comps' as in the real estate business – the prices for which comparable properties have recently sold. This isn't a step you can skip.

Until recently, it was hard to assemble data for making comparisons, and you might have paid a dealer double or triple for a work he bought six months earlier at auction. Today, online databases like Artnet make auction research easy. They offer various search functions, so you can search by "title," to learn if the work came up and what it brought. If you learn that the work brought $500,000 and the dealer's asking $1 million, you should ask him why he's doubled up. He may tell you that he took the risk and bought a dirty painting and cleaned it, and that it's worth three times what he paid. The thing is that he's probably right and does deserve the profit, but that's hard for many collectors to swallow. But know that sales results from small houses don't appear on major online databases.

You can also search by "size," "year," and "price descending," which will help you find similar works you can compare with "yours." Since there are lots of variables, such as condition, you can only consider online auction comps as useful ammunition for your negotiations — not the last word. What you can get, though, is a good sense of rarity. If very few works like the one you're considering have come up, you'll understand why the dealer feels justified in asking a premium price. But if 147 similar works have sold in the last two years, you'll have more negotiating power. And if you sort by "price descending" and "sales date descending" you'll learn if the artist's market is trending up or down. If you're buying in a rising market, you might stretch for the work. If the market's declining, you can make a low offer or decide against buying. But the climate can change overnight, and a competent advisor can reliably predict which way the wind is blowing.

Since auction sales tell only half the story, it would be nice to know how your artist has performed in private sales. Unfortunately, that kind of information isn't readily accessible. You can ask your dealer or other dealers, but they may only know what they've had. A good advisor will be far more likely to have or can find the relevant information.

If you ask an auction house for their opinion, they'll give you an estimate, let's say, $1,200,000-$1,800,000, too wide a range to be helpful. If a steel company told you the price of a ton of steel was "between $120 and $180," you'd think someone was crazy, when you could google the price and know down to the penny what you'd have to pay. That's not true of art; estimates are fairly meaningless.

Once you've determined the right price to pay, and added a percentage for the "love factor," you're ready to put on your best poker face and negotiate.

NEGOTIATION

I can already hear some of you muttering, "Negotiate? I could teach *her* a thing or two ..." and you're probably right. Anyone who runs a successful business needs no tips from me on negotiating. But there are some subtleties peculiar to the art world worth noting.

Since most negotiations have many moving parts, it makes sense to take a few minutes before you start and write down your idea of a good, medium, and bad outcome. Opposite, put down what you think your opponent's ideas are of the same. That way, if you have to make a quick move during the negotiation, you can refer to these benchmarks.

Below are some tactics to get you started:

Know your stuff. Knowledge is power. Your seller knows the value of the object he's offering you, what he can realistically expect to receive, and his bottom line. If you've done your homework, he won't be the only one with such knowledge.

Let's say, for instance, that a dealer is asking a million dollars for a Matisse drawing. If you didn't know better, you might make an offer of $700,000, settle on $850,000 and think you did well. But, if you've learned that the right price is between $650,000 and $700,000, you'd have to start with a much lower offer.

Listen Carefully. Try to figure out why your seller wants what he wants and use that information to your advantage. If he's got the work on consignment and has to take your offer back to the owner, he'll need to be able to "sell" them on it. Give him reasons.

Explain your reasoning. Explain why you think an asking price is too high or why you can't pay more than you're offering. Maybe you're on a tight budget or you're deciding between this work and one offered by a competitor. Try not to seem arbitrary, and making it personal sometimes helps: "My wife doesn't really like the painting, but she agreed that if I could get it for $250,000, she'll go along." This works better than coldly digging in your heels and saying, "Not a penny over $250,000."

Timing is everything. The length of time a dealer has had a work can affect his willingness to accept an offer. If he just got it, he may hang tough, but if he's shown it to many collectors without success, he'll be more susceptible to a low offer.

Put on your game face. Like a card shark who shows no emotions, a good negotiator starts working it the second he sees a work of art he wants to buy. Swooning, declarations of love, and even minor shows of enthusiasm in front of dealers are out. Even if you think the seller can hear your heart pounding, stay calm and keep him guessing.

Years ago, I took a famous writer client into a gallery's viewing room, where I'd set aside five paintings for him to see. As soon as the first painting was placed on the easel, his face lit up, "I love it! I'll take it!!" I was shocked. I'd never seen anyone make a decision that quickly. When the second painting was brought out, he enthused, "I want that one, too!" The same with the third and the fourth. Finally, I pulled my writer/client out of the viewing room into the hall and whispered that he was ruining my ability to negotiate. There was one last painting to see, I explained, and I begged him to dummy up if he liked it. He apologized and went back into the room, where the painting had been placed on the easel. He sat quietly for a few minutes, and I silently breathed a sigh of relief. Then he blurted out, "I guess I'll take them all!" I didn't get to negotiate that day, but I did get to experience what dealers consider to be a dream client — that rare creature who says, "I love it. I'll take it. How soon can I pay?"

Be courteous. Never be arrogant or discourteous. It seldom helps, even in the art world...even when you're tempted.

Never say, "Take it or leave it," unless you really mean it.

If you make an offer, say it's only good for 24 hours. This puts you in the driver's seat. It's never good to leave an offer floating out there and allows a seller time to use it to solicit higher offers. But if you say it, you better mean it.

Don't bid against yourself. Avoid increasing your offer without the other side countering. Otherwise, you'll seem too anxious.

Leave something on the table: Pigs get slaughtered. The best deals are those that make both the buyer and the seller happy or at least only slightly unhappy. If you push a dealer so far that he makes nothing, he'll either never offer you his best things again or he'll raise his prices when he sees you coming.

Factor payment terms into the negotiation. Payment terms are typically thirty days. To wrangle a lower price, offer to pay immediately. On the other hand, if you're stretched, you may need 'terms.' Paying in thirds — 30, 60, and 90 days — is not uncommon. A famous collector used to tell dealers, "You name the price, I'll name the terms."

Concede on things that don't cost you anything. If the dealer wants to borrow the painting for a future show, let him. You want to be perceived as one of the good guys, so that the dealer will offer his best things to you, first, before anyone else.

Beware of making a lowball offer. Even though making low offers is common practice, you can overdo it. The art world is small, and, unless you're a bottom fisher and don't care, it's self-defeating to alienate a potential supplier. A too-low offer is insulting, and you risk the dealer telling you to get lost — and really meaning it. Therefore, start your negotiation with an offer that's at the low end of what's reasonable. The seller may feign insult but ultimately accept something close.

Bluff. Most people don't lie about substantive matters, but they lie in a negotiation. The seller always starts by asking more than he wants and buyers offer less than they're willing to pay. Negotiating is always about the two parties gauging how far they can push each other.

Split the difference. The seller says, "I can't take a penny less than X," and the buyer wails, "Here's my last offer." But, after much back and forth, they get closer. One sound tactic to close the deal is to say, "Let's split the difference." That's hard to resist and often gets the job done. If the seller springs this tactic on you to get you to a place you don't want to go, don't be afraid to tell him. And it's a good idea to calculate what price results from splitting the difference before you propose the split or accept it.

Go for the burn. If you love the work, the negotiation is close, and you're only a small percentage apart, don't be foolish to let the work slip away because the final price is a little higher than you hoped. Since art prices are a moving target, and the general direction for great things long-term has always been *up*, ten years from now, when the value of the work has tripled, you won't remember that you paid a bit more than you'd wanted. You'll only remember the pleasure you've had living with it all this time.

Collector Eli Broad's 'gentlemanly' approach. In his book, *The Art of Being Unreasonable*, Broad says that toward the end of a negotiation, he asks, "Is that the best you can do?" That polite question can make the seller clutch and feel that you're ready to walk away if he can't do better. Maybe they'll lower the price a tad more. They do for Eli.

The Columbo Thing. Remember the TV detective *Columbo*, played by Peter Falk? Just when the perp thought he'd gotten away with the crime, Columbo would slap his forehead and say, "Oh, just one more thing...." Then, he'd nail the guy. Try it in negotiations. After a price has been agreed upon, try to request something you haven't talked about but isn't inconsistent with the deal. It might be, "Just one more thing. I assume you'll pay for the shipping."

Don't try to use the *Columbo* tactic too many times in the same transaction. There are times when a deal falls apart, even when price and terms are agreed upon. I call it "little murders." If you ask for one concession after another, there could be a break point at which the seller snaps, demands his painting back, and calls off the deal.

Negotiating is all about a willing seller and a willing buyer finding their sweet spot together. Sure, there are times you'll have to walk out, but don't let your ego get in the way, and think hard before you turn your back and shut the door. There may be plenty of fish in the sea, but if you love a particular work, don't let it be the one that got away.

AFTER YOU OWN IT

YOU'VE FOUND A PAINTING YOU LOVE, done your due diligence, paid a fair price, and now all you want to do is take it home and enjoy it. Not so fast. With ownership comes responsibility. The good news is that unlike yachting or breeding race horses, art collecting is low maintenance. However, since expenses and obligations come with the territory, it's best to know what they are going in.

To begin, there's often psychological fall-out that comes with purchasing a work — buyer's remorse. Don't panic. It happens, especially to beginners. After all, you've just dropped a sizable sum on a work of art you've only seen once or twice, so it's fairly normal to question your decision — and maybe your sanity.

Years ago, I was in a skybox at Sotheby's with Sam, a California real estate developer, bidding on a Picasso, his first major purchase. As the auctioneer advanced at an agonizingly slow pace, Sam's face turned redder, until I was afraid he was having a heart attack. Finally, the Picasso was 'knocked down' to us (lingo for winning the bid) at the top limit we'd set. Drenched in sweat, Sam looked like he'd just run a marathon. Suddenly, he gasped, "Is it too late to back out?" Just then, a waiter appeared with champagne. After a few sips, Sam's face returned to its natural color. By he time he downed a second glass, his laughter could be heard in the auction room below. After the sale, we went out for a celebratory dinner, which Sam capped off by devouring an enormous slice of chocolate cake. He immediately buried his head in his hands, moaning, "Why did I eat that?" I guess Sam is just a remorseful kind of guy. Luckily, he's gotten over it when it comes to paintings, but not dessert.

Remorse can cut two ways. You can also suffer emotional pain from *not* buying something you wish you had. Arthur Altschul, the Post-Impressionist collector I've discussed, always joked that if he wrote an autobiography, he'd call it *Paintings I Have Missed*. He regretted not stepping up and buying works late in his collecting career, when he was so spoiled by the low prices he paid early on. He could have used a good case of price amnesia. In fact, one of the best characteristics a long-time collector can have is the ability to forget what things used to cost. Altschul couldn't do that. Abstainer's remorse dogged him all his life.

INSURANCE AND SECURITY

As soon as you pay for a work, make sure you insure it for "in transit and at all locations." And if you live in earthquake country, you might also consider earthquake insurance. General art insurance isn't particularly expensive, and it will give you peace of mind. Specialized art insurers, such as AXA, Chubb, and Chartis, will use your bill of sale as the "agreed value" for replacement, and, recognizing that the art market is fluid, will pay 15% more than your insured value if a claim is made. It's not a bad idea to include a buy back clause in your policy which gives you the right, should the work be stolen and recovered after you got paid out, to buy it back at the settlement sum plus a negotiated amount. And because of market fluctuation, especially in the field of contemporary art, be sure to update your insurance periodically. You'll want to increase coverage on works that have gone up in value and reduce it on works that have gone down. Why pay higher premiums than you need to?

Not everybody wants insurance. Since most accidents happen when pieces are moved, some collectors opt not to lend and not to insure. They're betting against theft and disasters. I was surprised to learn that a client who owns an insurance company doesn't insure his own collection of large-scale Abstract Expressionist paintings. "Just let someone try to walk off with an eight-foot canvas," he laughed. If your paintings aren't as big as a highway billboard, however, theft may loom large on your list of concerns.

Other collectors leave their paintings uninsured to avoid a paper trail for the IRS. Either they paid cash for the paintings and want no records, or they want to avoid paying estate tax by having the children quietly remove them from the walls and take them home. People used to get away with these moves, but not so much anymore. And though I shouldn't be anyone's conscience, I can only suggest you don't do anything illegal.

Whether you insure your collection or not, you might want to consider installing a home security system. It's amazing what James Bondian security devices are available for domestic use, including infrared alarms, sensors, motion detectors, closed circuit TV, and even GPS systems that can be embedded in your paintings. No matter what precautions you take, however, your art can get stolen. Until recently, only 5% of stolen art was returned, but now, because of Interpol and Art Loss Register, the percentage is much larger. Owners report thefts to these agencies, and dealers and collectors check their databases before buying. A Salvador Dali drawing, worth $150,000, stolen from Adam Lindemann's New York gallery in 2012, made its way to Europe and back via express mail days later. Evidently, the thieves assessed their chances of "fencing" the work as poor and chickened out. And when thieves stole a Johns, a Piet Mondrian, and some Cornell boxes from LA bond fund manager Jeffrey Gundlach's home and drove off in Gundlach's red Porsche, he got the paintings back, but not the car.

If your works are stolen, you may never see them again. A Vermeer, Rembrandt, Degas, and other masterpieces taken from Boston's Isabella Stewart

Gardner Museum in 1990 have never been recovered. That's also true of a huge $5 million outdoor bronze which disappeared from the Henry Moore Foundation in England. It's hard to hide a giant sculpture, so it's probably a good guess that it was melted and sold for scrap metal. If that happened, the thieves made about $2300, even though the Moore Foundation offered $10,000 reward for the sculpture's return. Evidently, there were no Mensa members in this gang.

MOVING AND SHIPPING

Please don't move any art yourself, even if the insurance company allows it. It's tempting to grab a cab home from the gallery where you bought the painting, holding it on your lap or putting it in the backseat of your car. But *don't do it*. It doesn't take much of a bump for a painting to slip in its frame, causing flaking or more serious damage. Let professional art movers — not general movers — pack and move your works. If it's not going far, they'll soft-pack it. If it's going a distance, they'll crate, "museum" crate, or double-crate it and ship it by truck or air. If by air, art movers may even hand carry out to the tarmac and put it in the cargo hold themselves, so that no other 'hands' are involved and there's no risk of damage caused when a crate drops the inch or two from the loading platform to the conveyor belt.

The most economical way to ship a work is to put it on an art mover's scheduled shuttle truck with works owned by others. If you're in a hurry, or your work is extremely valuable and you want it moved by itself, FedEx's "Custom Critical" service provides a dedicated climate-controlled truck and two drivers. From the time the work is picked up, until it reaches its destination, the truck doesn't stop. What I especially like about this service is its anonymity. If you use an 'armored' car service like Brinks, you're practically screaming, 'Valuable object inside!!' possibly setting yourself up for a robbery. Nobody looks twice at a FedEx truck.

FRAMING

The saying "Clothes make the man" could just as easily apply to frames and paintings. A great frame can make a mediocre painting look like a million bucks, and a bad one can kill a great painting. Many times, I've thought that we've gotten works at auction on the low side because the frames were so hideous they distracted other potential buyers. Auction houses are onto this now and borrow antique frames to show off their more expensive lots.

Terry Stent, an Atlanta collector of American art, acquired a painting he felt was the jewel of his collection and hung it over the fireplace in his living room. He waited, but for two years, no one who came into his house said a word about it. He finally realized the frame was the problem. He had it reframed, and now, when people come into the house, it's the first work that commands their attention.

Plenty of artists don't want their paintings to be framed. "Let the painting speak for itself," they say. One of the things Ann Temkin did when she took over as Chief Curator at Painting and Sculpture at MoMA, in 2008, was to take frames off paintings that weren't meant to be there. Before Temkin, the museum had removed a lot of the frames on paintings and put them all in the same white box frame. Now, a walk through MoMA is a lesson in framing. Whereas a number of paintings are frameless, some are in simple mahogany L frames or white box frames, and others are in elaborate gilded antique frames. Works painted to the edge of the canvas are in island frames, with space between the paintings and frames so that the painted sides can be appreciated. The takeaway is that there's no one frame that works on all paintings, but there is *the* right frame for a specific work. You just have to figure out what that is.

Good framers like Lowy and Eli Wilner in New York and Jerry Solomon in Los Angeles are like hairdressers to the stars. Their frames, repros and antiques, are fabulous, and they offer tremendous experience and expertise. They have corner samples you can hold up on a work to judge, and they use computer programs that allow you to see exactly how your work would look in various frames.

If you've got the budget, and your painting would look good in an antique frame, you should go that route. Like period furniture, antique frames have a patina that new ones don't have and details that can't be reproduced. And it's not only old paintings that look good in antique frames; modern and contemporary paintings can look phenomenal. The right Picasso in an antique Spanish frame is a wow. But don't think old frames are cheap. A great Renaissance or Baroque frame can cost tens of thousands of dollars. If you've already spent hundreds of thousands of dollars or more on a painting, however, why not go the distance and spend a little more for the perfect frame? Be warned: buying antique frames can become an addiction. Floridian Justine Simoni has spent millions of dollars on frames which she displays, *totally empty*, all over her house. That's right — no pictures, just frames.

INSTALLATION

Once you bring your new painting home, you quickly realize that where you hang it and what you put next to it are important. A thoughtful installation will increase your enjoyment. As Victoria Newhouse points out in her book, *Art and the Power of Placement*:

The simple act of hanging a painting requires important decisions: the choice of room, the positioning within the room, the juxtaposition of other objects, lighting, wall color, and wall texture. Even the floor is a factor; a hard shiny surface reflects light, sound and color quite differently from soft, sound and light absorbing materials.

No wonder that collectors find installing works a challenge and why advisors spend so much time doing it. I'm sure my mother wouldn't understand. "You got a Ph.D. so you could hang pictures?" "You bet, Mom — it goes with the territory, and I love it."

A successful installation depends on your spaces, how you live, and how you think about your collection. Some collectors buy art to decorate their homes, others build their homes as backdrops for their art. New collectors tend to hang expensive paintings front and center, seasoned collectors often hang their priciest works where they spend most of their time, such as in their bedroom. Some collectors install their collection so that they're color coordinated, and others create a dialogue so the works play off one another in terms of style or subject matter. There's no one right way, of course. A client once called, excited. One night when she couldn't sleep, she went into the living room where we'd hung a Picasso next to a Matisse. She claimed she overheard the two artists talking. "After all," she said, "they were friends."

The late Marcia Weisman, Norton Simon's sister and a well-known LA collector in her own right, believed in creating drama by hanging paintings in unexpected places. She liked putting paintings high on a wall or near a threshold, rather than in the center of a wall, which she found boring. Even if you're not ready to make such a leap, if, after while, you're too used to your paintings where they are, move them around. You may find that you fall in love with them all over again.

For many collectors, rehanging their collection is an exciting creative part of collecting. Years ago, in Washington, DC, I visited two collecting couples on the same day. The first had a great collection of Latin American artists, beautifully installed. But the couple was restless. Later that week, all the art in the house was going into storage, and a whole new group of works from storage would be installed. The second couple, the Podestas, now divorced, had just rehung their collection. Once a year, they enlisted an outside curator to pick a theme and choose works from their holdings to install in their home. Seeing the works in a new context was important to the couple.

Bottom line, when you're installing art, most pros follow a few key rules:

1. For the proper height, shoot for the comfort zone in which the eyes of an average person will be looking at the painting a third of the way down from the top. Be especially careful in dining rooms not to hang them too high, since diners will be viewing them from a seated position.

2. Avoid hanging big paintings in packed, high-traffic hallways or anywhere else where they can be damaged by kids, guests, or pets rubbing against them.

3. If you insist on hanging the art yourself (and I beg you not to), use professional 'art hooks' designed to distribute the painting's weight evenly, making them less likely to fall.

A client of ours had a devastating accident the day his first art purchase arrived. He was too excited to wait for an installer, so, after he found the perfect place to hang it, he leaned it against the wall while he went searching for a hammer and hooks. When he returned, he backed into the painting and kicked a hole in it. Professionals have hung every work he's bought since. It makes sense, as professionals can deal with the structure of every wall and wall covering, and, because they're keenly aware of the fragility of paintings, they wear white gloves to prevent fingerprints from marring the work's surface. Since many installers are artists, they also have excellent aesthetic judgment about placement. Most also have the patience of Job in handling collectors, designers, and advisors, all of whom may be giving conflicting orders, such as "Over there and higher," vs. "Hang it here, but lower." To poke fun at the frailties of art installation, a group of handlers and ex-handlers organized an Art Handling Olympics. This included events such as "Bubble-Wrapping" and "The Static Hold," in which one of the organizers shouted conflicting orders and took leisurely phone calls while the competing handlers held 50-pound lead weights against a wall.

LIGHTING, TEMPERATURE CONTROL, AND CLEANING

You're probably not going to have banks of multi-colored lights at home, as galleries do, but good lighting is critical. Collectors of 19th-century and old master paintings often opt for picture lights, the kind that screw into the stretcher and arch over the work. A narrow bulb bathes the painting's surface in warm light, particularly flattering to older paintings. By contrast, contemporary art collectors generally prefer ceiling lights. If you go this route, please avoid installing fixtures that create a scalloped effect on the wall. No painting and no wall looks good with scallops. And while I'm voicing preferences, may I suggest using LED low voltage lights? While every collector knows that works on paper must be kept away from too much light, fewer collectors realize that the same is true for some paintings. Curators at the Van Gogh Museum in Amsterdam have noticed, for example, that exposure to certain lights has caused a chemical reaction and darkening of some of the yellows in Van Gogh's *Sunflowers*.

To prevent works on paper from becoming light-struck, they should be kept out of direct sunlight and framed with glass that filters harmful UV rays, like Optium or Museum glass. It's also a good idea to install UV filters on your windows. Even if you do all those things, try to get into the habit of lowering your shades during peak sunlight hours and when you're leaving home. Some of our clients make covers of sun-resistant fabric they drape over the works when they're away for long periods. And if you're still concerned, you can invest in a device that measures the light and alerts you when it's too strong. I could make suggestions from here to Sunday, but since the proper lighting depends on so many variables — the art you collect, your ceiling height, the pigments used, etc. — it's probably a good idea to have a lighting expert and conservator come to your home and create a bespoke system.

The right environment also depends on paying proper attention to temperature and humidity. The optimum temperature for paintings is 64 to 77 degrees Fahrenheit (18 to 25 degrees Celsius) and the humidity should be between 40-50%. So watch your thermostat, and if your house tends to be dry, humidifiers can help. Above all, try to keep the temperature and humidity constant. Fluctuations can cause oils and works on paper to become wavy, which may or may not be a problem. Recently, a client was considering a Morris Louis painting at auction in New York and because it was wavy, I asked a conservator to have a look. The conservator explained that the painting had gone from one environment, likely Florida, to New York, and if our client bought it, there was a good chance after it was in his house a while, the waves would disappear. He was right. Other times, a canvas may have to be re-stretched or a work on paper re-mounted to flatten it.

Finally, paintings should be kept dust-free, which is actually not as easy as it sounds. If you're too vigorous, you can damage the work, and if you dust too softly, dirt can stick to the varnish and gradually make the work look dingy. Moderation is key. One of our clients, a captain of industry, pays his housekeeper extra not to touch, let alone dust his art. He does *that* himself. And as one conservator told me, "I've made more money on housekeepers..."

You'd like to think that once you install a work in your home, it will stay in the same condition forever, but that seldom happens. Think of paintings like organic living things. They're going to change, and the changes may need a conservator's intervention. For that reason, it's probably a good idea to have a conservator come to your house every couple of years to examine the collection and see if anything needs attention. It's better to face small problems sooner than big ones later. Outdoor sculptures require more frequent inspections, cleanings, and waxings — especially if the work is in sea air. Ray Stark had his 13-foot Giacometti *Standing Woman I* cleaned every few months because neighborhood birds used her head as a combination lookout post and outhouse, causing a peculiar white halo. (Stark's

Giacometti and twenty-some other sculptures are at the Getty, where they were donated.)

ACCIDENTS HAPPEN

Of course, the specter of a freak accident is always looming. One Sunday morning, I got a frantic call from a client with a "painting emergency." I don't get many "house calls," so I raced to his apartment, where I found him pacing the floor, looking like he'd pulled an all-nighter. When he took my hand and started leading me toward the bedroom, I stiffened. We were both single then, and I wondered if the 'emergency' wasn't a new twist on 'come up and see my etchings.' From the bedroom door, though, I could see a tear near the bottom of a ravishing 1960s Tom Wesselmann nude we'd placed over his bed six months earlier. "How'd it happen?" I gasped. He looked down and sheepishly mumbled, "Ahem — toe hole." I didn't know whether to laugh or cry.

Accidents have even happened in my own family. Many Christmases ago, Bert's late wife gave him a David Hockney print, a portrait of Henry Geldzahler, a famous curator and a great mutual friend of Hockney and my husband. Unframed, it was rolled in wrapping paper. Unaware of its contents, my husband tore off the paper and, unfortunately, ripped the print. A conservator was able to fix the tear so it was virtually invisible, but it's unsalable. It could have been worse: the preceding Christmas, my husband's giant poodle saw a 'tree' in the living room and peed all over the presents. The Hockney could have been one of them.

Don't think that professionals are immune to accidents. When a friend, an auction house expert, was doing an appraisal in an English country house, he found the library too dark to see the paintings hanging there. The butler went off and returned with an old-fashioned gas torch. Holding the torch up to a painting with his left hand, while making notes with his right, the expert soon became alarmed by the smell of fire. He asked the butler to check the house. The butler politely observed, "The painting, sir. It's on fire." A few months later, the same expert was on another appraisal in another big, dark country house. This time, taking no chances, he carried a painting into the front driveway to look at it in daylight. Propping it up against a bush, he went back inside the house to find someone to hold it up so he could see it properly. Meanwhile, a delivery truck pulled into the driveway and ran over the painting. Ever since, my friend has referred to himself as "the Inspector Clouseau of art." Because accidents like these happen, companies like Gallery Support Group have come into existence to teach individuals, museum and gallery staffers, and shippers how to handle art.

COLLECTION MANAGEMENT

Collecting art generates more paperwork than you might imagine — invoices, letters of authenticity, photos, correspondence, records of payment, insurance policies, condition reports, framing and conservation bills, and copies of relevant literature. And if you lend works to museum exhibitions, the amount mushrooms. Before you know it, you'll have drawers and computer files filled with documents, and you'll be spending far more time than you bargained for keeping it all organized.

Fortunately, good computer collection management systems are available and easy to use. You can scan everything and never need paper clips and manila files again. Needless to say, though, you should store important original papers in a safety deposit box. You'll need them if you sell. If you have an advisor, he or she will oversee all this.

TO LEND OR NOT TO LEND

If you buy an important work of art, museums will want to borrow it for special exhibitions. There are pros and cons to lending, and there's seldom a simple "yes" or "no" answer. On the plus side, having a work in an important show signifies that it's highly regarded in scholarly circles. And since the 'exhibition history' on a doc sheet works like the list of extra-curricular activities under your high school yearbook photo, the more shows listed, the more luster your piece acquires. Lending, therefore, not only can add to the fame of the work while you own it — but also to the bottom line when you sell.

Some collectors, like famed Venezuelans, Patty and Gustavo Cisneros, lend because they feel strongly that it's the moral imperative of every art collector to make their works available for the public. I agree. Others lend, neither out of a sense of duty, nor for the credentials it adds to the work, but because they like the status and perks that go with it. They love travelling to other cities, seeing new museums, getting the first-class treatment of being invited to opening dinners, and mingling with other collectors. There's nothing that can make a collector puff his chest out farther and faster than to be asked, "Which one is yours?" It proves what a good eye he has.

Yet, many collectors flatly refuse to lend. They feel that the risk of damage in transit and at shows outweighs any upside. During the "Los Angeles 1955-1985" exhibition at the Pompidou in Paris in 2006, three works were damaged — two, simply by falling off their mountings. The no-lenders say, "Why put a painting in harm's way?" As well, many hate the fact that their beloved work of art will be out of the house for months or years on end. Once, when I told a client that the Getty *and* the Musée d'Orsay in Paris wanted to borrow a painting he owned for a year-long traveling show, he nearly cried: "I've just separated from my wife, and that would be like another separation." In the end, he agreed to a loan to one venue — the Getty — if he could have his painting home for Christmas.

Though it's rare, vandalism is a risk. The man who hacked the toe of *David* in Florence said that a female model of Veronese, the 16th-century painter, told him to do it. And the perpetrator who spray-painted Picasso's *Guernica* with the words "KILL LIES ALL" ironically became an art dealer specializing in graffiti art. Once, an entire exhibition of Sherrie Levine's checkerboard paintings at the High Museum of Art in Atlanta, including one I owned, was defaced when someone walked around the room with a sharp instrument, like a key, and etched a line across every painting. Luckily, the artist agreed to repair all the works, but I felt violated. So, I'm super-sympathetic when clients express trepidations about lending.

You also can't overlook the slim possibility that your work may be stolen. I know it's the stuff of novels, and the chances are infinitesimal, but it does happen. The unsolved 1990 theft at the Gardner Museum, which I've already mentioned, still makes collectors queasy. Two thieves, dressed as police officers, tricked the guards into letting them enter the museum at 1:30 am. They tied up the guards, who didn't even struggle. According to Ulrich Boser, in his book, *The Gardner Heist: The True Story of the World's Largest Unsolved Art Theft*, one of them, a student working the night shift, whined to his captors, "Don't worry... They don't pay me enough to get hurt [on the job]."

Most of the time, lending goes well and your work will come back to you just as you sent it. As Michael Govan, Director of LACMA, wisely points out, "It's like a plane crash. Would you never fly on an airplane? It's a relatively safe business." If you decide to lend, however, be prudent. If the show's organizers want your work badly enough and you've determined that the security is sufficient, you have the leverage to insist that it be put under glass, behind a rope, that it travels in a museum crate, or that it only goes to one venue. And, you don't have to give the same answer for every request. You can decide which exhibitions are worth lending to and which you can skip.

LIVING WITH YOUR COLLECTION

Since collecting can be addictive, it won't take long before you'll cover every wall in your house, want more art, and have nowhere to put it. What do you do then? Build an addition. But too often those extra rooms quickly fill up, and you're back to square one.

Some collectors lend to relatives or museums, or rent or buy spaces to hang their surplus works. Michigan collectors Maxine and Stuart Frankel show their cutting-edge contemporary art in a warehouse, and in Miami, the Rubell Family Collection/Contemporary Arts Foundation, and the de la Cruzes open their collections to the public, switching art in and out of buildings they own in the design district. Many galleries and collectors buy buildings where it's cheap, and install their collections. Business and real estate get tied up with the business of collecting, and the two go hand in hand in wealth appreciation.

Lack of space isn't the only reason collectors open exhibition spaces and museums. The late Japanese real estate developer, Minoru Mori, opened a space for temporary exhibitions on the 53rd floor of his 54-floor mixed-use skyscraper in Tokyo. It was a branding tool for drawing tourists and adding prestige and traffic to the building. Mori wasn't the first to do something like that. He and others have taken a page from real estate developer Marty Margulies's book. Decades ago, Marty installed a sculpture garden on the grounds of Grove Isle, Miami, an apartment complex he developed. The collection was a way of making his complex stand out against the competition. Recent reiterations have gone way beyond. A recent Miami development, Oceana Bal Harbour, offered apartments which came with shares in two Jeff Koons sculptures, ordered but not expected to be delivered for a few years. The fate of the sculptures will fall into the hands of the apartment owners, by vote.

WORST-CASE SCENARIO: YOU BOUGHT A FAKE

There's always the possibility that you'll discover a work that you've bought is a fake. What do you do then? Laws differ state to state on the statute of limitations and other issues, but, generally, a bill of sale from a gallery or private dealer (a professional) to you (a non-professional), listing the artist and name of work, is a warrant of authenticity. If you can prove that the painting is wrong, within a certain length of time, and the burden of proof is on you, you should be able to get your money back. The major auction houses give you only five years to return a work, but even within that time, expect them to be difficult since they've paid their consignor, and the prospect of chasing the consignor down for money isn't something they want to do. If you form serious doubts about a work's authenticity up front — don't buy.

An illustrative lawsuit revolved around two porphyry vases in ormolu mounts that were consigned to Christie's by the 7th Marquess of Cholmondeley (pronounced "Chumley"), a friend of the British royal family. (He's the guy who used to walk backwards at the opening of Parliament in front of the Queen, carrying the scepter of state.) Christie's catalogued the vases as French 18th century. A Canadian heiress bought them for $3 million and learned after that word had circulated in the trade before the sale that the vases weren't "period," i.e., they weren't 18th century. She asked for her money back, but Christie's refused. She sued, won in the trial court, but lost on appeal. The appellate court bought Christie's argument that because there was a 70% chance the vases were authentic, the sale should hold. The court missed the point that everyone in the art world knows; no one in their right mind would buy vases or anything else knowing there's a 30% chance they were *wrong*. The Canadian should have won.

If you buy a work from a collector, rather than a dealer, you have to be especially cautious, because, in many states, a non-professional isn't responsible for warranting authenticity if he issues you a simple invoice, unless the invoice expressly says so. Let's say you meet a little old lady who sells you what she says is a painting by Edward Hopper she inherited from her father, Hopper's next-door neighbor. Surprise! The painting turns out to be by somebody else's next-door neighbor. Although the invoice she's given you clearly states the painting is by Hopper, you may have to prove that the LOL made a deliberate or negligent representation, and, by the time you do that, she may have left town or died. So, if you buy collector-to-collector, get a lawyer to draft a contract that protects you from future legal nightmares.

EXIT STRATEGIES

If you own valuable art, there may come a time when you won't want to possess it any more. You might want to give it away or trade it for something better, or different. Or maybe you'll *need* to sell. Face it, inevitably one day you're not going to be here to own it anymore. Think of it this way, we're all just temporary custodians of our art. Since s$@t happens, it's best to be prepared so you can disconnect yourself from your collection in a way that's advantageous to you.

GIVING IT AWAY

Giving away beloved works of art is a brave thing to do. You've studied them, selected them, developed a relationship with them, and, frankly, you're going to miss them. You probably want your children or someone else near to you to have them, so you need to know how to pass the works along while generating the fewest bucks for Uncle Sam. See a lawyer to get it right. He'll probably tell you that, if such a gift falls within the maximum allowed lifetime tax-free gift, you can go that route. You should document it, however, and, if you want to live with the art until you die, you have to rent it from the recipient. If that doesn't work, there's a veritable laundry list of tax-saving vehicles that may do the trick. These include family foundations, family partnerships, charitable remainder trusts, remainder purchase charitable trusts, donor advised funds as part of community foundations or other financial institutions, flip unitrusts, net income trusts, standard unitrusts and liquid life insurance (I know... it's quite a list). Your attorney can explain these and design an instrument that suits your needs. The goal is that, by the time you die, your heirs are sitting with art worth far more than you paid with as little taxes due as possible. Meanwhile, you'll have the pleasure of knowing that someday the art will be hanging on your dearests' walls.

If you're thinking of passing the art along to your children, realize that it may be more of a burden on them, than a blessing. Some of your children may like the art, others may not, making it hard to divide the collection. Or every one of them may claim the same work, which can cause much drama and tear a family apart. One day not long ago, without any advance notice, a shipper delivered a client's valuable Fernand Léger painting to my office with a note from her asking me to sell it. The owner, a 70-ish woman, loved the painting and was convinced that it would double or triple in value over the next few years. So why was she selling? I called, terrified she'd fallen ill. She laughed off my concerns. "It's simple," she explained, "three doesn't go into one." She had three children and one expensive painting. She'd decided to sell the work and divide the cash among the three kids, rather than risk postmortem squabbling.

Some collectors want their paintings to go to a museum. That way, they get the whole enchilada — a tax deduction, kudos for being civic-minded philanthropists, and the public gets to see great art. But which museum? Obviously, if you have a major Picasso or other high-caliber work, every museum will want it, and you're probably being courted already. If you have good but not great things, big museums may be less enthusiastic, and a small museum may be more appreciative. John Paxton, father of the actor Bill Paxton, decided to leave his modest collection to the Nevada Museum of Art in Reno, a museum he'd never visited but only read about. He reasoned that his works would be shown and valued there, not de-acquisitioned or sentenced to the basement, as they would be in a larger institution. Other collectors buy with a museum and community in mind. In Dallas, four families — the Rachofskys, Hoffmans, Roses and Youngs — have formed a joint venture committing donations of works to the Dallas Museum.

The first step in giving away your art is to call the director or curator of your museum and have a chat. If they want it, ask an art appraiser to do a fair market appraisal and discuss it with your accountant or lawyer, so you know what you can deduct from your tax bill. Timing your gift can be important: If you think the value of your art is going up, and you can afford to wait, you might hold your fire. Jim Dicke, a well-known collector and philanthropist, regrets giving away his Basquiat too soon; had he waited a few more years, the painting would have gone up millions, along with his tax deduction.

Before you say 'farewell' and close the crate, you might want to have one more talk with your museum director about your work's long-term future. It's hard to resist the pleasure of imagining your grandchildren and their children on visits to the museum reading the wall label noting that the work was a gift from you. If your gift is important enough, you may be able to stipulate that it can never be de-accessioned or that it will always be on public view. If you're giving an entire collection, you may even be able to require that the museum keeps it intact and shown together. The next step up would be arranging for an entire museum wing to be named after you; but even if your collection is world-class, you may have to come up with a major cash gift to get naming rights. Try to get the best deal, then say goodbye. You're doing the right thing.

SELLING AND TRADING

You can get lots of advice on buying art, but selling is just as hard, and there's not much out there in terms of help. Deciding whether to sell at auction or privately and how much to ask depends on how fast you need the money, the nature and quality of what you're selling, and the market sector's response.

DEATH

In discussing the many reasons why individuals sell, we might start with the Grim Reaper, since he comes to us all and, when he does, art changes hands. That's because you can't take it with you. Or can you? We all know the old saying, "Bury me in my Cadillac." Frankly, I don't know anyone who's buried himself with art except for the artist Ed Kienholz, who was interred in one of his installations, a 1940 Packard tricked up with all kinds of Keinholz "confections," including the ashes of his dog. Japanese businessman, Ryoei Saito, who bought Van Gogh's famous *Portrait of Dr. Gachet* in 1990 for over $82 million, once said he wanted the painting buried with him when he died. Curiously, since Saito's death in 1996, there's been no sighting of the painting. It's likely that he sold it due to business reversals, but let's hope if he did take it with him, he wasn't cremated.

Years ago, David Nash paid a condolence call on a retired colleague, Jacob Weintraub, whose wife had died. Weintraub, a sculpture dealer, walked Nash through his apartment, showing off his collection, which was far from distinguished. When the two finally sat down on the sofa for a drink, the older man asked Nash which work he liked best. At a loss for what to say, Nash pointed to the closest object, an Arp on the coffee table. The dealer smiled and nodded, "My late wife liked it so much, I put her ashes in it."

For most collectors, the greatest control from the grave is to organize the dispersal of their paintings before they die. A celebrity client in her sixties called last year to ask us to arrange her estate sale. She was in fine health, but she wanted to make sure that everything would be just the way she wanted it. She'd organized her funeral, down to the music, and now she wanted us to negotiate with an auction house and have the catalog designed and ready to go. We decided which items would be sold, picked photos of her to be included, and a writer friend of hers penned an extremely flattering essay about her superb taste. The auction house we chose even made a stunning mock-up of the sales catalogue. Her only criticism? She wanted a blue cover to match her eyes.

DIVORCE

When couples get divorced, and paintings are a major asset of the marriage, they're often forced to sell. In the late 1950s, Edward G. Robinson owned one of the finest private Impressionist and Post-Impressionist collections ever assembled, including Cézanne's *The Black Clock*. When he separated from his wife, Gladys, Robinson needed to sell the collection to pay her off, something Gladys adamantly refused to allow. At the time, my husband was a very young lawyer at a law firm that represented Robinson. His senior partner reasoned that, if they could somehow get the paintings out of the house, Gladys' emotional ties to them would be severed, and she'd be more amenable to selling. The court's temporary order prevented Robinson from selling any art without Gladys' consent; but it said nothing about lending. So they enlisted the cooperation of LACMA, and one Saturday at midnight, while Gladys was in Palm Springs, two trucks pulled up in front of the Robinson house. My husband, a colleague of his, and Rick Brown, then Director of LACMA, moved the entire collection — 58 utterly sublime works of art — out of the house and onto museum trucks. Bert will never forget staggering to the curb carrying Degas' iconic bronze *The Little Fourteen-Year-Old Dancer*. And the plan worked! After her initial rage at coming home to empty walls, Gladys agreed to sell. But she exacted one last bit of revenge: Robinson could sell the collection to anyone in the world *except* LACMA. In the end, the entire collection went to Stavros Niarchos for the then-fantastic sum of $3 million. Today, those same paintings are worth billions.

Pop Art collectors Robert and Ethel Scull also had an acrimonious divorce in which their collection played a central role. Robert, under the guise of redecorating their apartment, put the 35 paintings that were in their apartment in storage in *his* name, and filed for divorce. He claimed that he built the collection alone and that the paintings were his. Ethel claimed they collected together. Ten years later, the court finally awarded her a third of the paintings, some property and cash from art sold in the interim. Robert and Ethel met at a warehouse to divvy up the remaining paintings, and with a toss of a coin, Ethel got first pick. She chose Johns' famous 1959 *Out the Window*, which she sold within a year for $3.63 million. She continued to sell the works she got to support her lifestyle. In the end, although there was nothing left of the collection, she got immortality through Warhol's 1963 portrait, *Ethel Scull 36 Times*. What started innocently, with Ethel getting dolled up to go to Andy's studio to pose for a portrait, turned into an extraordinary adventure when Warhol took her to a Times Square photo booth. He had her sit in various positions while he deposited coins. From those photos, he painted the magnificent, breakthrough portrait, which Ethel later donated jointly to The Met and the Whitney.

DEBT

For owners who are suffering financial distress, art is often the first possession to go. Rather than sell their houses, cars, or plate-sized Rolex, which friends and colleagues would more readily notice, collectors under fire liquidate their art. That's why most distress sales happen quietly and privately. Some of Bernie Madoff's victims seemed to be an exception, wearing their losses like a badge of honor, selling their art very publicly through dealers and at auction. It's hard to know how much art was actually sold by that unfortunate group. I suspect that half the dealers who said they were selling on behalf of Madoff victims weren't; they were just trying to make buyers feel like they were getting a steal. It worked; bottom fishers were salivating from New York to LA.

DOWNSIZING AND THE DEAL

When collectors get older and move to smaller homes and apartments, their wall space shrinks, and they often have to sell. Doug Cramer, the producer of TV's The *Love Boat* and *Dynasty*, moved a few times, and each time, feeling the need to do "artistic downscaling," as he called it, he consigned bunches of works to auction.

A collecting couple we advise retired and decided to move from a large home in Greenwich, Connecticut to a smaller New York apartment. The casualty was their beloved 12 foot-wide Joan Mitchell diptych. They were disconsolate, but cashing a check for more money than they expected eased the pain, and they did go on to buy many new, smaller things for their new digs.

Other collectors may not *need* to sell but do it because they receive an offer they can't refuse. A client had no intention of selling his Orientalist masterpiece by Gérôme — until we lent it to a show at the Getty and a collector from the Emirates came knocking with a gigantic offer. He'd bought it through us only a few years earlier, and he figured it had been one of his best investments. But would the market for the artist continue to go up at the same high rate? What would happen if Middle Eastern collectors were no longer interested in Orientalist subjects, or the price continued to fall? It was a risk he decided not to take.

Some collectors with a great work pick a high number, and if anyone offers that much, they sell. A collector of Post-Impressionist paintings always sold when he could sell it for ten times what he paid. Later, when the things became worth a hundred times what he paid, I wonder how he felt. And then, there are collectors who sell when the value of a painting becomes a disproportionately high portion of their net worth. Years ago, I took a cold call and drove out to Long Island to see a man who wanted to sell a Mary Cassatt. When I pulled up at his address, a small Levittown tract house, my expectations dropped to zero. Inside, however, hanging over a plastic-covered sofa was a huge, breathtaking masterpiece by the artist. When I asked the owner why he wanted to sell, he shrugged, "I can't afford to keep a painting that's more valuable than my house."

FALLING OUT OF LOVE

Your tastes may change over time, and the art you bought when you were thirty may not be what you want to live with when you're fifty. Or perhaps you still like the artist, but you've found a better example. If you've made wise decisions, you won't have to live with yesterday's choices. You can sell or trade for something different and/or better.

In the early 1980's, Peter Lewis, a collector and philanthropist, bought a painting by Basquiat on my say-so, without seeing it. He paid $3,000. A few years later, he called to say that he didn't like it and wanted to sell. When I told him the piece was no longer worth what he had paid, he was unfazed, "Don't worry. I'll take a loss. I just want out." I laughed, "It's not that. It's worth much more. Right now, about $150,000." He fell silent for a moment and then exclaimed, "I *love* my painting!" He kept the Basquiat and sold it several years later for a huge profit. Many years later, on Peter's 80th birthday, he asked me to sell another painting, a Joan Mitchell. He'd had me buy it for him thirty years earlier, when he was fifty and wanted to buy himself a present for $50,000. We got him over $5,000,000, a hundred times his investment.

On occasion, sellers suffer 'seller's remorse.' Friends who collected American paintings found the perfect Georgia O'Keeffe after decades of looking. The asking price was 2 million dollars, which gave them sticker shock since they'd never spent that much on a work before. They decided to do a 1031C, a tax-free like-kind exchange, named after its section number in the Internal Revenue Code, and trade two paintings from their collection plus cash for the O'Keeffe. Ironically, after they got the O'Keeffe, they decided that they couldn't live without the two paintings and bought them back, giving the dealer a big profit.

HOW TO SELL

In contrast to dealers who are constantly short on funds and have to turn over their inventory to pay bills, most collectors have the luxury of holding long-term and selling when the time is right. A wealthy eighty year old Boston dowager who's collected for over fifty years would be bored stiff if she wasn't on the phone every day, buying, trading, and selling. It's her passion, her fun, and certainly her retirement income.

The first challenge a seller faces is figuring out the work's fair market value, i.e. what a willing buyer would pay a willing seller in the current market. That requires taking a long, hard, objective look at the work. You can search online auction databases like Artnet, as you did when you were buying, to come up with the fair market value. Be truthful with yourself and don't automatically think that yours is better than all others that sold. Advisors can be helpful by being objective in assessing what's sold at auction as compared to yours and telling you what private sales of similar works have taken place and whether the market for your artist is trending up or down. You don't want to sell low and learn a few months later that prices for the artist have tripled. Also be truthful in assessing the work's presentation. Selling a work of art is like selling a house; a little upgrading, like a new fence or a kitchen backsplash, can increase its salability. For paintings, a cleaning or a new frame can make a difference to the bottom line.

Deciding how to sell the work is a crucial step. Not long ago, I received an email from a collector which shows how fraught it is:

Suppose a friend of yours had a wonderful painting, say a Francis Bacon, that might fetch $30 to $40 million, and she was deciding how she might sell it. Would you advise her to select an advisor who can help establish a price or a dealer she respected and had experience in the field who would offer it privately and discreetly, or have a dealer exhibit it at an art fair and feed off the frenzy that accompanies those events, or consign it to an auction house that will display and promote it? I know there are pros and cons to each, but I'm interested in your learned and wise perspective on this so I can advise my friend.

I love this letter. It's so earnest and transparent. It reminded me of the off-color joke about the man who tells his doctor he's got a friend who may have gonorrhea, to which the doctor replies, "Take your friend out of your pants, and we'll have a look at him."

Of course, the "friend" in the email was the writer himself. The questions he asked were good ones, so, preserving the fiction, I told the writer to tell his 'friend" that sending the work to an art fair was a bad idea, because works at that price level usually don't sell at fairs. Besides, if a painting is seen at a fair and passed over by the world, it's no longer fresh on the market. Also, auctions didn't make sense unless he could get a guarantee, which I doubted would happen since it wasn't everyone's idea of a great Bacon. If he consigned with only a reserve, he risked it getting bought-in. That left the possibility of giving it to auction for private treaty or an advisor or dealer to sell. Unfortunately, my friend's "friend" didn't take my advice and not long after, the painting came up at auction without a guarantee. The picture failed to reach its $30 million reserve, and the owner had to take it home, where it probably will have to languish a few years before he can offer it again.

If you think that auction may be the way to sell your painting, email customer service departments or experts an image of the work along with a 'doc' sheet. If the material's desirable, you should be able to negotiate a great deal. If your work is extremely valuable but the house won't give you a guarantee, don't consign it. Tim, a friend, suffered worse consequences than my friend with the Bacon. In August 2008, he asked my advice in selling his entire contemporary art collection. I gave him the same spiel I gave my collector friend with a "friend," imploring him not to put the works in an auction without a guarantee. I went to the auction houses, and both offered a guarantee. Tim's lawyer informed me that having sat through at least a dozen auctions (that made him an expert?) he insisted that Tim consign everything without a guarantee. That way he wouldn't have to split the overage with the house.

Sadly, Tim followed his lawyer's advice and consigned his collection to the November 2008 auction with no guarantees. The market tanked in September, and the sale took place at the lowest point of the financial crash. Most of his paintings didn't sell, and the few that did brought low prices. It was tragic — and avoidable.

If the painting you're selling is less than fantastic, you won't have the option of a guarantee, though the auction houses may offer you an aggressive estimate to lure you in. It's natural to want to go with the house that offers you the highest estimate, but compare other concessions they're willing to make, like waiving the seller's premium, or offering you trade terms. Other factors should affect your decision, such as the number of works already consigned by your artist. If there are others better than yours, it's likely yours won't do well. If other good works by other artists have been signed up for 'your' sale, that bodes well. Great estate material or a consignment from someone famous attracts attention and pumps up the pre-sale interest on everything in the sale. Lackluster material will bring the energy and prices down. Many savvy consignors would rather go with the house that has better things signed up even if the competing house offers better terms.

Don't be disappointed to learn that once your work is signed, sealed, and delivered, the house may stop making promises and start retracting them. They often come to consignors and tell them that they've looked more carefully at the work, or the market has shifted and the estimate and reserve they gave you are too high. Their goal is to have low estimates on every lot so that the prices realized will be higher than the printed estimate. As I've mentioned, day-after-the-sale headlines reading "Record Sale Doubles Estimate!" make the auction house and the art market look good. Therefore, once you're hooked, they may ask you to lower the estimate and reserve with lines like, "The market's shaky right now," or "The painting's in worse condition than we thought." The house may also try to convince you that lower estimates attract more bidders. A lot of people go along with that. But then, a few days before the sale, don't be surprised if the house asks you to lower the reserve again.

If you've looked at the databases and/or know what the auction houses think your painting is worth and want to explore the dealer route, you're ready to have an educated conversation. Choose a dealer who has experience in selling works by your artist. Ask what he'd pay outright or, if he took it on consignment, what your minimum net would be, what he'd ask for it, and what percentage he'd expect for himself.

Let's say that a dealer wants to buy your nice but not great Lichtenstein painting of an apple, one of a series by the artist, and offers you $300,000. You agree, and he buys it outright. Whatever he gets above that is his. That's fine for many collectors. Others want sellers to work on a percentage. And still others want to participate in the upside, as a form of "schmuck" insurance. That way he safeguards against a seller making multiples of what he makes, and feeling like a schmuck.

On rare occasion, you may hear of a dealer running away with consignors' money, so insure your work on your own policy or have the seller insure it and send you a copy in which you're named as loss payee. When private dealer Michel Cohen disappeared in 2001, he owed between 40 and 100 million dollars to some pretty savvy dealers, including Ernst Beyeler, for works they gave him to sell. Cohen had been in the business a long time, he was a good dealer, but apparently in the wake of the 2000 dot.com bust, he needed money to cover market losses. He also sold shares in paintings multiple times. For example, he sold a half share of a Monet to a New York dealer and 100% to a London dealer. He went on the lam but was caught and imprisoned in Rio. While awaiting extradition, he escaped and is still missing.

In 2010, Larry Salander, a respected American Art dealer, pleaded guilty to a number of different crimes, including not paying consignors for works he sold. All told, this group was out $120 million. Salander did one better than Cohen and sold shares in works of art that didn't exist, which reminds me of the way Max Bialystock in Mel Brooks' *The Producers* sold more than 100% of the stock in a play, sure it would flop and he wouldn't have to return any money. The most painful part was that Salander scammed friends, and the heirs to many artists' estates, including Stuart Davis, Elie Nadelman, and Robert De Niro's father, a painter — all of whom he'd dealt with for years. Although the risk of anything going wrong like that is small, you can take steps to make sure that doesn't happen. You can send your painting to your own account at a warehouse, give a seller access to show it there, and release it only after you're paid.

Unscrupulous dealers also do something that may not be grand larceny but it's plenty annoying; they 'shop' your painting by e-mailing a photo of it to other dealers and collectors. In no time, your painting goes viral and is no longer fresh on the market. Collectors lament all the time that within days of sending a photo to a dealer, they're offered their own work by other dealers.

One last suggestion (and you knew this was coming) — your art advisor can be a valuable piece of manpower when it comes to selling. If consigning to auction sounds complicated, and it is, an advisor, who's been through it many times, can help you avoid the pitfalls and negotiate terms you never thought possible. And if auction seems too risky or too public, or you need to sell quickly and can't wait for the next round of sales, your advisor will explore other avenues — auction "private treaty" sale, consigning or selling to a dealer, or selling straight to another collector. Advisors know which way your work will sell better. They're familiar with all the players, they know what to expect from them, and how to push their buttons.

Everyone will need an exit strategy someday, and when that time comes, it can be an extremely emotional experience. Once, after a long, hard negotiation, a client who was selling a painting he inherited from his grandfather called asking for "one more thing." I was worried he was going to blow the deal, but all he wanted was to take his family to the warehouse where the painting was being held to say goodbye. After all, he said, letting go of the work was like losing a family member. When that time comes for you, should you find yourself a little teary-eyed, remember that it's better to have loved and sold than never to have loved at all.

CONCLUSION

ART DELIVERS. Despite admonitions about its pitfalls and dangers, the art world offers unlimited pleasure to its participants. I've written this book to demystify this serpentine world and make it easier for you to traverse as an observer or collector, I've encouraged you to get deeper involved in the art world, and if you feel less intimidated and more comfortable in knowing how the art world works and how its players operate, I've accomplished what I set out to do.

Everyone's reasons for collecting are different. For some, the end game is nothing more than owning a few nice paintings to enhance their home. For others, collecting offers escapism, an opportunity to leave their day-to-day lives behind. For still others, the satisfaction comes from the thrill of the chase, the status that owning art confers, or the leg-up in society collecting provides. And even if they don't need it, many find the possibility of making a financial killing irresistible. At the very least, almost everyone responds to the intellectual challenge, enjoys meeting fascinating people, and is enchanted by the art itself. If you buy art prudently, you're not only making a good investment in dollars and cents, you're making an important investment in yourself.

I couldn't sum it up any better than John Medveckis, a Philadelphia collector, who, with tears in his eyes, described how collecting changed his life. "Without the journey collecting has taken me on, the intellectual stimulation, and the people I've met along the way, I wouldn't be half the person I am today." Collecting can be the same for you.

My own journey has been much like John's. My life has been enriched by art, the world of art, and my experiences. No matter what happens tomorrow, thanks to my life in art, I'm ahead of the game.

ILLUSTRATIONS

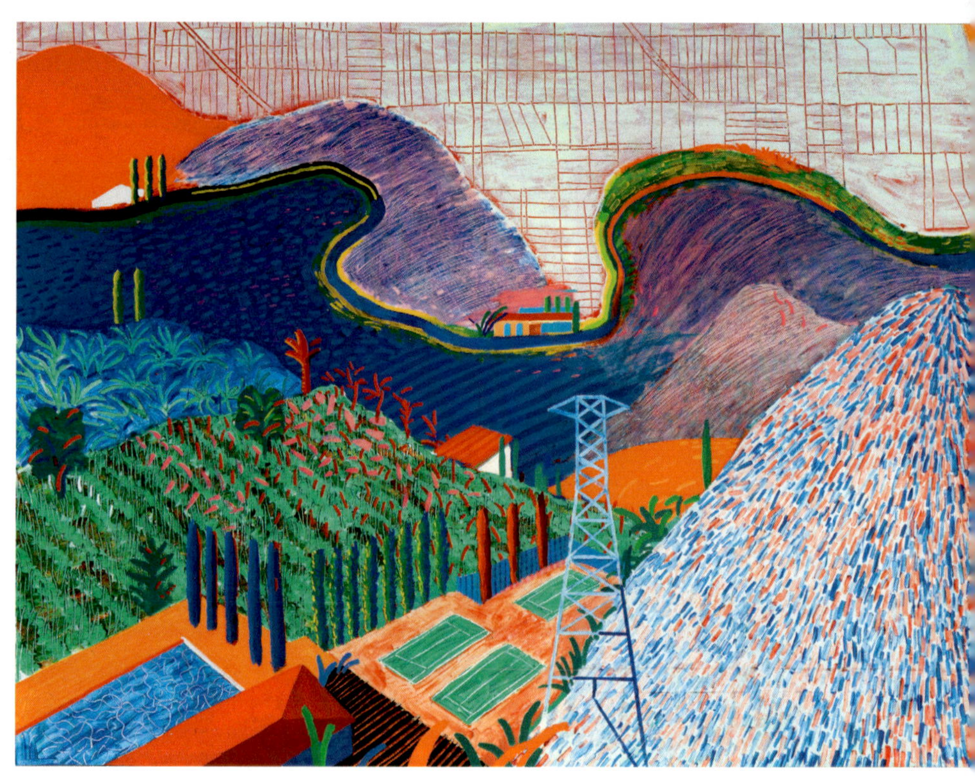

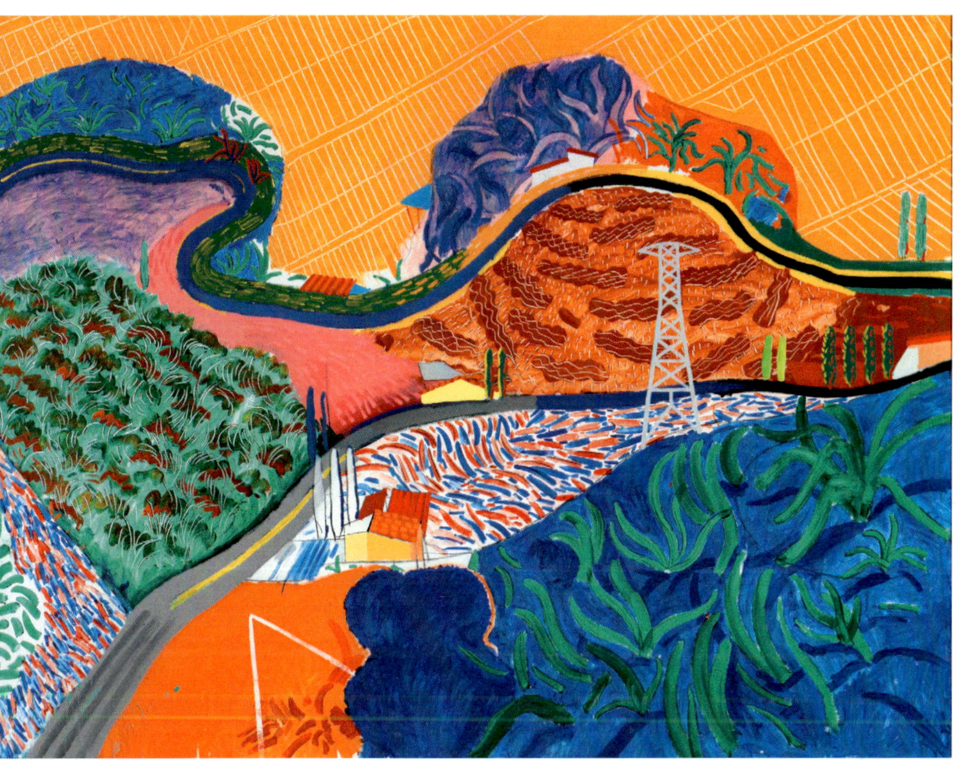

ill. 1
David Hockney (1937-)
Mulholland Drive: The Road to the Studio
1980 Acrylic on canvas 86 x 243" (218.5 x 617 cm)

Collection Los Angeles County Museum of Art (LACMA)
Photo: Richard Schmidt

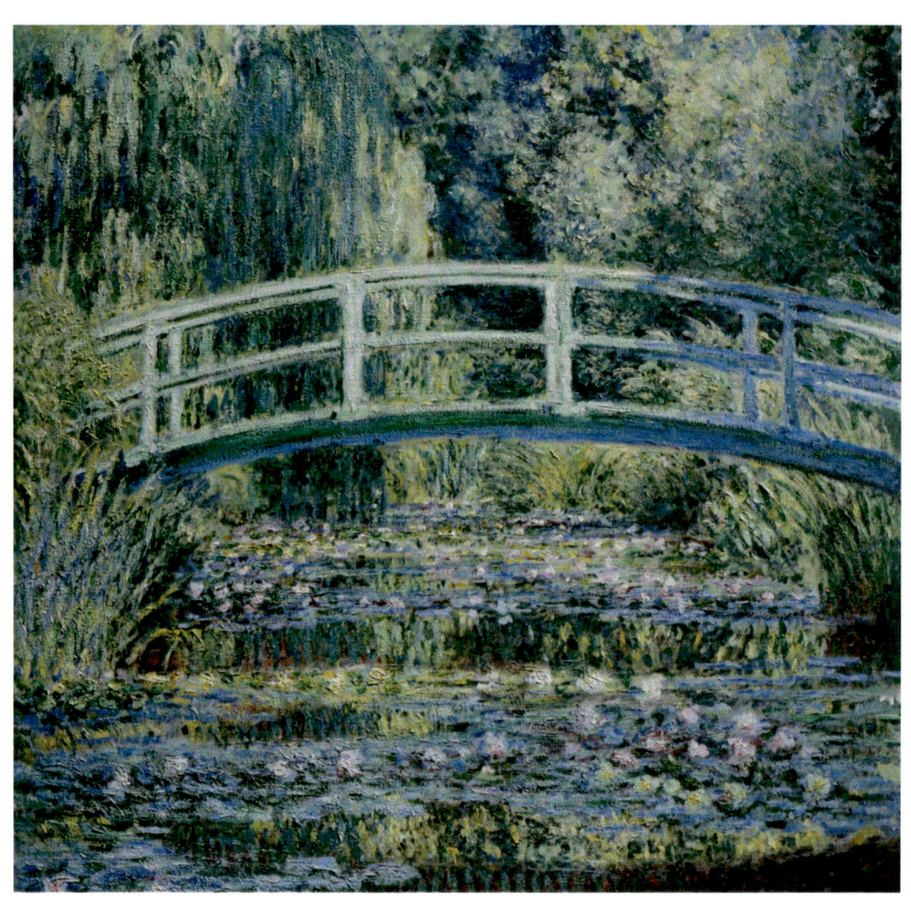

ill. 2
Claude Monet (1840-1926)
Water Lilies and Japanese Bridge
1899 Oil on canvas 35.625 x 35.25" (90.5 x 89.7 cm)
Princeton University Art Museum / Art Resource, NY

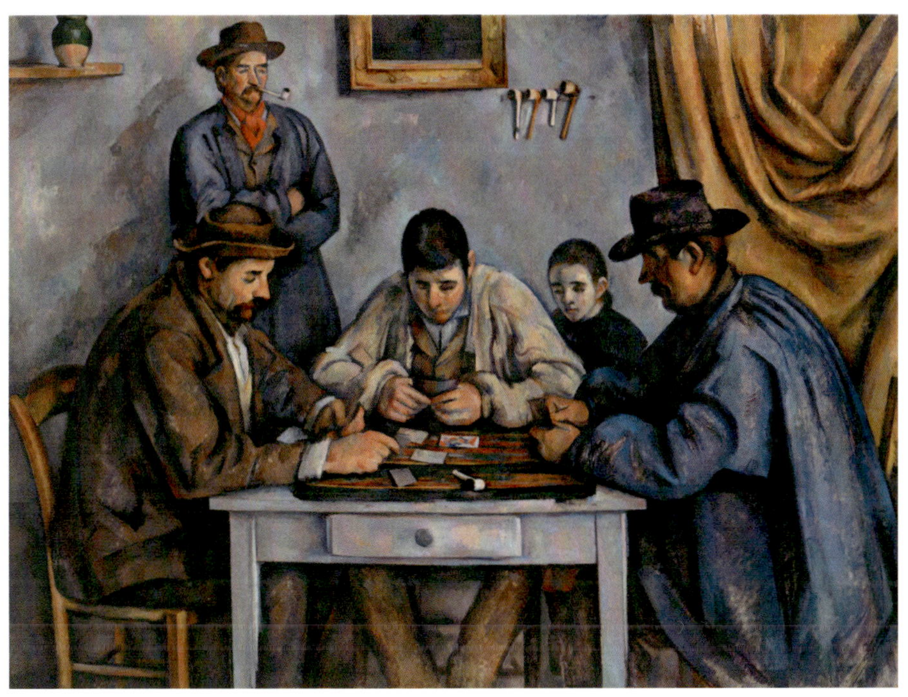

ill. 3
Paul Cézanne (1839-1906)
The Card Players
1890-92 Oil on canvas 53.25 x 71.625" (135.3 x 181.9 cm)
The Barnes Foundation/ Bridgeman Images

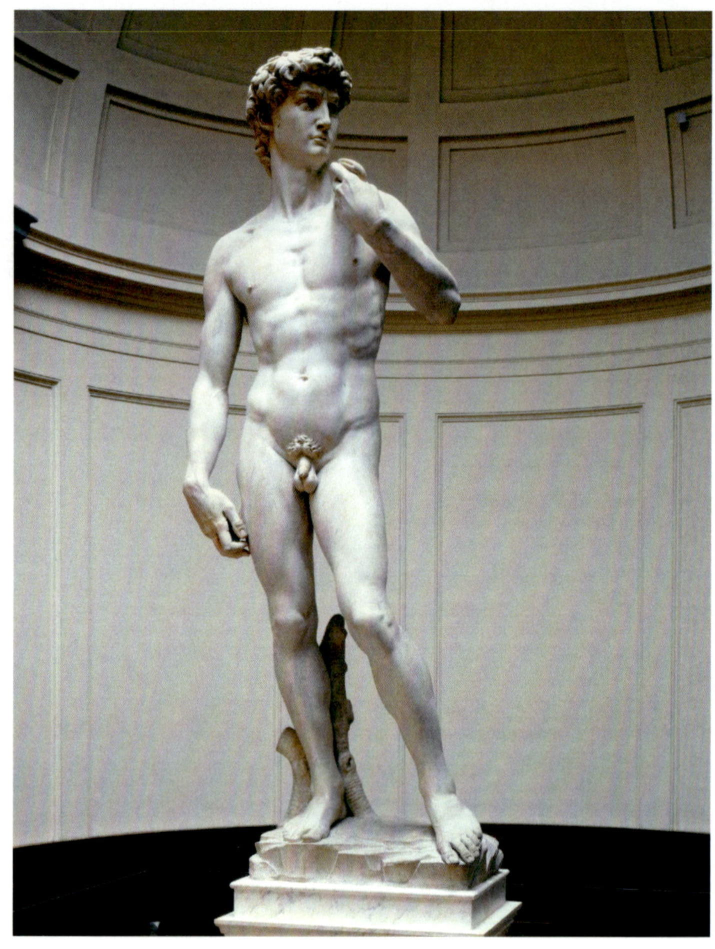

ill. 4
Michelangelo Buonarroti (1475-1564)
David
1501-1504 Marble 17' (5.17 m)
Scala/Ministero per i Bene e le Attività culturali / Art Resource, NY

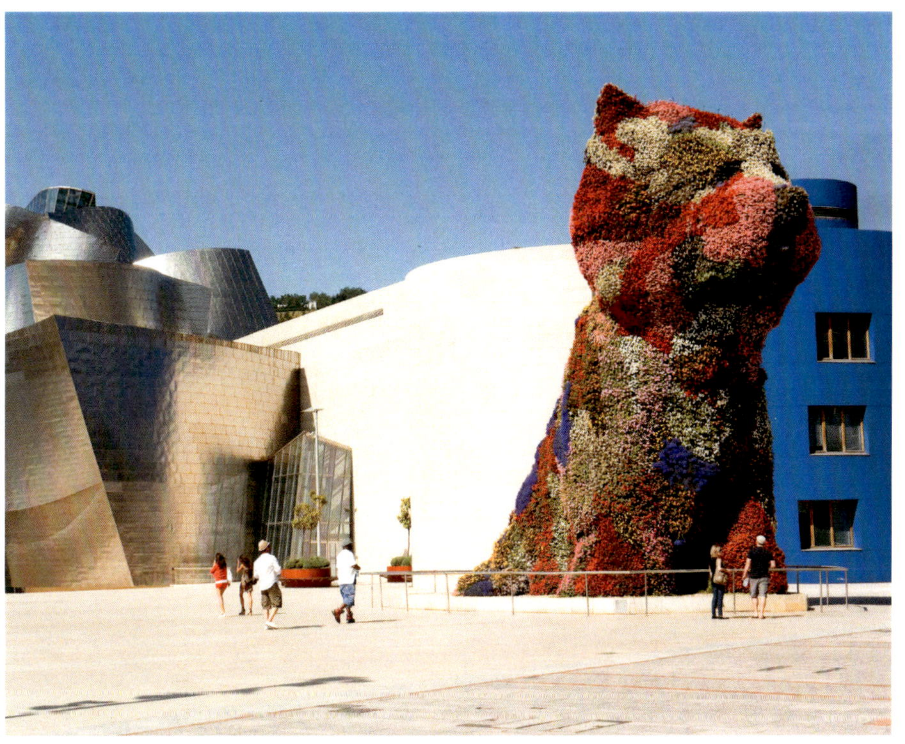

ill. 5
Jeff Koons (1955-)
Puppy
1992 Stainless steel, soil, geotextile fabric, internal irrigation system, and live flowering plants 486 x 486 x 256" (1234.4 x 1234.4 x 650.2 cm)

Photo: Erika Barahona Ede

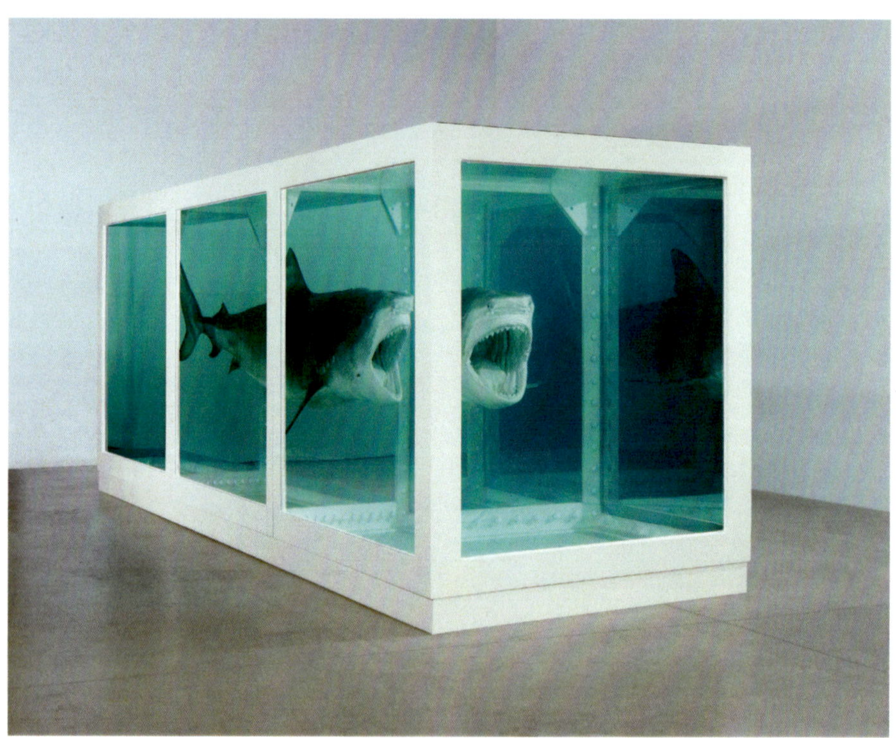

ill. 6
Damien Hirst (1965-)
The Physical Impossibility of Death in the Mind of Someone Living
1991 (three-quarter view)
Glass, painted steel, silicone, monofilament, shark and formaldehyde solution
85.375 x 213.375 x 70.875 " (217 x 542 x 180 cm)

Photo: Prudence Cuming Associates Ltd
VIII

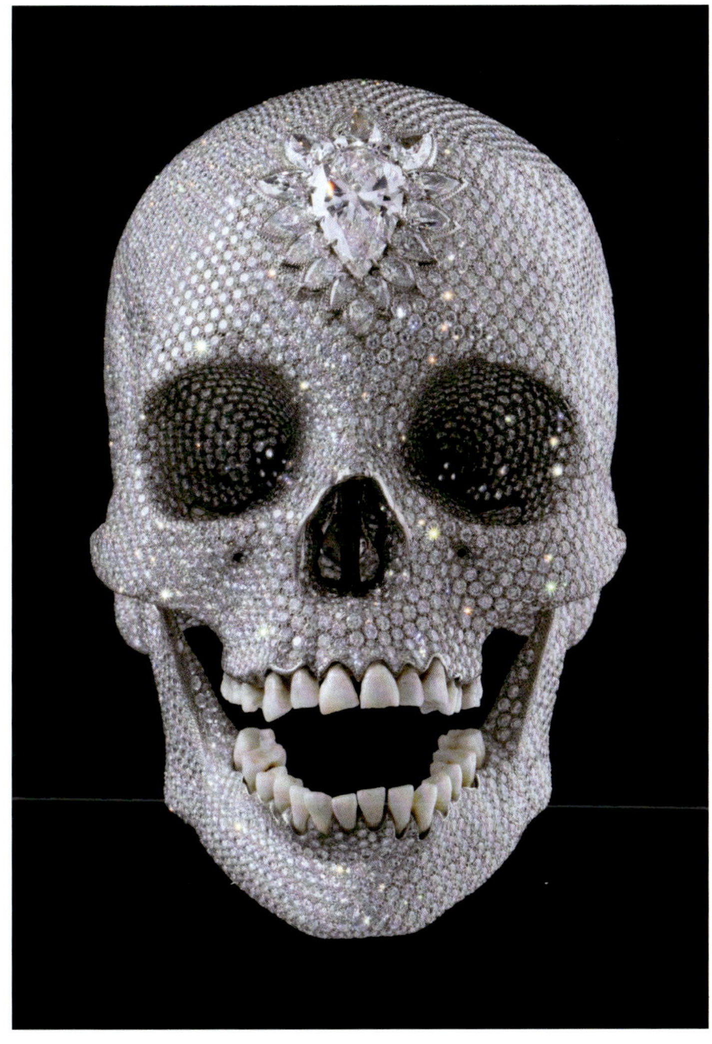

ill. 7
Damien Hirst (1965-)
For the Love of God
2007 Platinum, diamonds and human teeth 6 .75 x 5 x 7.5" (17.1 x 12.7 x 19.1cm)

Photo: Prudence Cuming Associates Ltd.

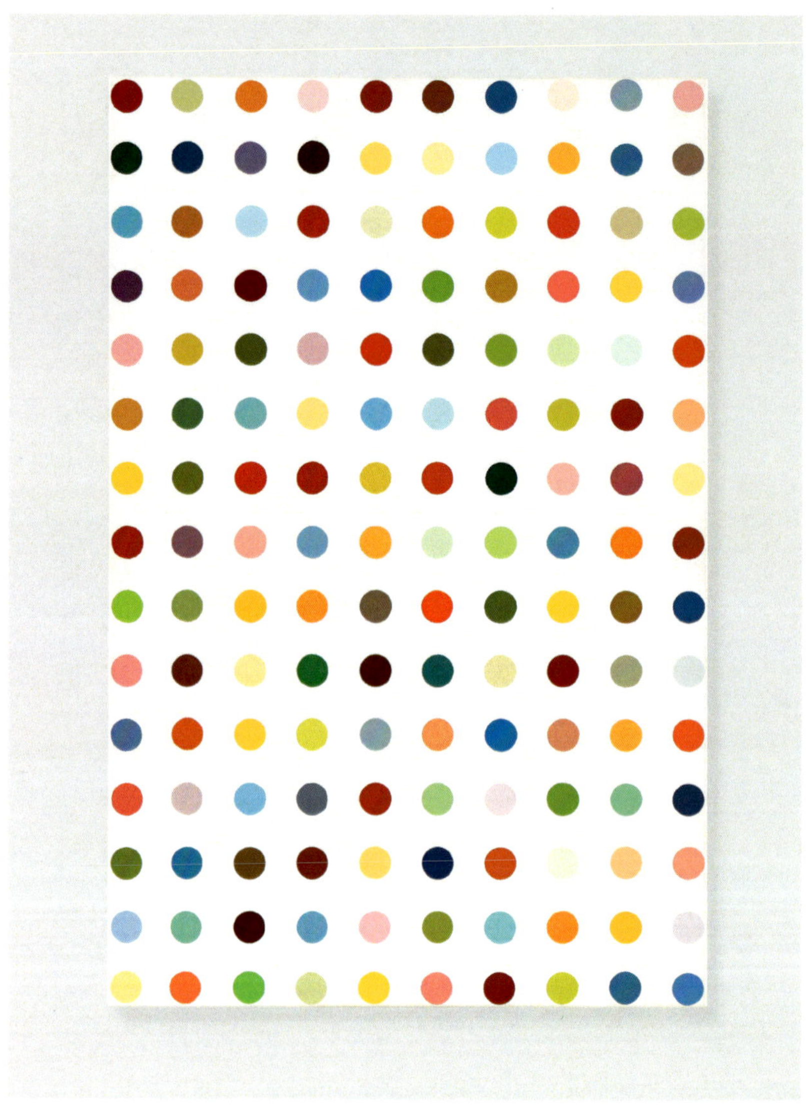

ill. 8
Damien Hirst (1965-)
Notechis Ater Niger
2000 Household gloss on canvas 29 x 19" (73.7 x 48.3 cm)

Photo: Prudence Cuming Associates Ltd.

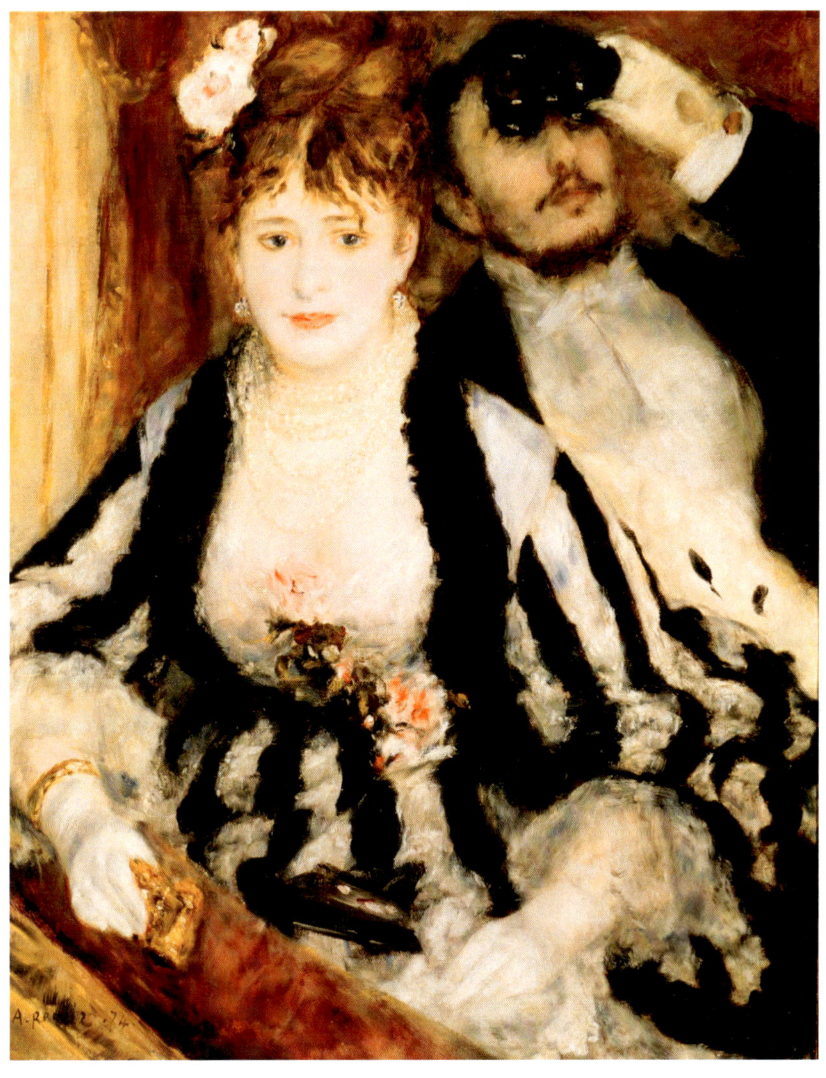

ill. 9
Pierre-Auguste Renoir (1841-1919)
La Loge (The Theater Box)
1874 Oil on canvas 31 x 24" (80 x 64 cm)
Scala / Art Resource, NY

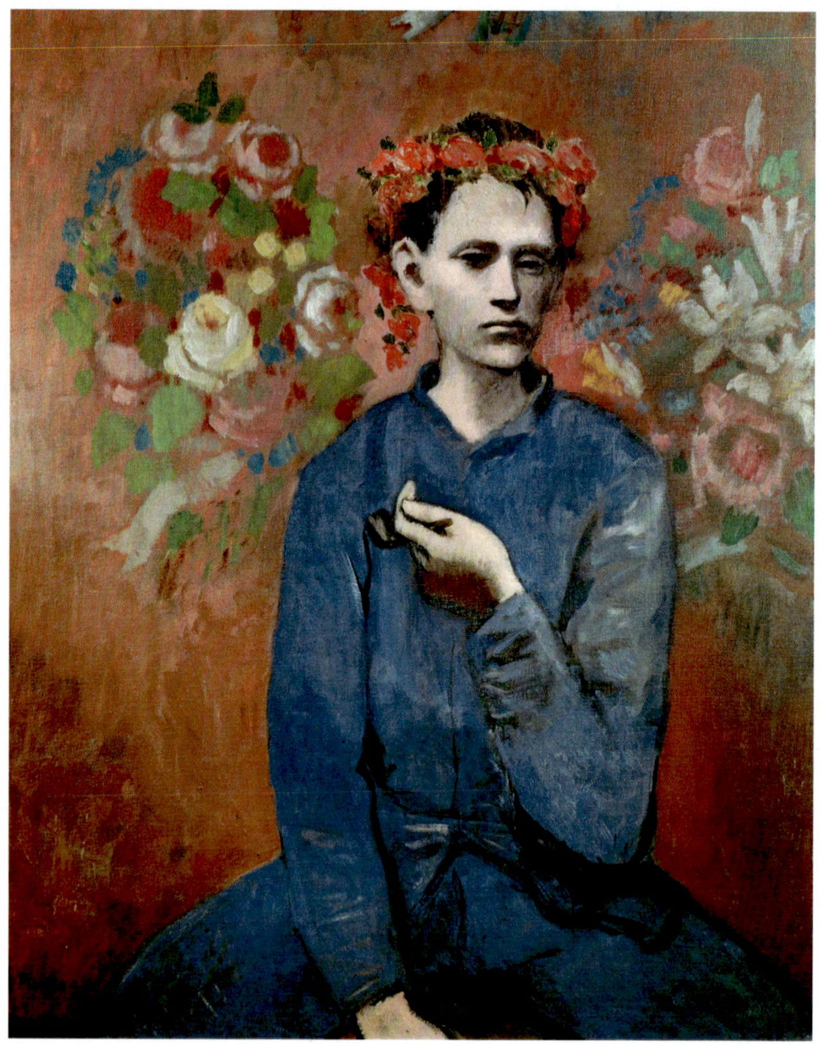

ill. 10
Pablo Picasso (1881-1973)
Garçon à la Pipe (Boy with a Pipe)
1905 Oil on canvas 39.3 x 31.8" (100 x 81 cm)

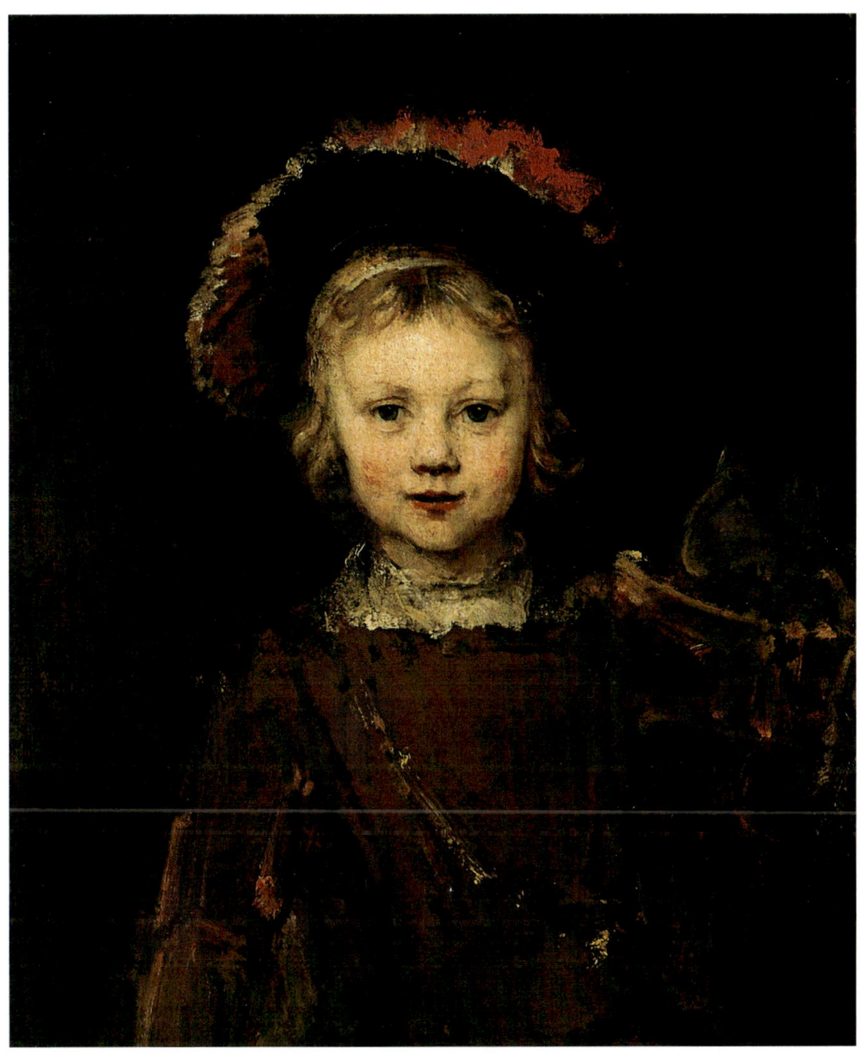

ill. 11
Rembrandt van Rijn (1606-1669)
Portrait of a Boy
1655-60 Oil on canvas 25.5 x 22" (64.8 x 55.9 cm)
The Norton Simon Foundation

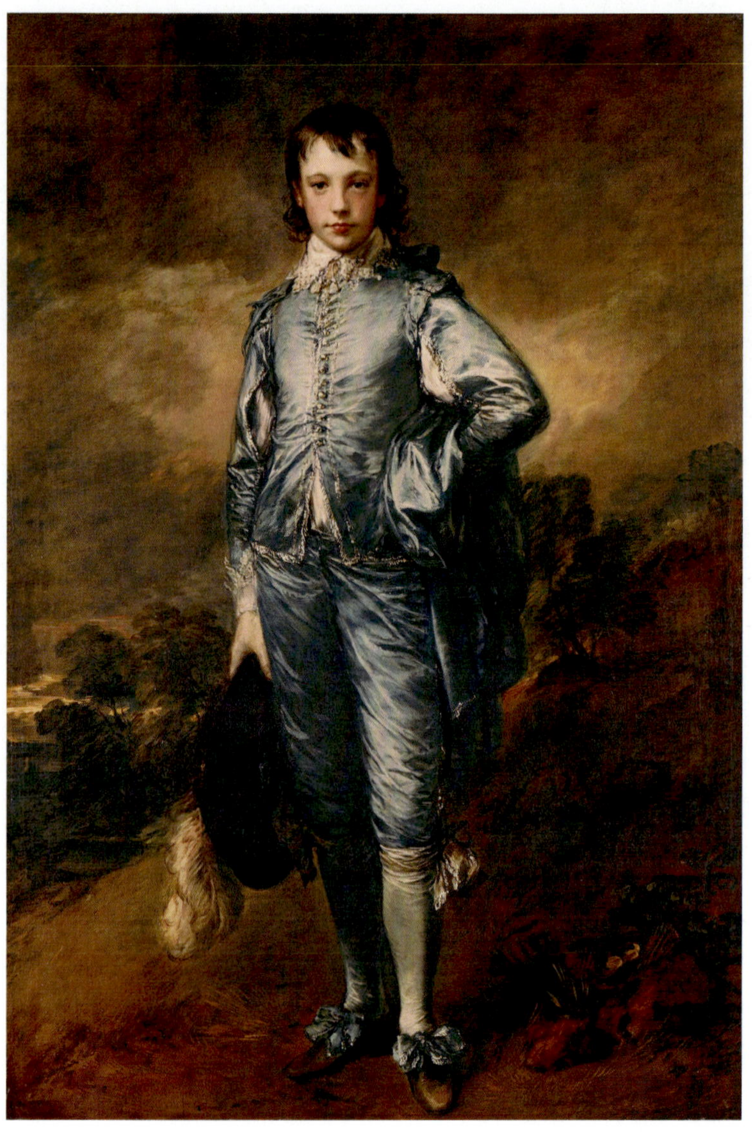

ill. 12
Thomas Gainsborough (1727-1788)
The Blue Boy
1770 Oil on canvas 70 x 44" (178 x 122 cm)
bpk, Berlin / Art Resource, NY

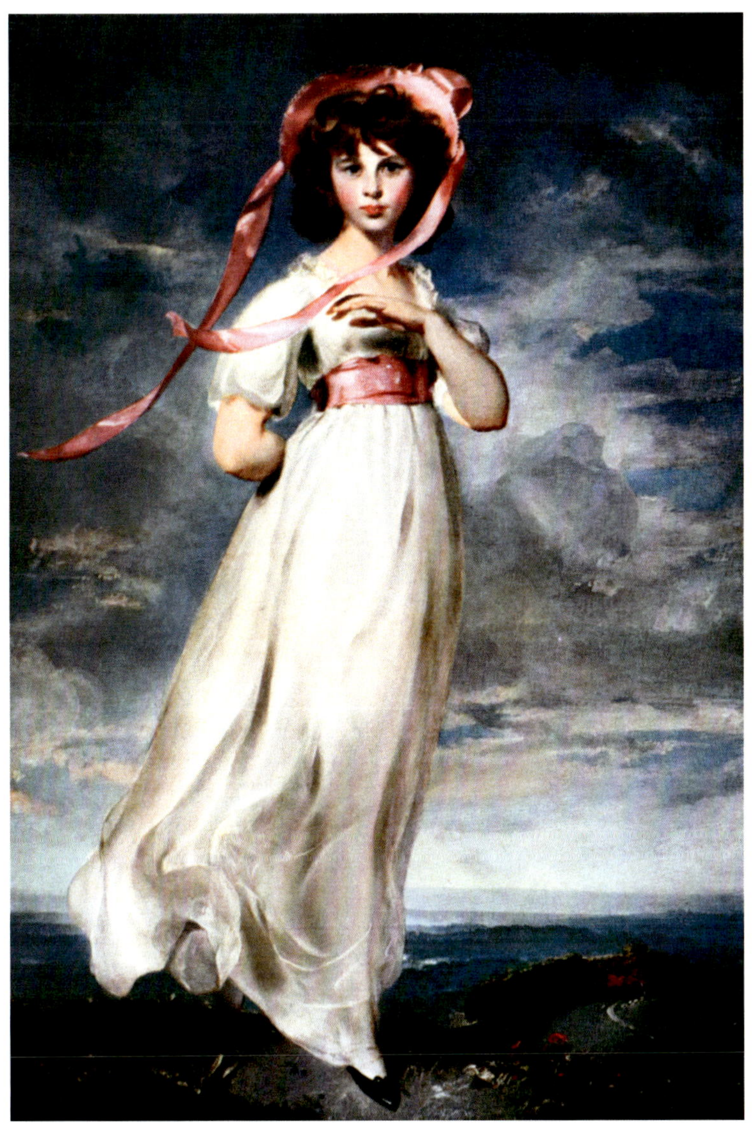

ill. 13
Thomas Lawrence (1769-1830)
Sarah Barrett Moulton: Pinkie
1794 Oil on canvas 57" x 39" (146 x 100 cm)
HIP / Art Resource, NY

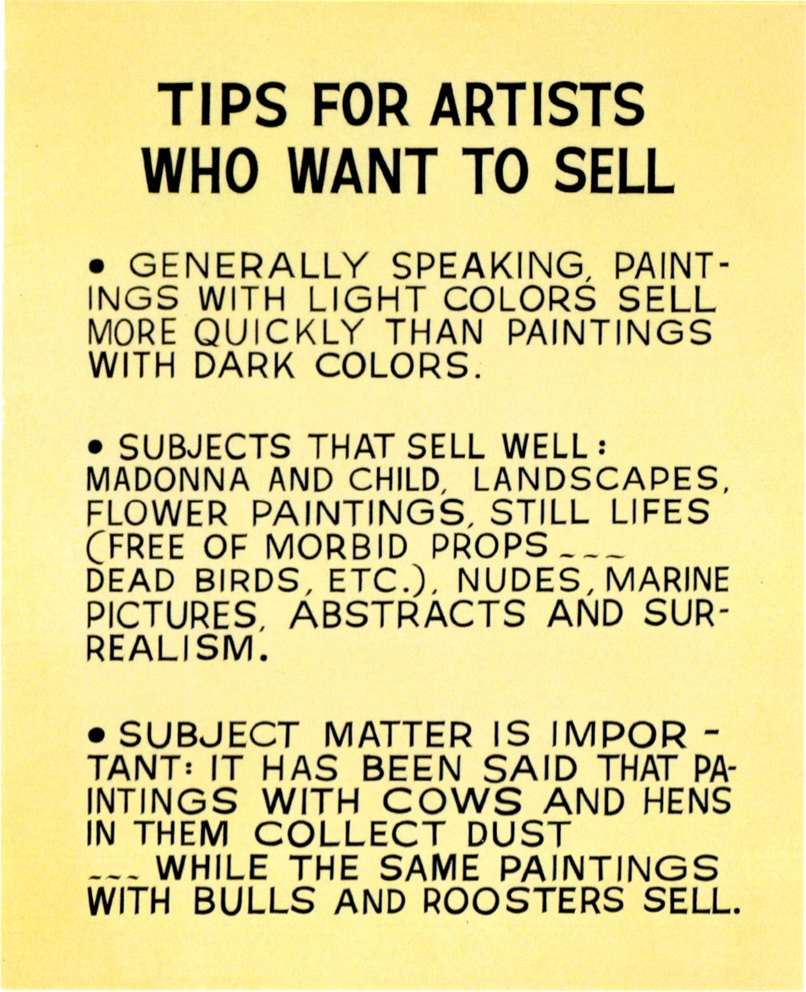

TIPS FOR ARTISTS
WHO WANT TO SELL

• GENERALLY SPEAKING, PAINTINGS WITH LIGHT COLORS SELL MORE QUICKLY THAN PAINTINGS WITH DARK COLORS.

• SUBJECTS THAT SELL WELL: MADONNA AND CHILD, LANDSCAPES, FLOWER PAINTINGS, STILL LIFES (FREE OF MORBID PROPS --- DEAD BIRDS, ETC.), NUDES, MARINE PICTURES, ABSTRACTS AND SURREALISM.

• SUBJECT MATTER IS IMPORTANT: IT HAS BEEN SAID THAT PAINTINGS WITH COWS AND HENS IN THEM COLLECT DUST --- WHILE THE SAME PAINTINGS WITH BULLS AND ROOSTERS SELL.

ill. 14
John Baldessari (1931-)
Tips for Artists Who Want to Sell
1966-68 Acrylic on canvas 68 x 56.5" (172.72 x 143.5 cm)
The Broad Art Foundation, Santa Monica
Image courtesy of the artist and Marian Goodman Gallery

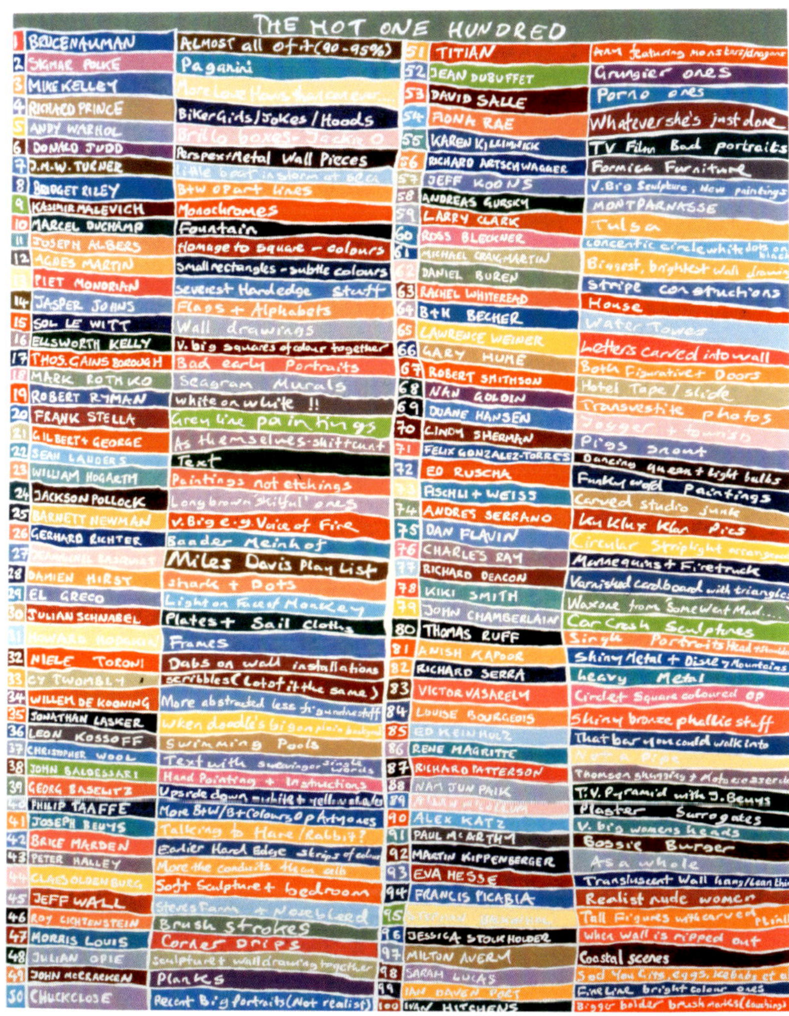

ill. 15
Peter Davies (1970-)
The Hot One Hundred
1997 Acrylic on canvas 100 x 80" (254 x 203.2 cm)
© Peter Davies, 1997
Image courtesy of the Saatchi Gallery, London

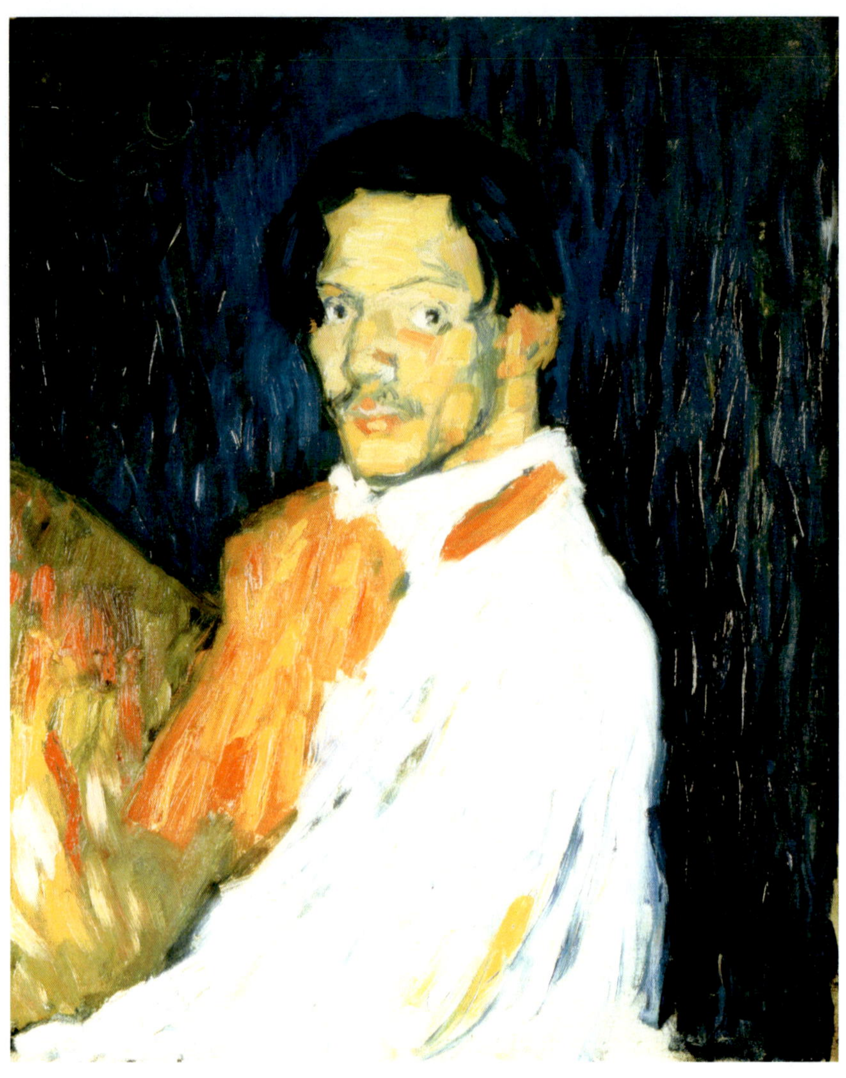

ill. 16
Pablo Picasso (1881-1973)
Yo, Picasso (Self-Portrait)
1901 Oil on canvas 29 x 23.875" (73.5 x 60.5 cm)

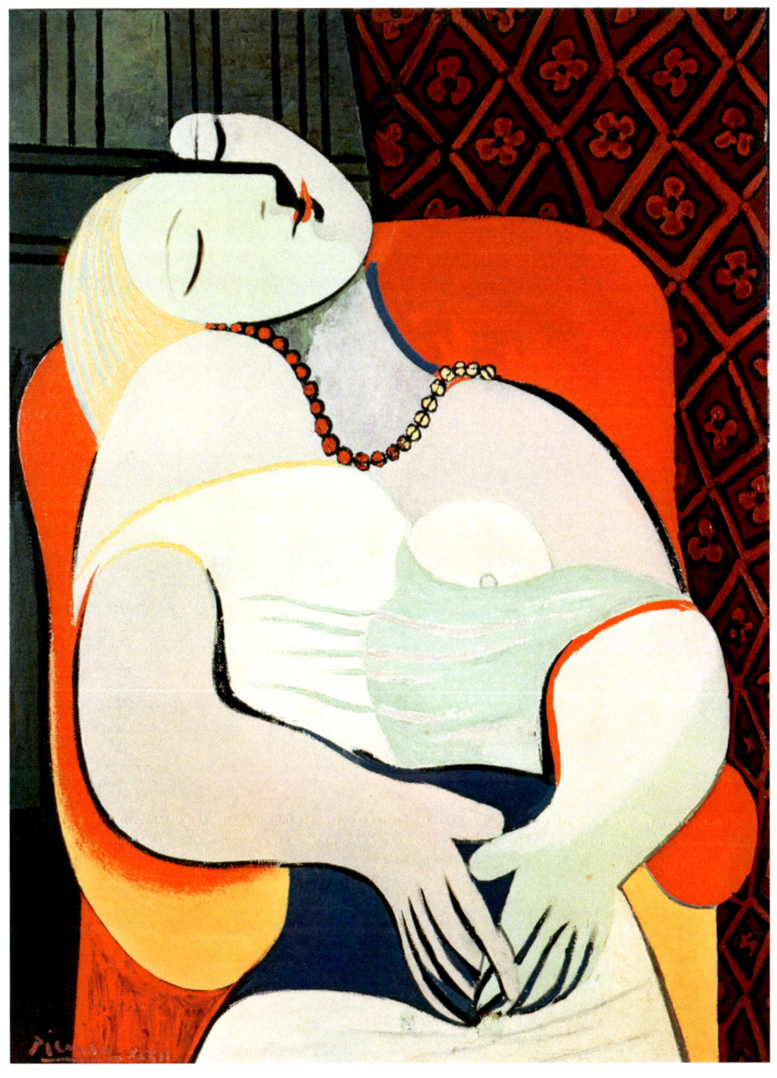

ill. 17
Pablo Picasso (1881-1973)
Le Rêve (The Dream)
1932 Oil on canvas 51 x 38" (130 x 97 cm)
© 2014 Estate of Pablo Picasso / Artists Rights Society (ARS), New York / Bridgeman Images

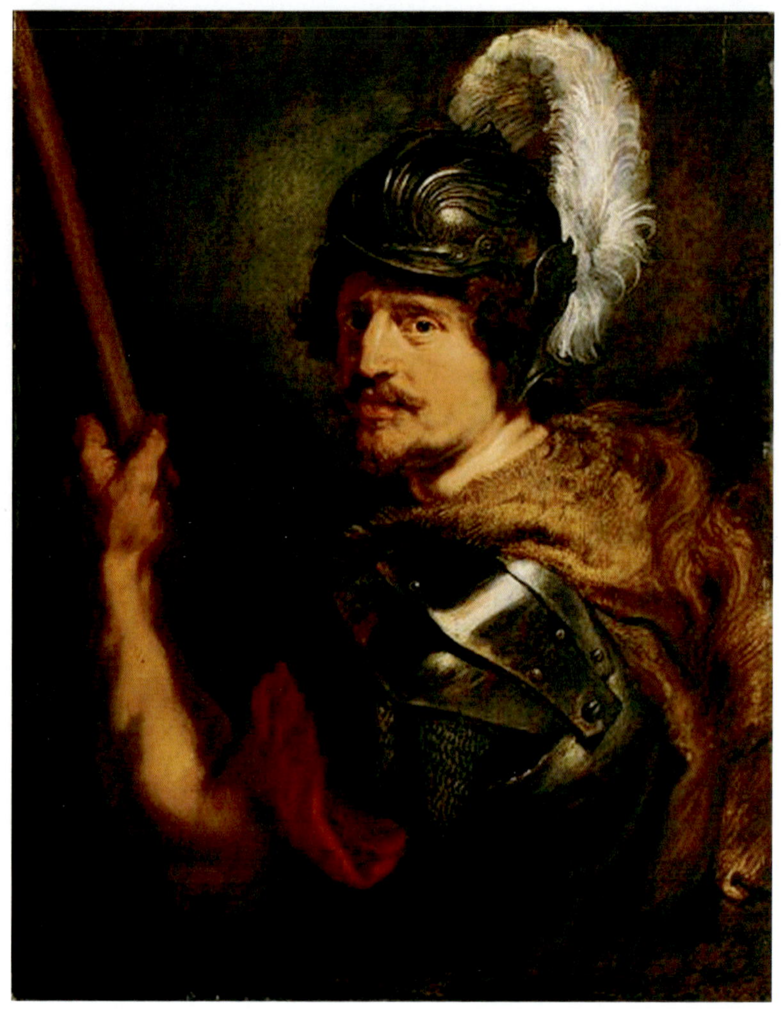

ill. 18
Peter Paul Rubens (1577-1640)
Portrait of a Man as the God Mars
Circa 1620 Oil on canvas 32.5 x 26" (82.6 x 66 cm)
Image courtesy of the Art Renewal Center – www.artrenewal.org

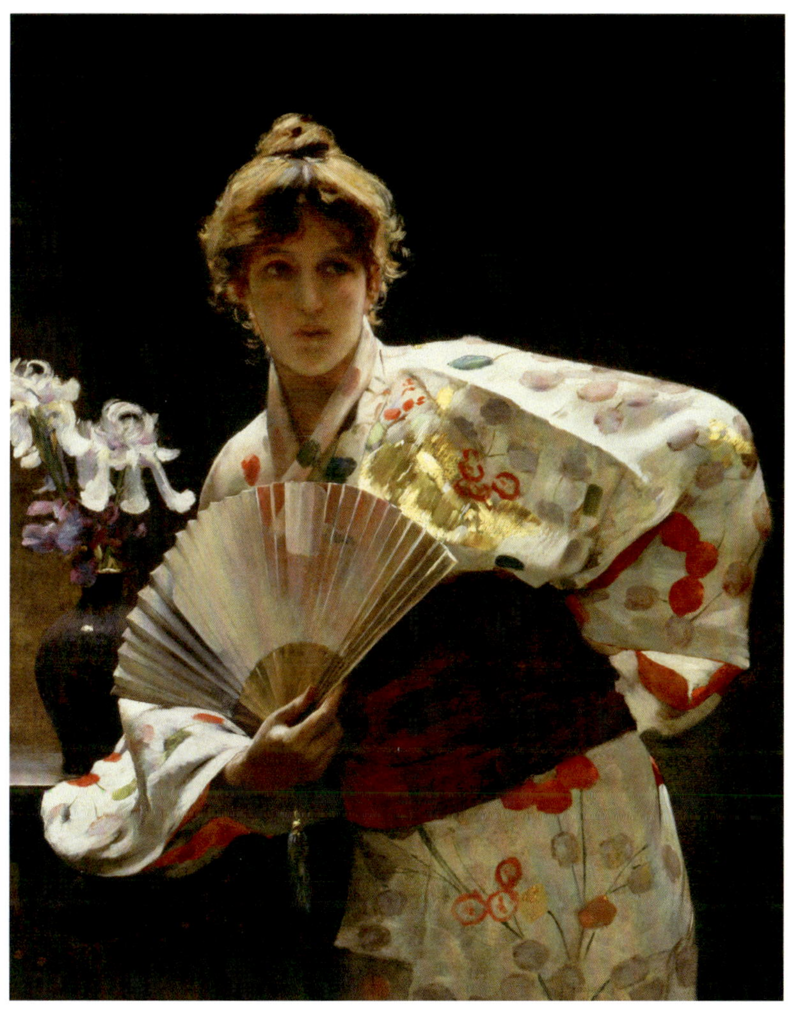

ill. 19
Charles Sprague Pearce (1851-1914)
Lady with a Fan
1883 Oil on canvas 27.75 x 22.5" (70.5 cm x 57.2 cm)
Image courtesy of Marie Halff

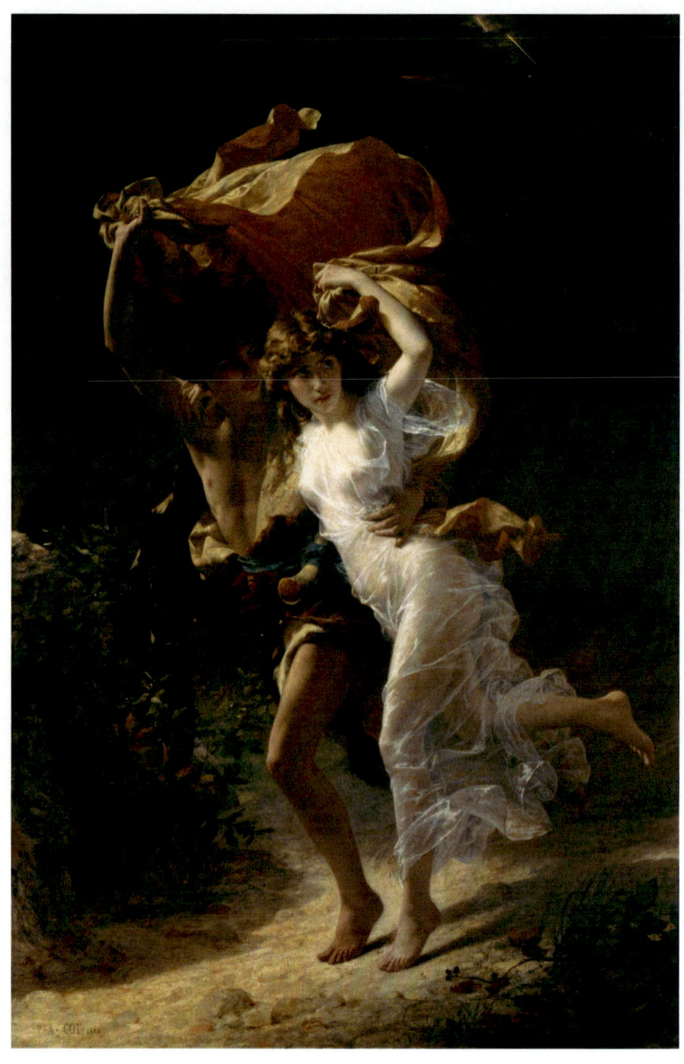

ill. 20
Pierre August Cot (1837-1883)
The Storm
1880 Oil on canvas 92.25 x 61.75" (234.3 x 156.8 cm)

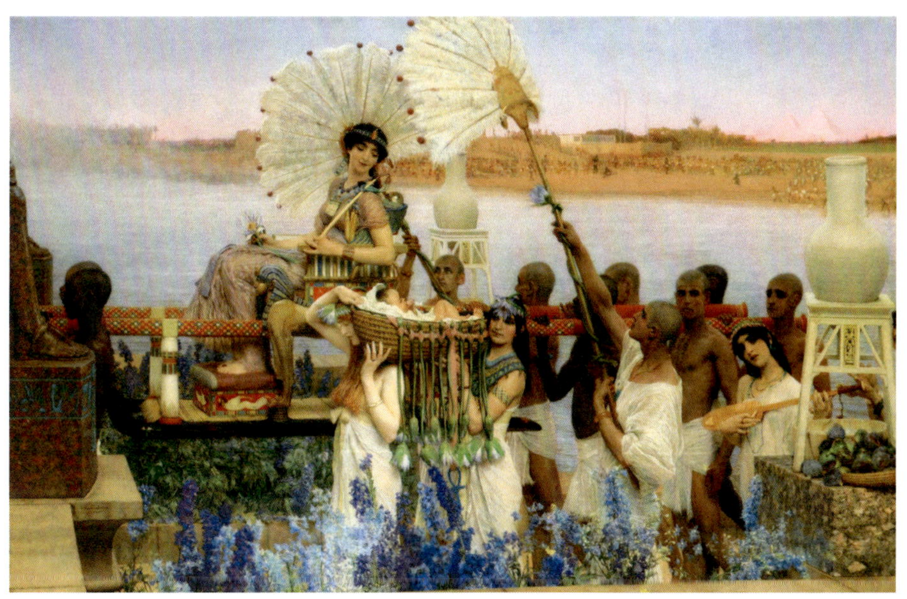

ill. 21
Sir Lawrence Alma-Tadema (1836-1912)
The Finding of Moses
1904 Oil on canvas 54.13 x 84.02" (137.5 x 213.4 cm)
Image courtesy of the Art Renewal Center – www.artrenewal.org

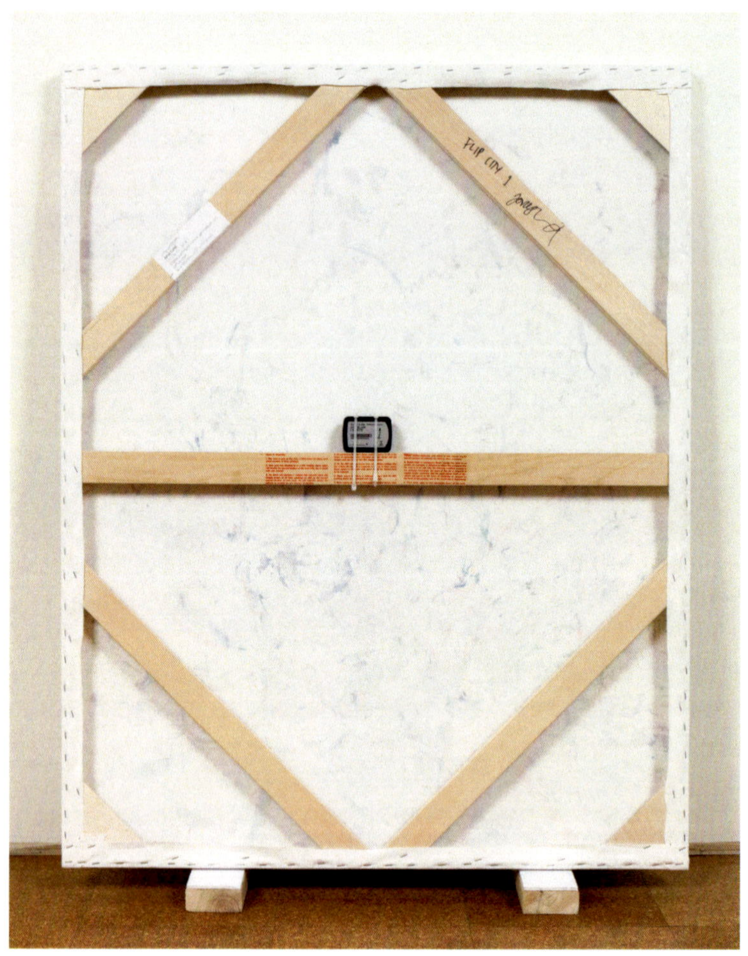

ill. 22
Jonas Lund (1984-)
Flip City 01
2014 Digital painting on canvas, gel medium and GPS tracker, 50 x 40" (127 x 101.6 cm)
Image courtesy of the artist and Steve Turner, Los Angeles
Photo: Don Lewis

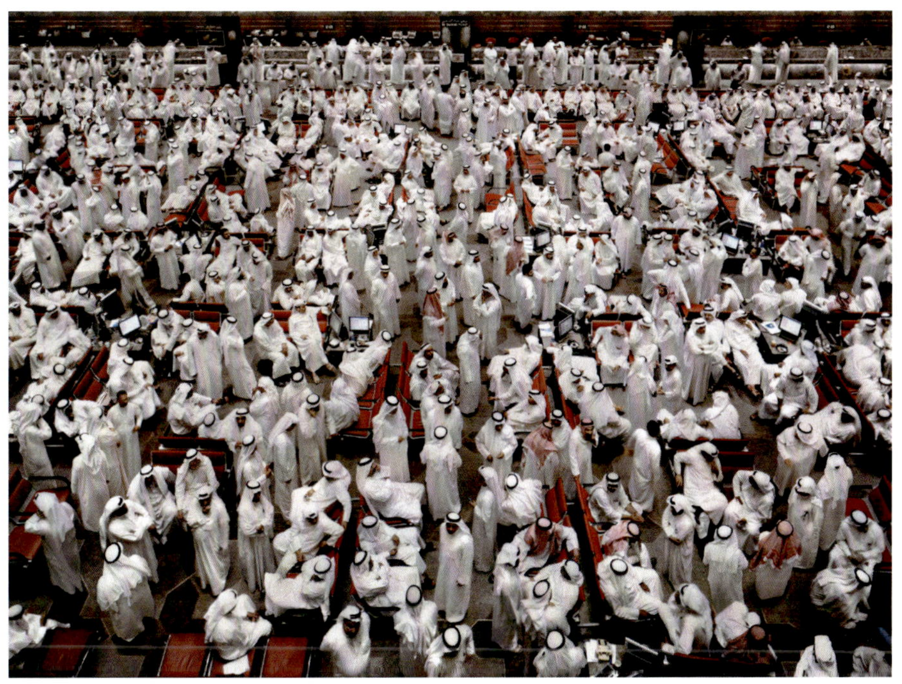

ill. 23
Andreas Gursky (1955-)
Kuwait Stock Exchange II
2008 91 x 120.8" (231.5 x 307 cm)

Image courtesy of Matthew Marks Gallery, New York and Monika Sprüth / Philomene Magers, Cologne/Munich

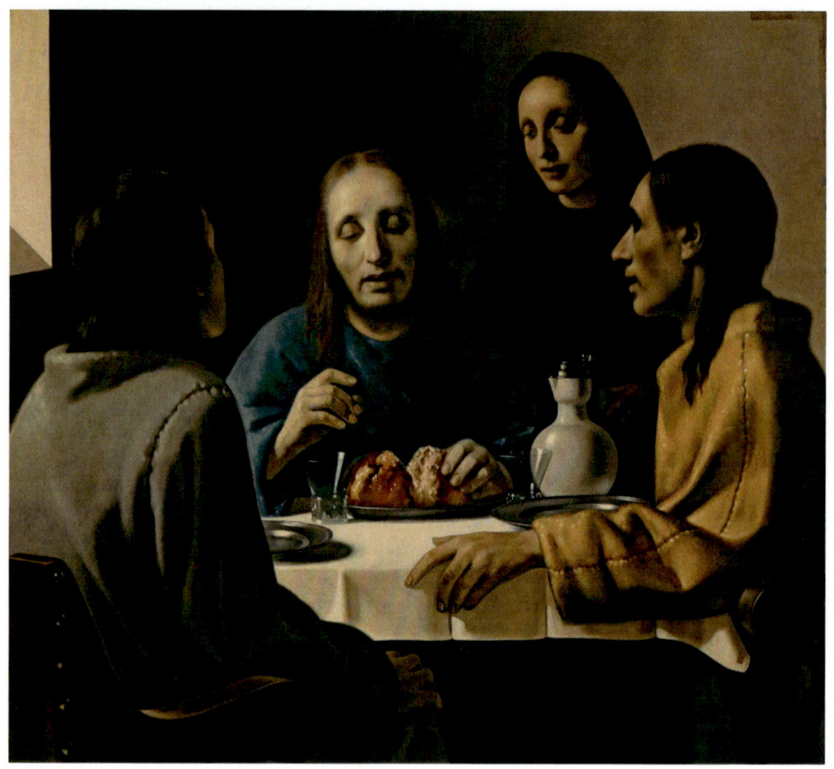

ill. 24
Han van Meegeren (1889-1947)
The Men at Emmaus
1936 Oil on canvas 46.5 x 51" (118 x 130.5 cm)
Museum Boijmans Van Bueningen, Rotterdam
Loan Museum Boijman Van Beuningen Foundation
Photo: Studio Tromp, Rotterdam

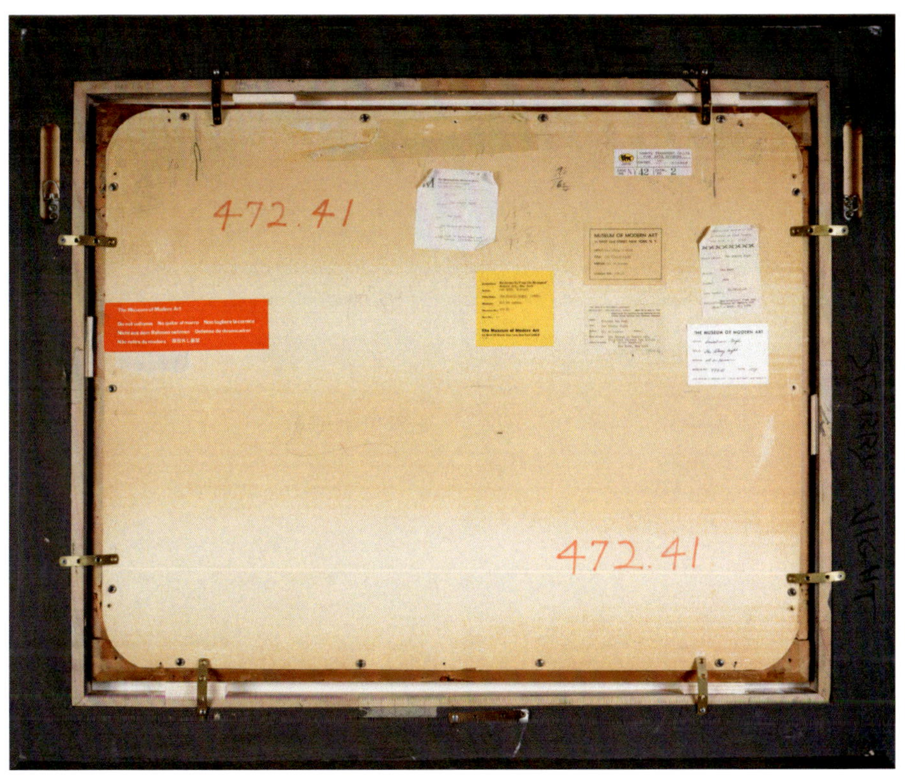

ill. 25
Viz Muniz (1961-)
Verso (Starry Night)
2008 Mixed media object 29 x 36.25 x 12" (73.6 cm x 92 cm x 30.5 cm)
Art © Vik Muniz/Licensed by VAGA, New York, NY

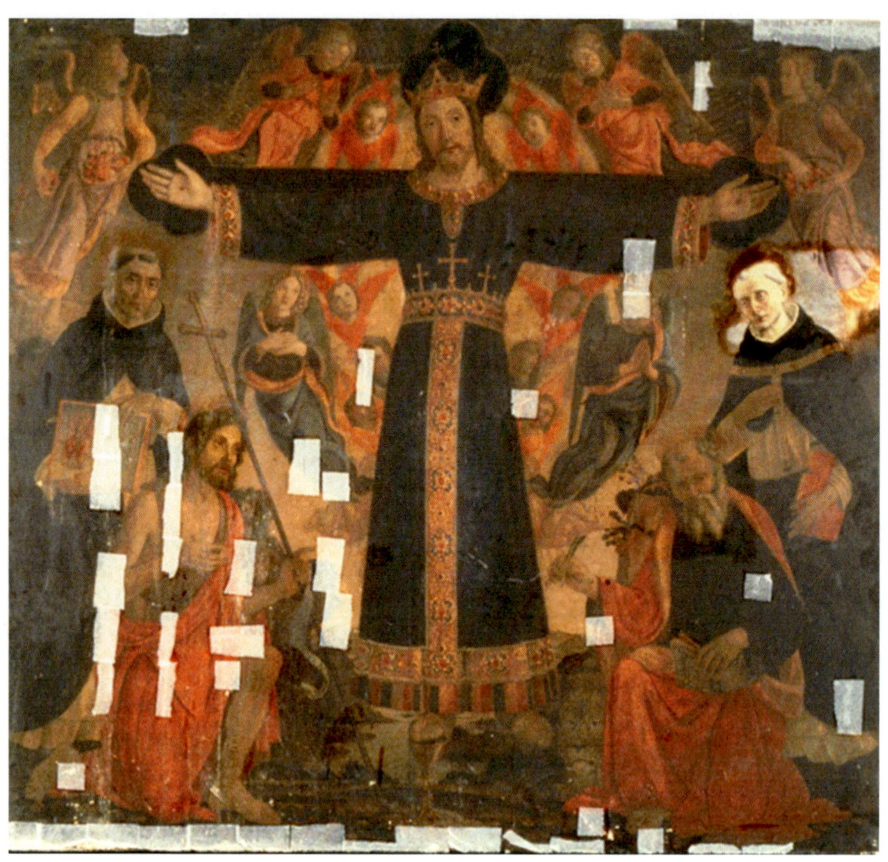

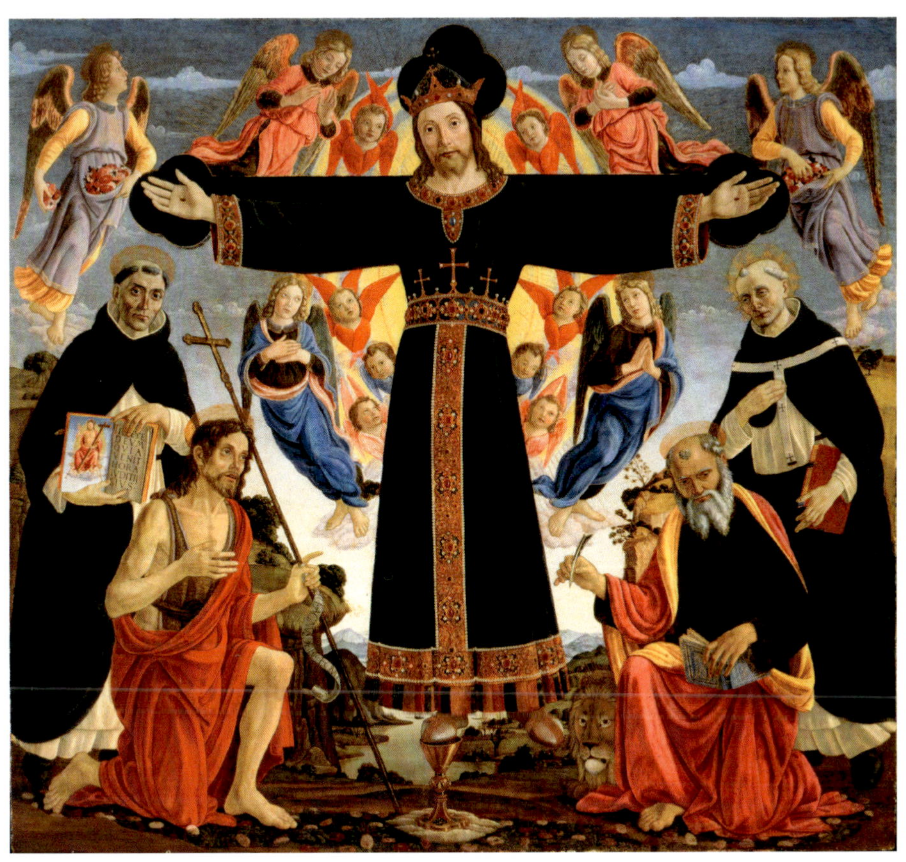

ill. 26 - ill 27
Master of the Fiesole Epiphany (1450-1500)
Christ on the Cross with Saints Vincent Ferrer, John the Baptist, Marc and Antoninus
Circa 1491/1495 Tempera and possibly oil on panel 72.75 x 79.75" (184.79 x 48 cm)

Before and after restoration

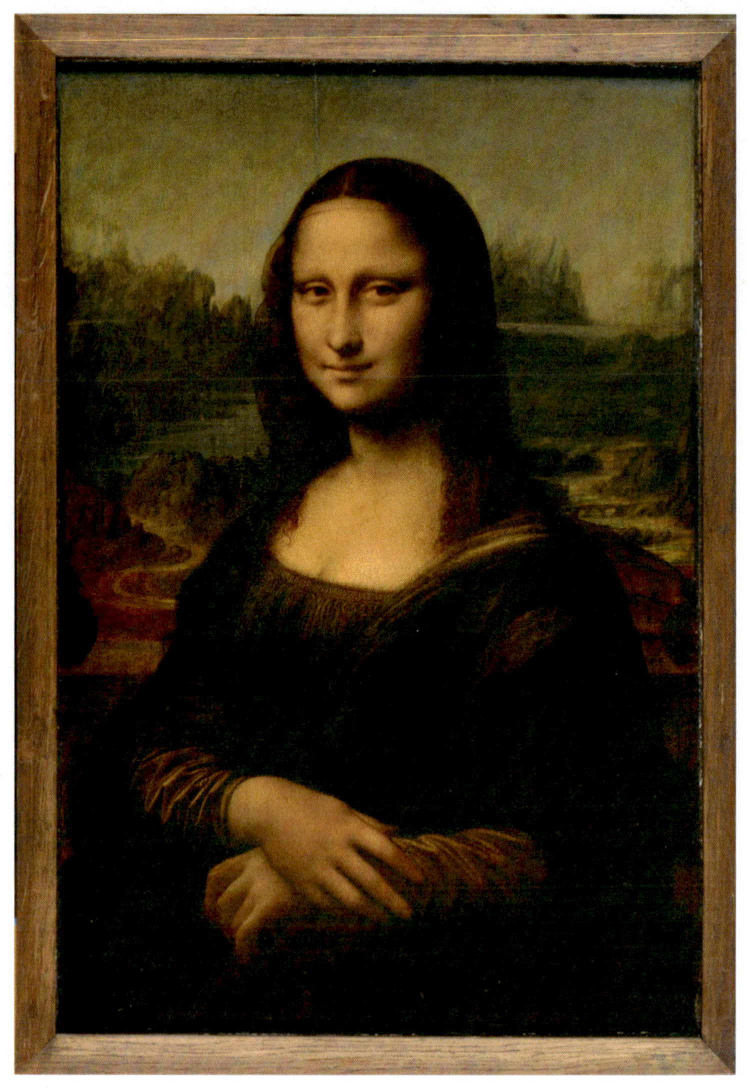

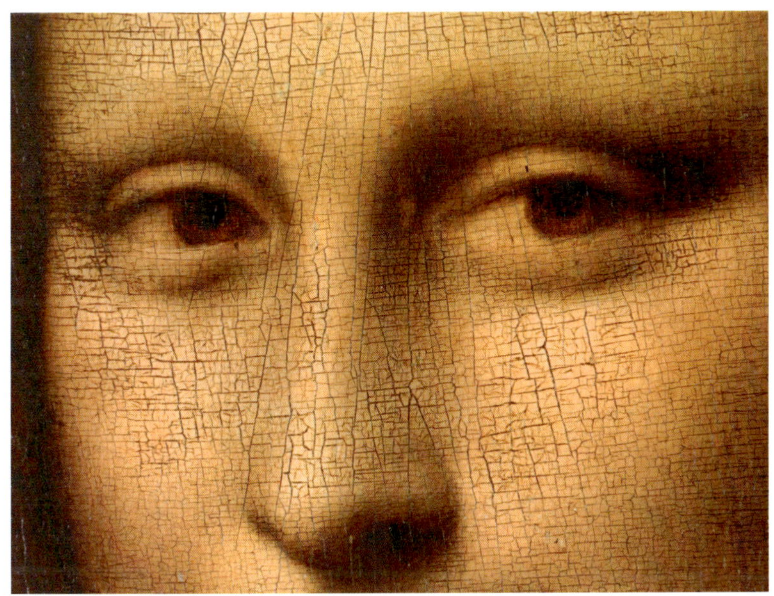

ill. 28 - ill. 29
Leonardo da Vinci (1452-1519)
Mona Lisa (La Giaconda)
1503-1519 Oil on wood 30.31 x 20.86" (77 x 53 cm)
Photos: Lewandowski/LeMage/Gattelet & Michel Urtado
Musée du Louvre

Example showing craquelure

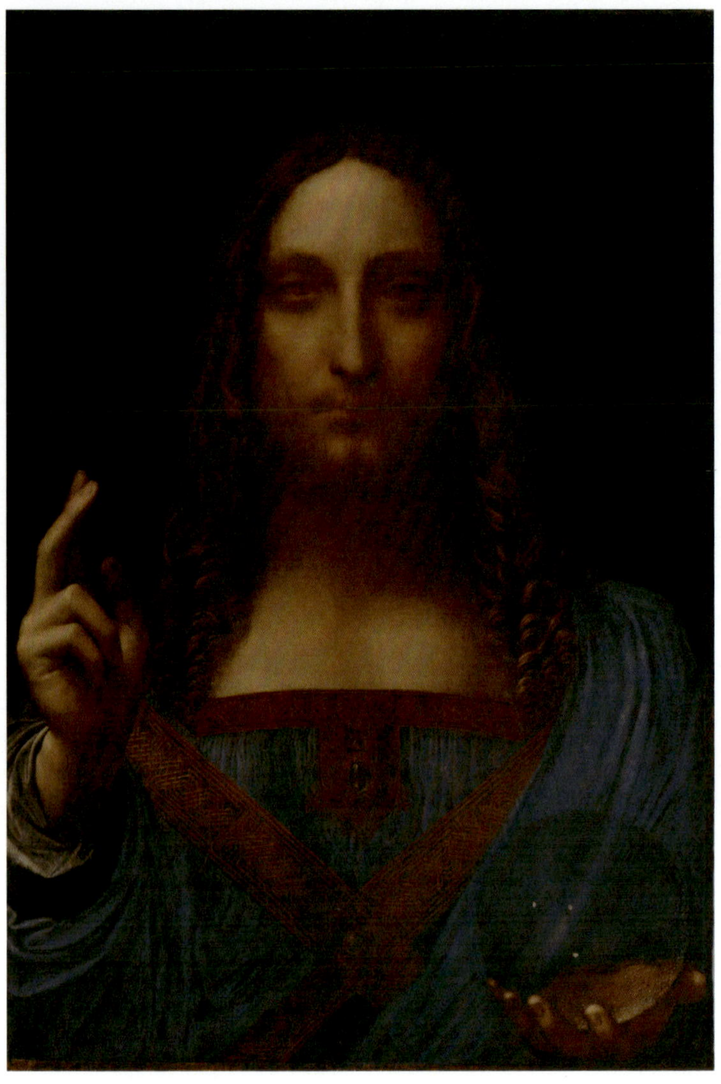

ill. 30
Leonardo da Vinci (1452-1519)
Salvator Mundi
Circa 1499 Oil on walnut 17.75 x 25.75" (45 x 66 cm)
HIP / Art Resource, NY

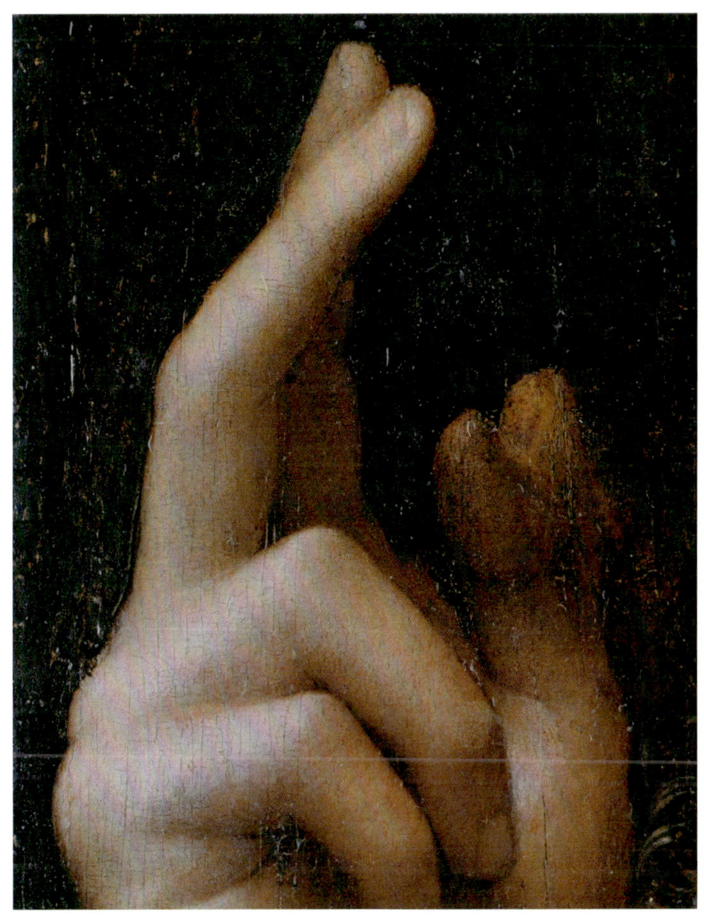

ill. 31
Leonardo da Vinci (1452-1519)
Salvator Mundi (Detail)
Mid-treatment photograph of Blessing Hand, December 2007

Photograph: Josh Nefsky

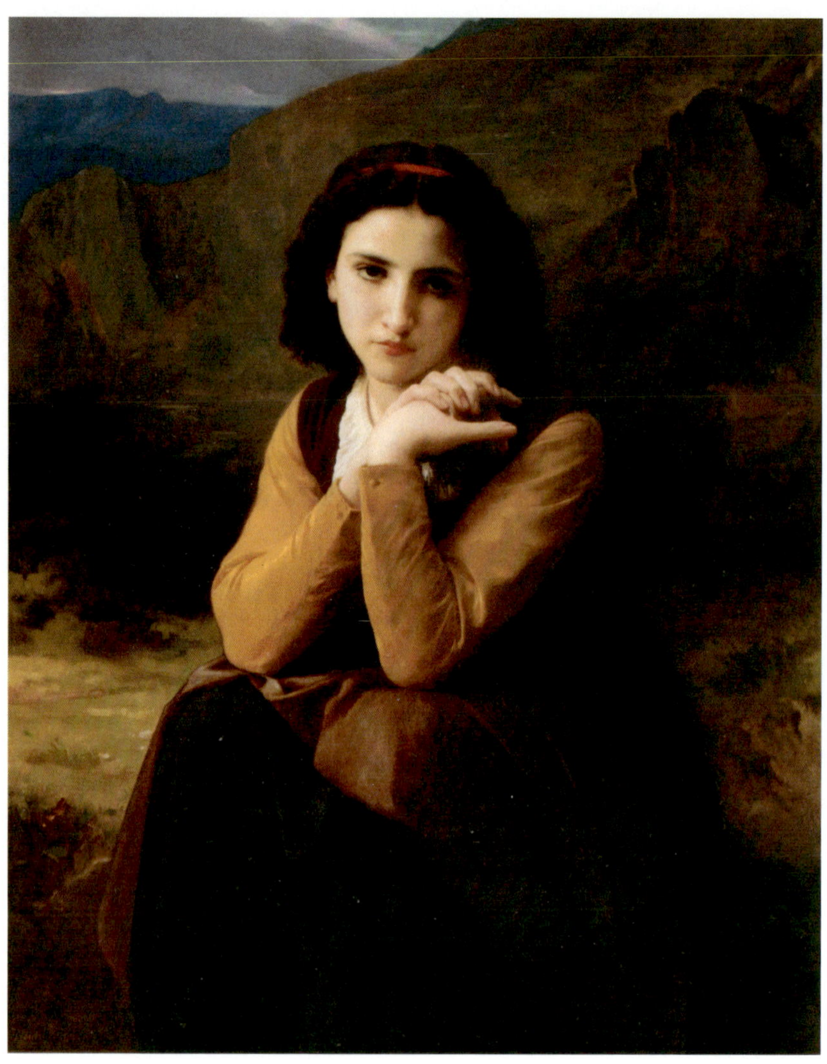

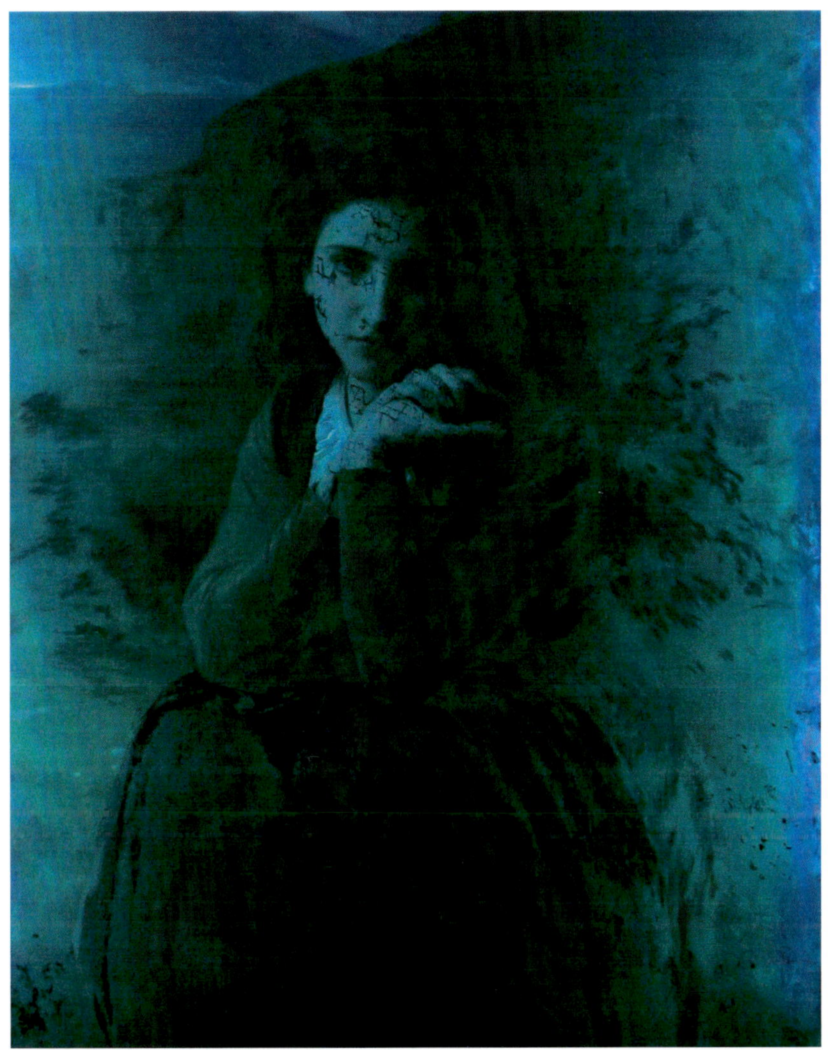

ill. 32 - ill. 33
William Bouguereau (1825-1905)
Mignon
1869 Oil on canvas 39.53 x 32.01" (100.4 x 81.3 cm)
Images courtesy of the Art Renewal Center® – www.artrenewal.org

Comparing original and while viewed under UV light

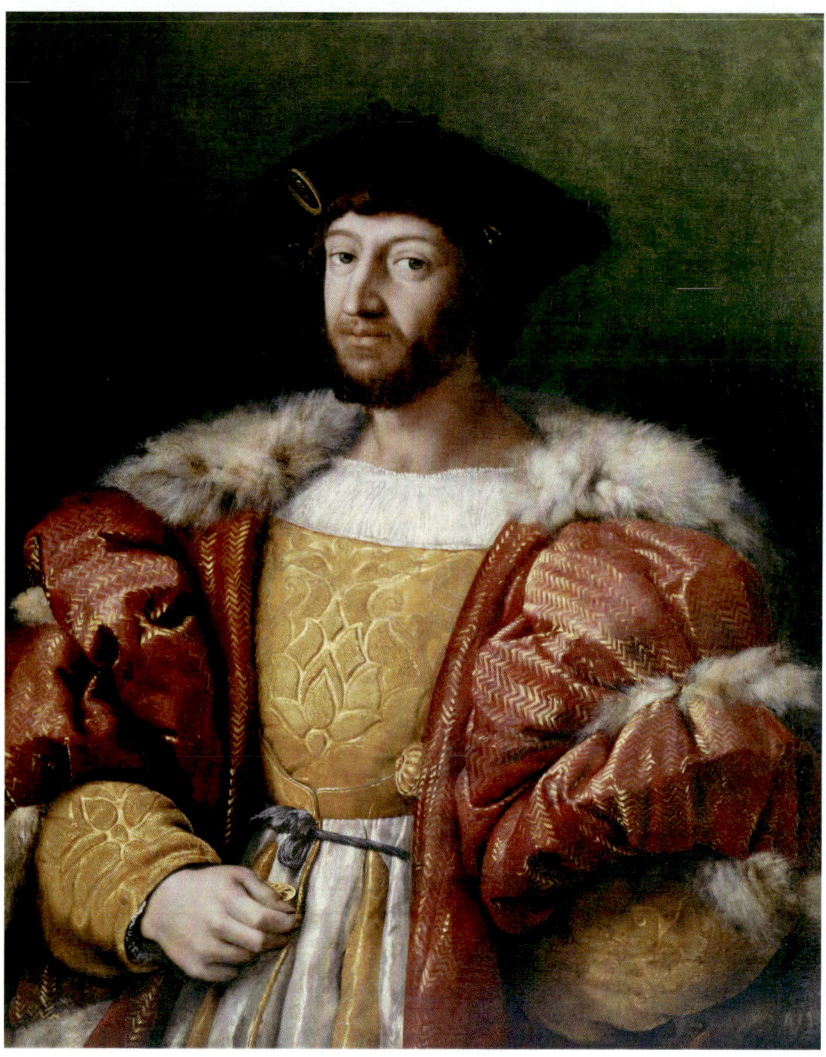

ill. 34
Raphael (Raffaello Sanzio of Urbino) (1483-1520)
Portrait of Lorenzo de Medici
Circa 1492-1519 Oil on canvas 38 x 31" (97 x 79 cm)
Private Collection /Bridgeman Images

ACKNOWLEDGEMENTS

As my mother always said, "If you're looking for someone to blame, it's the Mama." And indeed, it's only because my mother schlepped me through museums that I'm in the art world. No one before or since opened my eyes to the wonders of art as she did.

Love came first, then education. My professors at Columbia University were sensational, and I owe them a great debt. But when I went into business, there were no playbooks or rules, so I had to rely on friends and colleagues for guidance. Many who helped me throughout my career, such as Ira Spanierman, David Nash, and Derek Johns, helped me again with this book. They generously shared their observations of this byzantine world by way of anecdotes, some of which I've included. Other friends, including David Norman at Sotheby's and Patty Hambrecht, added valuable insider's insight on auction procedures.

Millicent Wilner shared her knowledge of Damien Hirst, Reba White Williams and Dave Williams, their expertise on prints, and Peter Fetterman, his vast knowledge of photographs. Frederick Ilchman, Curator of European Paintings at the MFA, Boston was a great resource for all things Renaissance. Joe Fronek, head conservator at LACMA, and Tanya Thompson, an independent conservator in LA, were kind enough to answer questions I had about conservation. Ellen Baskin, a brilliant researcher, pulled rabbits out of hats finding documents, and Stephanie Quinn Westphal shone as an informal life-coach for writing. Lucrecia Sachs, Marissa Bidner, Morgan Weiner, and Chloe Spitalny helped tremendously as well. I offer special thanks to Susan Estrich, who generously gave her time to read early drafts and offer constructive criticism and to Ann Berman, a brilliant art journalist, who embraced the book, shared her ideas, humor, and organizational skills. Without the counsel of Bobby Woods, publisher of Marmont Lane Books, I would have never made it to the finish line.

While writing this book, I thought of all the collectors I've worked with, and a number of stories I relate come from experiences we've shared. I'm thankful for the opportunity to have met them and am fortunate to count many as friends. They make my work my life's greatest pleasure.

I am also indebted to my partner in life, my husband, Bert Fields. Husbands usually get thanked for standing by their gal, and mine certainly deserves that and more. He's the best sounding board and editor a writer could have. So, Bert, for all those Saturdays I dragged you to galleries and all those weekends you edited my book when you could have been writing your own, I deeply apologize. I love you dearly.

SPECIAL THANKS

My profound gratitude goes to a unique individual, Abigail Asher, who's made our over twenty years together at Guggenheim, Asher Associates, a fantastic adventure.

ABOUT THE AUTHOR

Barbara Guggenheim is the founder of one of America's best-known art advisory firms, Guggenheim, Asher Associates, with offices in New York and Beverly Hills. She holds a doctorate in Art History from Columbia University, has taught on the college level, worked at Sotheby's, headed two departments at Christie's, and lectured for years at the Whitney Museum.

Ms. Guggenheim has written commentaries on the art world for many journals, including *The New York Observer* and the *Robb Report*. She lectures widely on collecting art and the art market and has been the subject of numerous magazine articles, including profiles in *Vanity Fair* and *Forbes*. Guggenheim also writes humorous short stories which have appeared in such magazines as *W*, *Elle*, and *Harper's Bazaar*. She's published four books, including *Decorating on eBay: Fast and Stylish on a Budget*.

Guggenheim lives in Malibu with her husband, Bert Fields, a renowned lawyer and author of several non-fiction books on English History and numerous novels.

GLOSSARY

A

Absentee bid: called a "commission" or "order" bid, this offers a mechanism for individuals who do not wish to be present at sales to bid
Acrylic: a fast-drying paint in which the pigment is suspended in acrylic polymer
Appropriation: borrowing elements from other art objects to create a new work

B

Black light: ultra-violet (UV) light used in assessing condition of paintings to detect repairs and changes made after the varnish has been applied
Buyer's premium: at auction a percentage of the hammer, arrived at by a sliding scale, all buyers must pay to the auction house
Buy-in: when a work doesn't reach its reserve at auction, it goes back to the owner

C

Catalogue raisonné (CR): a reasoned documentation of all works made by an artist done by an expert who has only included works he is certain is by the artist. Provided are images, dimensions, dates, details of signature, provenance, exhibition history and literature.

Chandelier bidding: imaginary (bogus) bids auctioneers call out in hopes to getting real bidders to jump in so that the work reaches the reserve
Conceptual Art: art in which the idea takes precedence over the results or traditional methods
Condition: the physical state of a work of art
Condition report: an analysis prepared by a conservator which documents the physical state of the work, listing damages, changes, and repairs, and perhaps a prescription for further conservation
Craquelure: the pattern of cracking in paint

D

Dendrochronology: method for analyzing age of wood
Doc sheet: fact sheet listing the work, details (title, date, measurements, and medium), provenance, literature, and exhibition history

E

Edition: in making prints, the number of prints struck from a plate

F

Foxing: usually reddish age spots or stains on paper

G H

Gallerist: an individual who owns or runs an art gallery
Gesso: a white mixture of chalk and other binders which prepare the canvas or wood for the application of paint
Gouache: a kind of paint in which, although the pigment

is suspended in water, it's thickened with a glue-like substance so as to appear thicker, like poster paint
Guarantee: committed sum the auction house or a third person, called the 'third-party guarantor,' will pay the seller for an object that comes to auction, whether or not the object reaches the agreed-upon guaranteed sum during the bidding

I J K

Impasto: paint that's laid on a composition so thickly, one can see brush or palette-knife strokes

L

Light-struck: the fading of colors which occurs, especially to works on paper, after prolonged exposure to sunlight

M N

Maquette: scale model
Medium: material or substances which comprises a work
Minimal Art: a movement which grew in the 1960s in reaction to Abstract Expressionism. Its proponents focused on impersonality and simplicity of form. The sculptures often used heavy industrial materials.
Monograph: a detailed book on a single artist written by an expert
Monotype: a unique print

O

Oil: pigment suspended in oil, such as linseed or chestnut

P Q

Pentimento (plural *pentimenti*): change(s) made by the artist in the process of painting evidenced by previous work showing through
Pigment: the powder or other substance that constitutes the color in paint
Primary market: when a work of art leaves the artist's studio (or estate) and is sold for the first time
Private dealer: vendors of art who are not encumbered with galleries
Private Treaty Sale: the term auction houses use to refer to sales they make not through auction
Provenance: the history of a painting from the time it leaves the artist's studio to the present

R

Relining: adding a new canvas to the back of an existing one to add support or to save a deteriorating canvas or when there's damage to paint layer
Reserve: minimum a seller agrees to accept at auction
Retrospective: an exhibition of works from the artist's past
Ring: a group of buyers who collude not to bid against each other during an auction and after the auction, by way of another auction, determine who gets the items. Those who do not win the object share in the profits.

S

Secondary market: a work from any era that has already been sold once

Seller's Premium: a percentage of the hammer price a seller must pay
Stretcher (or *Stretcher bar*): a wooden framework support on which the artist fixes a canvas, typically using nails or staples

T

Tempera: a medium for pigment comprised of egg yolks and water

U

Underbidder: at auction, bidders who do not win the lot

V

Varnish: protective transparent coat some painters use which can appear shiny or matte
Vedute: views of cities or vistas, particularly those of Venice, brought back to England by British aristocrats who made the Grand Tour in the 18th century as souvenirs and to impress their peers

W X Y Z

Watercolor: paint comprised of pigments suspended in a water-soluble binder, such as gum arabic and thinned with water, providing a transparent appearance

BIBLIOGRAPHY

INTRODUCTION

Reyburn, Scott. "Christie's has Art World's First $1 Billion Week." *The New York Times*, 13 May 2015, p. A1.

FIRST THINGS FIRST

Pisa, Nick and Catherine Humble. "Now culture shock has an official name: David Syndrome." *The Telegraph*, 11 Nov. 2005. Web.
http://www.telegraph.co.uk/news/worldnews/europe/italy/1502882/Now-culture-shock-has-an-official-name-David-Syndrome.html

"Painting meets its femme fatale." *BBC News*, 21 July 2007. Web.
http://news.bbc.co.uk/2/hi/6910377.stm

Blumenthal, Ralph. "A Celebratory Splash for an Enigmatic Figure." *The New York Times*, 04 June 2005. Web.
http://www.nytimes.com/2005/06/04/arts/design/04twom.html

PLAYERS

Betts, Kate. "Top 10 Everything 2003." *Time*, 18 Dec. 2003. Web.
http://www.time.com/time/specials/packages/article/0,28804,2001842_2001830_2002055,00.html

Lindemann, Adam. *Collecting Contemporary Art*. New York: Taschen, 2010. Print.

Smith, Roberta. "Hirst, Globally Dotting His 'I'." *The New York Times*, 12 Jan. 2012. Web. http://www.nytimes.com/2012/01/13/arts/design/damien-hirsts-spot-paintings-at-gagosian-in-eight-cities.html

Petry, Michael. *The Art of Not Making*. London: Thames & Hudson. 2011. Print.

Hirst, Damien and Gordon Burn. *On the Way to Work*. London: Faber and Faber. 2001. Print.

"Obituary: R.B. Kitaj." *The Independent*. 25 Oct. 2007. Web. http://www.independent.co.uk/news/obituaries/r-b-kitaj-397791.html

Feinstein, Roni. "The Scull Collection." *Art in America*. 04 June 2010. Web. http://www.artinamericamagazine.com/reviews/the-scull-collection/

Cohen, Patricia. "Federal Judge Strikes Down California's Art Royalties Law." *The New York Times*, 21 May 2012. Web. http://artsbeat.blogs.nytimes.com/2012/05/21/judge-strikes-down-californias-artists-royalties-law/

Auden, W.H. "In Memory of W.B. Yeats." *Auden: Collected Poems*. New York: Modern Library. 2007. Print.

Kazanjian, Dodie. "House of Wirth: The Gallery World's Power Couple." *Vogue*, 10 January 2013. Web. http://vogue.com/865264/house-of-wirth-the-gallery-worlds-art-couple/

Behrman, S.N. "The Days of Duveen," *The New Yorker*, 29 Sept. 1951. Web.
http://snbehrman.com/library/newyorker/51.9.29.NY.htm

Kennedy, Maev. "Hirst's Skull Makes Dazzling Debut." *The Guardian*, 01 June 2007. Web.
http://www.guardian.co.uk/artanddesign/artblog/2007/jun/01/hirstsskullmakesdazzlingde

La Ferla, Ruth. "Figures at an Exhibition." *The New York Times*, 24 May 2015: 7-9. Print.

Perl, Jed. "The Irredeemably Boring Egotism of Cindy Sherman." *The New Republic*, 14 March 2012. Web.
http://www.tnr.com/article/the-picture/101646/cindy-sherman-moma-pop-culture-camp-kitsch-aura

Berenson, Bernard. *Homeless Paintings of the Renaissance. 1st ed.* Bloomington: University of Indiana Press. 1970. Print.

"Christie's Contemporary Does a Record $388 million." *artnet.com*, 09 May 2012. Web.
http://www.artnet.com/magazineus/news/artmarketwatch/christies-contemporary-5-9-12.asp

Kazakina, Katya and Philip Boroff. "Lichtenstein's 'Sleeping Girl' Brings Record $45 Million." *Bloomberg Business Week*, 09 May 2012. Web.
http://www.businessweek.com/news/2012-05-09/lichtenstein-s-sleeping-girl-brings-record-45-million

Muchnic, Suzanne. "Auction of Billy Wilder's Art Fetches $32.6 Million." *Los Angeles Times*, 14 Nov. 1989. Web.
http://articles.latimes.com/1989-11-14/news/mn_1941_1_billy-wilder-s-art

Vogel, Carol. "Rock, Paper, Payoff: Child's Play Wins Auction House an Art Sale." *The New York Times*, 29 Apr. 2005. Web. http://www.nytimes.com/2005/04/29/arts/design/29scis.html

Campbell, Sara. *Collector Without Walls: Norton Simon and His Hunt For the Best.* Los Angeles: Norton Simon Distribution, 2010. Print.
Sandelson, Michael. "UK Bookies Predict Record Munch Price." *The Foreigner*, 02 March 2012. Web. http://theforeigner.no/pages/news/uk-bookies-predict-record-munch-price/

Vogel, Carol. "'The Scream' Is Auctioned for a Record $119.9 Million." *The New York Times*, 02 May 2012. Web. http://www.nytimes.com/2012/05/03/arts/design/the-scream-sells-for-nearly-120-million-at-sothebys-auction.html

Grant, Daniel. "Rising Trend: Private Art Sales via Auction Houses." *Barron's*, 11 June 2012. Web. http://blogs.barrons.com/penta/2012/06/11/rising-trend-private-art-sales-via-auction-houses/

Kimmelman, Michael. "Havemeyer Collection: Magic at The Met Museum." *The New York Times*, 26 March 1993. Web. http://www.nytimes.com/1993/03/26/arts/review-art-havemeyer-collection-magic-at-the-met-museum.html

Cohen, Patricia. "A Collector Bets His Eye And His Gut." *The New York Times*, 02 December 2013. Web. http://nytimes.com/2013/12/07/arts/design/a-collector-bets-his-eye-and-his-gut.html

Orden, Erica. "Art Basel Off to a Fast Start." *The Wall Street Journal*, 02 December 2010. Web. http://online.wsj.com/article/SB10001424052748704594804575649182483014578.html

Lindemann, Adam. "Occupy Art Basel Miami Beach, Now!" *The New York Observer*, 29 Nov. 2011. Web. http://www.adamlindemann.com/occupy-art-basel-miami-beach-now/

Trebay, Guy. "Art Basel Miami Beach: Where Art and Commerce Come Together and Party." *The New York Times*, 10 Dec. 2010. Web. http://www.nytimes.com/2010/12/12/fashion/12Basel.html

Newhouse, Victoria. *Towards A New Museum.* New York: The Monacelli Press, 2007. Print.

Hoving, Thomas. *Making the Mummies Dance: Inside The Metropolitan Museum of Art*. New York: Touchstone, 1994. Print.

Vogel, Carol. "Impressionists Head South." *The New York Times*. 02 Nov. 2007. Web. http://www.nytimes.com/2007/11/02/arts/design/02voge.html

Pogrebin, Robin. "Resisting Renaming of Miami Museum." *The New York Times*, 06 Dec. 2011. Web. http://www.nytimes.com/2011/12/07/arts/design/jorge-m-perezs-name-on-miami-museum-roils-board.html

Gross, Michael. *Rogues' Gallery: The Secret Story of the Lust, Lies, Greed and Betrayal That Made The Metropolitan Museum of Art*. New York: Broadway, 2010. Print.

Thornton, Sarah. *Seven Days in the Art World*. New York: W.W. Norton, 2008. Print. (172)

Gibson, Eric. "The Lost Art of Writing About Art." *The Wall Street Journal*, 18 Apr. 2008. Web. http://online.wsj.com/article/SB120848379018525199.html

Gewen, Barry. "State of the Art." *The New York Times Book Review*, 11 Dec. 2005. Web. http://www.nytimes.com/2005/12/11/books/review/11gewen.html

COLLECTORS AND COLLECTIONS

King, William Davies. *Collections of Nothing*. Chicago: University of Chicago Press, 2008. Print.

Muensterberger, Werner. *Collecting: An Unruly Passion*. New York: Mariner Books, 1995. Print.

McAndrew, Clare. *The International Art Market: A Survey of Europe in a Global Context*. London: The European Fine Art Foundation, 2008. Print.

Gleadell, Colin. "Art Sales: David Roberts opens huge new arts centre in Camden." *The Telegraph*, 17 Sept. 2012. Web. http://www.telegraph.co.uk/culture/art/artsales/9548860/Art-sales-David-Roberts-opens-huge-new-arts-centre-in-Camden.html

Rice, Andrew. "Damien Hirst: Jumping the Shark." *Bloomberg Businessweek*, 21 Nov. 2012. Web. http://www.businessweek.com/articles/2012-11-21/damien-hirst-jumping-the-shark#p2

Martin, Douglas. "Herbert Vogel, Fabled Art Collector, Dies at 89." *The New York Times*, 23 July 2012. Web. http://www.nytimes.com/2012/07/24/arts/design/herbert-vogel-postal-clerk-and-modern-art-collector-dies-at-89.html

Waxman, Sharon. "A Producer Who Loved Both Art and Ribaldry." *The New York Times*, 11 May 2005. Web. http://www.nytimes.com/2005/05/11/movies/11star.html

Morrow, Lance. "Essay: the Shoes of Imelda Marcos." *Time*. 31 Mar. 1986. Web. http://www.time.com/time/magazine/article/0,9171,961002,00.html

Muchnic, Suzanne. "Rummaging Through the Andy Warhol Estate." *Los Angeles Times*, 21 Feb. 1988. Web. http://articles.latimes.com/1988-02-21/entertainment/ca-44010_1_andy-warhol-estate

Wolff, Craig. "Walter P. Chrysler, Jr., a Collector Of Modern Art and Artifacts, 79." *The New York Times*, 19 Sep. 1988. Web. http://www.nytimes.com/1988/09/19/obituaries/walter-p-chrysler-jr-a-collector-of-modern-art-and-artifacts-79.html

Clement, Russell T. and Annick Houze. *Neo-Impressionist Painters: A Sourcebook on Georges Seurat, Camille Pisarro, Paul Signac, Theo Van Rysselberghe, Henri Edmond Cross, Charles Angrand, Maximilien Luce and Albert Dubois-Pillet*. New York: Greenwood Publishing Group, 1999. Print.

Fowler, Glenn. "Wendell Cherry Is Dead at 55; Hospital Leader." *The New York Times*. 18 July 1991. Web. http://www.nytimes.com/1991/07/18/obituaries/wendell-cherry-is-dead-at-55-hospital-leader.html

Sutton, Larry. "Art Trove Fetches $206m, Masterpieces Go For Master Prices." *The New York Daily News*. 11 Nov. 1997. Web. http://www.nydailynews.com/archives/news/art-trove-fetches-206m-masterpieces-master-prices-article-1.783302

Fitzgerald, Michael. *A Life of Collecting: Victor and Sally Ganz*. New York: Harry N. Abrams, 1999. Print.

Adams, Stephen. "Roman Abramovich 'revealed as Freud and Bacon buyer'." *The Telegraph*, 18 May 2008. Web. http://www.telegraph.co.uk/news/uknews/1981367/Roman-Abramovich-revealed-as-Freud-and-Bacon-buyer.html

Vogel, Carol. "Inside Art: Joy and Tears for Sotheby's." *The New York Times*. 12 July 2002. Web. http://www.nytimes.com/2002/07/12/arts/inside-art.html

Veblen, Thorstein. *The Theory of the Leisure Class*. New York: Penguin Classics, 1994. Print.

Lewis, Tanya. "Record-breaking Wine: What Does $168,000 Taste Like?" *Wired.com*. Conde Nast Digital, 28 June 2012. Web. http://www.wired.com/wiredscience/2012/06/most-expensive-wine/

Kaplan, David A. *Mine's Bigger: The Extraordinary Tale of the World's Greatest Sailboat and the Silicon Valley Tycoon Who Built It*. New York: It Books, 2008. Print.

Vogel, Carol. "Landmark de Kooning Crowns Collection." *The New York Times*, 18 Nov. 2006. Web. http://www.nytimes.com/2006/11/18/arts/design/18pain.html

Frey, Bruno S. and Werner W. Pommerehne. *Muses and Markets: Explorations of the Economics of the Arts*. New York: Blackwell Publishing, 1989. Print.

Trucco, Terry. "British Pension Fund Sells $65.6 Million in Artworks." *The New York Times*, 05 April 1989. Web. http://www.nytimes.com/1989/04/05/arts/british-pension-fund-sells-65.6-million-in-artworks.html

Mei, Jiangping and Michael Moses. "Art as an Investment and the Underperformance of Masterpieces." *Abstract*. 2002. Web. http://people.stern.nyu.edu/jmei/artgood.pdf

Spiegler, Mark. "Five Theories On Why the Art Market Can't Crash." *New York Magazine*, 26 Mar. 2006. Web. http://nymag.com/arts/art/features/16542/

Gross, Daniel. "Painting for Profit: Is art a good investment?" *Slate*, 21 June 2006. Web. http://www.slate.com/articles/business/moneybox/2006/06/painting_for_profit.html

Woollard, Deidre. "Eli Broad Snaps Up Cheap Art." *The Luxist*, 12 Nov. 2008. Web. http://www.luxist.com/2008/11/12/eli-broad-snaps-up-cheap-art/

Reyburn, Scott. "Russians Fight Indian Billionaires for Old Master Records." *Bloomberg.com*. Bloomberg, 04 July 2013. Web. 5 July 2013.

Esterow, Milton. "From 'Riches to Rags to Riches'." *ARTnews*. 01 Jan. 2011. Web. http://www.artnews.com/2011/01/01/from-riches-to-rags-to-riches/
Lindemann, Adam. "Art Intel, 2011." *The New York Observer*, 05 Jan 2011. Web.
http://observer.com/2011/01/art intel 2011/

Lindemann, Adam, "Inside Out, Round and Round...: From Out-of-Whack Values to Artist Defections, This Art World Is Looking Topsy-Turvy." *GalleristNY*, 05 Feb.2013. Web. http://galleristny.com/2013/02/inside-out-round-and-round-from-out-of-whack-values-to-artist-defections-this-art-world-is-looking-topsy-turvy/

Ilnytzky, Ula. "Annie Leibovitz Settles With Art Capital Group." *The Huffington Post*. 12 Sept. 2009. Web. http://www.huffingtonpost.com/2009/09/11/annie-leibovitz-settles-w_n_283759.html

Montgomery, Trudy. "Tate Britain's Turner Prize 2010 Awarded to Sound Sculptor For the First Time." *The Huffington Post*, 10 Dec. 2010. Web. http://www.huffingtonpost.com/trudy-montgomery/tate-britains-turner-priz_b_794740.html

Belcove, Julie. "Feeding Frenzy: New Kid." *The New Yorker*. 03 Oct. 2011: 23. Print.

Meisler, Stanley. "Fake Paintings: 81 and Ill, Dali Still Confounds." *Los Angeles Times*, 16 Apr. 1986. Web. http://articles.latimes.com/1986-04-16/news/mn-4_1_dali-museum/2

Rowe, Peter. "Making Art and Making Money." *The San Diego Union-Tribune*, 04 Sept. 2010. Web. http://www.utsandiego.com/news/2010/sep/04/lessons-making-art-and-making-money/

DUE DILIGENCE

Esterow, Milton. "The 10 Most Faked Artists." *ARTnews*, 01 June 2005. Web. http://www.artnews.com/2005/06/01/the-10-most-faked-artists/

Reed, Christopher. "Wrong!" *Harvard Magazine*, September 2004. Web. http://harvardmagazine.com/2004/09/wrong.html

Frankenstein, Alfred. *After the Hunt: William Harnett and Other American Still Life Painters 1870-1900. 2nd ed*. San Francisco: University of California Press. 1975. Print.

F For Fake. Dir. Orson Welles. 1973. Specialty Films.

Irving, Clifford. *Fake! The Story of Elmyr De Hory, the Greatest Art Forger of Our Time*. New York: McGraw-Hill. 1969. Print.

Dolnick, Edward. *The Forger's Spell: A True Story of Vermeer, Nazis, and the Greatest Art Hoax of the Twentieth Century*. New York: Harper, 2008. Print.

Salisbury, Laney and Aly Sujo. *Provenance: How a Con Man and a Forger Rewrote the History of Modern Art*. New York: Penguin Books. 2010. Print.

"Fraud Art Dealer Who Fooled Galleries All over the Country Caught out When He Sold Fake Painting to Late Artist's Friend." *Mail Online*. Daily Mail, 27 Oct. 2011. Web. http://www.dailymail.co.uk/news/article2054200/Fraud-art-dealer-Rizvan-Rahman-caught-sold-fake-painting-friend-Cornish-artist-Jack-Pender.html

Deimlinge, Kate. "Forgery For Dummies: British Art Teacher Convicted of Selling Fake Picassos Had an 'Art Forger's Handbook'." *Blouin ArtInfo*, 14 Oct. 2011. Web. http://www.artinfo.com/news/story/38869/forgery-for-dummies-british-art-teacher-convicted-of-selling-fake-picassos-had-an-art-forgers-handbook

Vitello, Paul. Jacques Dupin, "Art Scholar and Poet, Dies at 85." *The New York Times*, 04 Nov. 2012. Web. http://www.nytimes.com/2012/11/05/arts/jacques-dupin-french-art-critic-and-poet-dies-at-85.html

Cohen, Patricia. "Ruling on Artistic Authenticity: The Market vs. the Law." *The New York Times*, 05 Aug. 2012. Web. http://www.nytimes.com/2012/08/06/arts/design/when-judging-arts-authenticity-the-law-vs-the-market.html

Shnayerson, Michael. "Judging Andy." *Vanity Fair*, Nov. 2003. Web. http://www.vanityfair.com/culture/features/2003/11/authentic-andy-warhol-michael-shnayerson

Guggenheim, Barbara. "Exit the Deciders: What Will the Recent Disbanding of Authentication Committees Mean For The Art World?" *New York Observer*. 07 February 2012. Web. http://observer.com/2012/02/exit-the-deciders-what-will-the-recent-disbanding-of-authentication-committees-mean-for-the-art-world/

Jha, Alok. "Software That Reveals Which Paintings Are Authentic." *The Guardian*, 11 Oct. 2006. Web. http://www.guardian.co.uk/technology/2006/oct/12/news.science

Kennedy, Randy. "Is This a Real Jackson Pollock?" *The New York Times*, 29 May 2005. Web. http://www.nytimes.com/2005/05/29/arts/design/29kenn.html

Waxman, Sharon. "Loot: The Battle Over the Stolen Treasures of the Ancient World." *The New York Times*, 2008. Print.

Reich, Howard. "$6.5 Million Will End Picasso Fight." *Chicago Tribune*, 10 Aug. 2005. Web. http://articles.chicagotribune.com/2005-08-10/news/0508100158_1_marilynn-alsdorf-art-loss-register-picasso

Ruiz, Christina. "C-prints Fade into the Light." *The Art Newspaper* Apr. 2010, issue 212 ed.: n. pag. 17 May 2010. Web. www.theartnewspaper.com/articles/C-prints-fade-into-the-light/20892

Ryzik, Melena. "Whitney Saves Douglas Davis's 'First Collaborative Sentence'." *The New York Times*, 10 June 2013. Web. http://nytimes.com/2013/06/10/arts/design/whitney-saves-douglas-daviss-first-collaborative-sentence.html

Sandler, Linda. "Art Dealer Sells Raphael For 100,000 Times the Price He Paid." *Bloomberg*, 06 July 2007. Web. http://www.bloomberg.com/apps/news?pid=newsarchive&sid=a6T.8.UI6wa0

AFTER YOU OWN IT

Newhouse, Victoria. *Art and The Power of Placement. 1st Ed*. New York: The Monacelli Press. 2005. Print.

Kurkjian, Stephen. "The Gardner Heist: Secrets Behind the Largest Art Theft in History." *The Boston Globe*, 13 Mar. 2005. Web.

Boser, Ulrich. *The Gardner Heist: The True Story of the World's Largest Unsolved Art Theft*. Waterville: Thorndike, 2009. Web. (5) http://www.boston.com/news/specials/gardner_heist/heist/

Reynolds, Christopher. "At Paris Exhibit, L.A. Art Is a Smash – Literally." *Los Angeles Times*, 03 Aug. 2006. Web. http://articles.latimes.com/2006/aug/03/entertainment/et-pompidou3

Bennett, Will. "Court Verdict in £1.9 Urns Case Will Be Crucial to Art World." *The Telegraph*, 26 Nov. 2003. Web. http://www.telegraph.co.uk/news/uknews/1447738/Court-verdict-in-1.9m-urns-case-will-be-crucial-to-art-world.html

EXIT STRATEGIES

Grace, Melissa. "Lawrence Salander...to plead guilty to $100M fraud." *New York Daily News*, 18 Mar. 2010. Web. http://articles.nydailynews.com/2010-03-18/news/27059356_1_fraud-scheme-art-work-john-mcenroe

Marmont Lane Books would like to thank Tom Andre, Andrew Golomb, David Gonzales, Ellen Baskin, Chloe Spitalny, Sylve Rosen, and Maureen Fewel for their assistance in the making of this book.

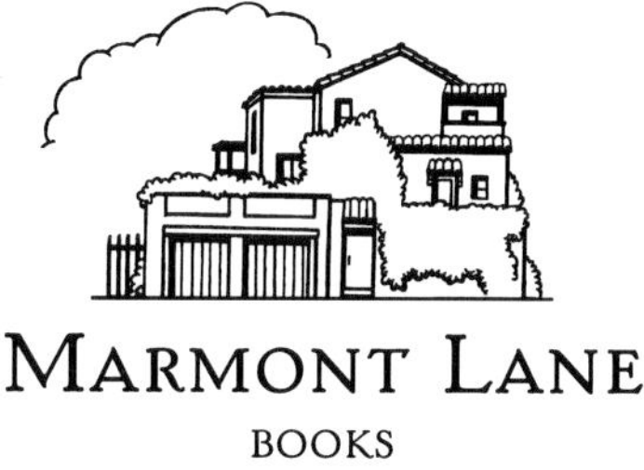

MARMONTLANE.COM